Exposed:

- **Secret Origins of Humankind**
- **The Serpent Race**
- **Mind Control**
- **The UFO Power Elite**

MW01487067

THE CONTROLLERS

THE HIDDEN RULERS OF EARTH IDENTIFIED

by Commander X
Retired Military Intelligence Operative

SPECIAL THANKS TO BARTON

Table of Contents

Editor's Note: At a press conference held in 1971, a top ranking astrophysicist acknowledged that his own personal research led him to believe that our planet was actually under the command of intelligent beings from space who have fantastic powers over us. These statements have since been forgotten. They should not be!!!

Leading Scientist Confirms Existence of "The Controllers"

Human beings are simply pawns in the games of alien minds that control our every move. Our whole life and the complete existence of this universe is at the whim of these creatures that hold fantastic mental powers over us.

So says Fred Hoyle, the famed British astrophysicist and author.

"They are everywhere," he said in a special press conference held in London, "in the sky, on the sea and on the earth. They have been there since the beginning of time and control nearly everything we do!"

Hoyle explained the many reasons why the majority of people had no idea of this.

"Panic is the major reason that no general announcement was ever made," he said. "But there have been some books out on the theory.

"But the books have really only circulated in scientific circles and academic markets. The theory and arguments around it are much too technical for non scientists.

"They seem to be totally free of any physical restrictions, such as bodies. They are like pure thought and can be anywhere at any time they please."

Hoyle then explained that they had the power to appear anywhere as anything.

"They can take any shape or form. They can appear as a tiger in one place or a person in another. They can appear as a gas or a cloud or anything that can be seen by the human eye and even by some forms that cannot be seen by the naked eye.

Hoyle pointed out that this intelligence probably controlled our complete evolution and continues to control our minds. All that man has built and become was done because of tinkering of these intelligent forces.

"And the weirdest thing about it," said Hoyle, "is that at times they actually appear in physical forms."

Hoyle told the press conference that a large art of the scientific establishment is convinced that another intelligence exists on this planet.

"It is not an intelligence from another planet. It is actually from another universe. It entered our universe at the very beginning and has been controlling all that has happened since."

This second universe, says Hoyle, where these powerful minds originally came from, is much like ours and yet on a totally different plane. "It is probably three dimensional like ours and may even have a fourth or fifth dimension which breaks the time and space barriers that restrict us. But their laws of chemistry and physics are no doubt completely different from ours because they are a much more advanced type of intelligence.

"In this way, they have been responsible for almost all of the legends in different countries which are scoffed at today. They also had a hand in the different things which were discovered in only some parts of the world and not others." Astrophysicist Hoyle, who is known throughout the world as one of the best, could not give concrete details about the intelligence. "They are so different what we know, that to try and describe them in a language that everyone would understand would be impossible.

"Hoyle said that the most recent documented incident of their appearance was at sea. Dozens of ships were following something on their sonar. It was traveling at 250 knots and 20,000 feet deep. There is nothing on earth that can go that far and that deep.

"Hoyle said he didn't expect many people to believe everything he said at the press conference. "Most people...will think that this is a hair-brained theory and just laugh it off. Others will be worried and check with police or governments.

"Naturally the government will deny everything. But most scientists know about it and agreed that it would be a good thing to get the story out and let the public chew on it. A little at a time, more facts will be released until everyone has access to all the information that is now only in the hands of scientists and government officials."

Chapter 1: UFOs & The Power Elite—Who's Really In Control of Planet Earth?

As we speed toward the year 2000, it has become more apparent than ever before that we are not totally in control of our lives; that there is a "power" that seems to be pulling us in a very negative and destructive direction. This applies not only to us as individuals, but to the planet as a whole. Most of us seem unable to point a finger in the direction of where this power originates from, yet we realize quite fully that there is a weight on our shoulders that seems to be getting heavier with each passing moment.

And while the vast majority of the public may not realize it, UFOs are here as an important role model in our development as a species, providing us with a sign from upon high (the "heavens") that there is much beyond the range of normal human development to strive for—both spiritually and technologically. For if we could but achieve all that which these craft and their occupants have demonstrated to us, if it is possible to accomplish, we would have a better standard of living for every man, woman and child on this planet regardless of race, religious belief or country of origin. Instead, those in power—going back thousands of years—have done all they possibly could to keep the truth about such matters as UFOs from reaching the "common person," thus allowing them to hold yet another ace in their hands when it comes to total domination over this planet.

The late Canadian scientist, Wilbert Brockhouse Smith, was one of the earliest pioneers during our lifetime whose job it was to upset as much as possible the applecart of the *negative forces* who continue to operate behind the scenes of science, politics, medicine, archaeology and all other matters that determine what we are allowed to believe about the history and structure of the planet and those residing on, below and above its surface. Though he has been remembered best for his discoveries pertaining to perpetual motion and alternative energy sources, many of his closest admirers do not realize that Smith often tapped into interdimensional and extraterrestrial sources for his knowledge and inspiration. In New Age circles, he would be known today as a "channel." According to his biography, Smith's investigations carried him into the fields of psychics, philosophy and religion. As an engineer, he was foremost in his field and the holder of numerous patents. He undertook a thorough study of gravity and devised several experiments that produced limited, but encouraging, results.

The Battle of Man's Mind

A prophet in his own right, Wilbert Smith foresaw a great danger that would engulf the world that would try to enslave mankind. And while he fully realized the danger that communism might bring with it if it spread, Smith envisioned a far worse foe that would attempt to control our minds as well as our hearts—but let us allow Smith to speak on his own behalf, so as not to color his words.

• • •

"I propose to give the reader a warning of a grave danger that we are all, consciously or unconsciously, facing in a world in which two great forces are striving to gain control of man's mind. This struggle has been going on from time immemorial, but never in the world's history has the conflict been more intense than it is in this present era of confusion and unrest. In the old days, mankind was often made to suffer physically, unspeakable things in the name of power, but today, with man's mind more developed and better educated, he is now facing the prospect of a refinement of even greater mental and spiritual cruelty—unless he is prepared to protect himself with right thinking.

The two great forces involved in trying to influence man's thinking may be described as *positive,* i.e., thoughts in harmony with the concept of a love of God and the brotherhood of man, and *negative,* those encompassing motives designed to gain control over man for the purpose of power. This battle for Man's mind is being waged on two fronts, the physical and the metaphysical, and the object of the fight is to bring about either the spiritual salvation or destruction of *homo sapiens.*

To deal first with the physical aspects, no matter how hard we may all strive to be strong-minded and individualistic, we are all subtly influenced by the spoken and written word and other forms of thought communication, particularly through the medium of books, newspapers, radio and television. In the latter field, as the sponsors know only too well, even the "commercials" play an important role in making up our minds to purchase certain products. In our business and social lives, we are often swayed by the thoughts of others, and some people too apathetic to form opinions themselves will accept the views of others more articulate, as their own. In all our daily contacts, a little of the good, bad or indifferent, as the case may be, is rubbing off and influencing our thinking.

In the field of politics, often an area of great misrepresentation in order to gain votes, even greater pressures are brought to bear and we are often influenced by the seemingly convincing rhetoric of clever politicians. But it is in the area of international politics that the gravest dangers lie, for here the stakes are high and the lust for power the greatest. Because of this, many of us have been through the horrors of at least one world war, if not two. But let us first analyze how these two wars came about in the first place.

In each case, a few men in power, with great personal magnetism, were able to influence and organize the minds of the common people to such a degree of mass hypnotism, that the entire nation believed it had a true cause to fight. Many of us watched and history books have recorded the militarist build-up of Fascism and Naziism, and, because of the evil it spawned that the free world had to fight against, we eventually witnessed the final downfall and disaster brought to these misguided people who allowed their minds to be warped by avaricious despots seeking only greater power. Unity in a country is a fine thing when it is directed into channels for the good of its people, but when it seeks to persecute others in order to gain its ends, it becomes a thing of evil and a triumph for the negative forces.

Crushing the evil forces of World War II, however, did not bring peace to the world, and very soon thereafter, and for exactly the same reason, i.e., a few men in power masterminding the masses, we found ourselves involved in the long, drawn-out "cold war" with the U.S.S.R., and hovering on the brink of a third global war that would well end in total annihilation of every living creature on this planet. We can perhaps take some comfort from the fact that the odds against *anyone* surviving a nuclear war are so great that it is very unlikely that either side will be the first to press the panic button, and maybe it is for this reason that the Russians are turning to a more subtle weapon—the manipulation of man's mind. Their success with the Pavlovian experiments and the subsequent "brainwashing" techniques, led them a step further—the establishment of an extensive physical research program, with the main emphasis on mental telepathy and ESP. How far they have gone with this program, we do not know, but one well-known American columnist found it necessary to warn the U.S. government that the newly-developed Russian technique of "cloud busting" (an expression used to describe the production of physical effects by intense mental concentration) would bear their close investigation. The Soviets evidently realize the potentialities of the power of thought far better than we do, and we must remember that power of any kind can be used for either good or evil.

These are some of the factors we are facing in the battle of Man's mind on the physical plane. But what of the metaphysical influences at work on us—the invisible but all-power full forces on the purely mental plane? Whether we realize it or not, we are equally susceptible, if not more so at the subconscious level, to these more subtle influences. Man's brain, which in reality operates on the metaphysical plane, is like a two-way radio that transmits and receives messages along the airwaves of the universe—and his receiving mechanism is open to thoughts both good and bad, which we either accept or reject according to our stage of evolution. Most of us are well aware of the truth of mental telepathy and many of us have had personal experiences of thought communication between loved ones often thousands of miles away. But what of special thoughts being beamed at us deliberately for a specific purpose, at both the conscious and subconscious levels, from another plane of existence?

Messages received through esoteric sources, purporting to come from Space Brothers who take an active interest in the spiritual welfare of the inhabitants of our planet, warn us that an even greater conflict is being fought on the metaphysical plane where intelligent beings of both a higher and a lower spiritual order than ourselves, are waging a fierce battle for Man's mind. The lower or negative forces, damned themselves by wrong thinking, are projecting strong thoughts Earthward in an attempt to bring about our spiritual downfall. On the other hand, the spiritual guardians of our planet are concentrating equally hard on sending out positive thoughts of goodwill and brotherly love. Thus we are being bombarded on the metaphysical plane by two conflicting schools of thought and, free will being the criterion of spiritual advancement, it is left to us which we choose to accept. However, from a purely logical point of view, if we want to save ourselves a lot of sorrow both in this life and lives to come, we should arm ourselves mentally against the onslaught of negative thoughts.

This is no time for confused or apathetic thinking—often the future breeding-ground of negative thoughts. Nor should we be just receivers and disseminators of the thoughts we pick up. Rather, we should get on the transmitting end and constantly project positive thoughts of goodwill to all. Every positive thought neutralizes a negative thought, so we shall be serving not only ourselves but all humanity.

In the final analysis, there are two simple, clear-cut maxims to be observed for complete protection from the negative forces at work on this planet: (1) acknowledgment and love of God as the Father of all Creation, and (2) brotherly love extended to *all* God's creatures throughout the universe. Anything else that interferes with these two beliefs should be vigor-

ously rejected. Further, if we return love for hate, hate will die of malnutrition, for it can only feed on returned hatred. Let us rather pray for spiritual enlightenment for these wretched souls who seek to harm us."

• • •
The Soulless Ones

It is only during the last quarter of a century that information regarding these sinister efforts to control the human race have come to our attention, due primarily to the likes of such dedicated "soldiers" for humankind as William Cooper, Dr. Antony C. Sutton, Riley Crabb, Alfred Bielek, Ray Palmer, Richard Shaver and a handful of others who have risked life and limb—setting aside all personal reward—to expose this global plot against humanity.

But who—you make ask, and have every reason to want to know—precisely is behind this attempt at mental and physical slavery and how is it possible they have gained such control over all of us?

The answer is manyfold and demands various explanations as set forth by those who have actually penetrated the inner workings of the *negative forces* who are referred to throughout the Bible as *The Beast* whose number is *666* (to be explained fully later).

Yahshua ben Yahweh identifies these demented individuals as "the soulless ones" who, he maintains, came here long ago "from another star system to become the uninvited inhabitants of earth. With technological wizardry, they influenced every aspect of our lives. They manipulated the genetic pattern. They altered the very fabric of thought. And they created a counterfeit race of soulless human automatons programmed to control us and our civilizations in the ways of death."

Yahshua further contends that "there is a small group of powerful, behind-the-scenes rulers who have been manipulating the affairs of Earth toward their own ends for years, if not centuries."

One of those, whom Yahshua of the Temple of Yahweh (Box 412, Ipswich, Old Queenslands, Australia 4305) calls upon in his writings for clarification is one Dr. Anthony C. Sutton who, as the author of a series of works, "claims to have come across secret documents that reveal a terrifying, long-range conspiracy that seeks to control our lives from cradle to grave, a goal that, if brought about, would turn this world into a closed system, a totalitarian nightmare as frightening as anything George Orwell could have imagined. Many people believe we are well down the track to just such a global nightmare, a New Dark Age."

Now let us allow this representative for all of us to describe this plot in his own words.

• • •

These evil elites, according to Dr. Sutton, already have control of education, the political parties, private banking firms, major law firms, the media and philanthropic foundations. They also have dominant influence in Western governments.

Is there a metaphysical explanation for the evil in our world? What is the real driving force behind such plutocratic groups that seek total world domination and control? What drives these oligarchs, scattered among every nation, race, people and culture, in their quest to enslave humanity to do their bidding? Is there a counterfeit race, parallel to the human race, that is metaphysically programmed to do evil?

Cosmic Conspiracy?

Anthony Roberts wrote in *The Dark Gods:* "The idea that the human race has been consistently plagued throughout its history by 'dark forces' is of course not a new one. All religions make reference to the 'powers of evil' and have elaborate hierarchies of spirits, angels and demons engaged in an endless struggle for mastery of the cosmic environment and, incidentally, human destiny. The great pagan religions that preceded Christianity and Islam were all possessed of an intimate knowledge of these spiritual forces, categorizing them as gods and goddesses, fairies and elementals, and various personifications of the diverse energies of nature. Far back in the depths of so-called 'prehistory' it is now known that the human race was aware of, and paid homage to, transcendent beings that existed outside the realms of temporary reality but manifested within it. All over the world these beings are variously represented among the detritus of religious experience, leaving a residue in philosophy, art, architecture and, most important of all, in the wondering souls of this planet's most dominant life-form. In nearly every culture, past and present, the religious ethos consistently takes on a polarizingly dualistic form."

In the old writings of the Essenes we read of a war between the "Children of Darkness" and the "Children of Light." The early Christian Church Fathers also wrote of the "seed [offspring] of the wicked one [Satan[." The following quotations may all be found in *The Anti-Nicene Fathers:* "Flee, therefore, those evil offshoots (of Satan), which produce death-bearing fruit,...These men are not the planting of the Father, but are an accused brood. And says the Lord, Let every plant which my heavenly Father has not planted be rooted up. For if they had been branches of the Father, they would not have been enemies of the cross of glory. Keep yourselves, then, from those evil plants which Jesus Christ does not tend, but that wild beast, the destroyer of men, because they are not the planting of the father, but the seed of the wicked one."

One of the greatest Christian evangelists of this century, William Branham, taught, based on *Genesis* chapter 3, verse 15, that there was a literal seed of the Serpent. A 'counterfeit creation' who, under the control of their father Satan, stood in opposition to the Children of God.

Where did this doctrine of the Serpent seed originate? Does the collection of ancient writings, known to us as the Bible, confirm that there are literal children of the devil in this world? In these Scriptures can we find an explanation for the evil in our world?

The Beginning

The Christian fundamentalist who insists on an extremely literal interpretation of the Biblical creation story, complete with fruit, green trees and a hissing snake, is sadly missing the profound metaphysical meaning. The origin of Man and the subsequent 'fall' described in *Genesis* is an allegorical explanation of what happened. Allegory is a way to describe something that is profound in terms of something simple. An extremely literal interpretation of the allegory makes the symbolic allegorical language more important than what it is meant to represent.

To understand what has been called 'the greatest question in the Holy Bible' we must turn to the opening chapters of *Genesis* in the Old Testament. By examining the meaning of the Hebrew words used in the first four chapters of *Genesis* we can arrive at the true meaning.

And Yahweh God said to the Serpent: "And I will put enmity between thee and the woman, and between thy seed and her seed; it shall bruise thy head, and thou shalt bruise his heel." (*Genesis* 3:125).

Now let us start at the beginning. Satan, of course, was not a Serpent. The thing that deceived Eve and seduced Eve was not a snake wriggling on the ground. The Hebrew word "nachash" means "enchanter" or "magician." A fallen angel, retaining still a lot of his angelic powers, no doubt could be very much an enchanter and a magician. Remember, God speaking to this Serpent said: "And I will put enmity between thee and the woman, and between THY SEED and her seed." Here the Yahweh is speaking to Satan, the fallen Archangel, and plainly states Satan is to have seed or offspring. Most Christians teach that this verse relating to the seed of the woman foreshadows Jesus Christ. However, they seem unable or reluctant to admit that God here declared that Satan, too, was to have a seed. They are willing to concede that Eve's seed was a physical human seed (that brought forth Christ); but they contend there is no physical offspring of Satan.

In many cases in the New Testament it is recorded that Jesus Christ referred to certain individuals as a "generation of vipers" (*Matthew* 12:34; 23:33), as "hypocrites" (*Matthew* 22:18; 23:13–39), and as "sons of Satan," addressing them in these words: "Ye are of your father the devil, and the lusts of your father ye will do. He was a murderer from the beginning, and abode not in the truth, because there is no truth in him. When he speaketh a lie, he speaketh of his own: for he is a liar, and the father of it." (*John* 8:44). This reference obviously does make a distinction between all men and some men. Note that Jesus clearly identified literal descendants of the devil. He did not say they were simply followers of the devil. Nor did he state they were wicked because of their particular religious viewpoint.

The Controllers

The author of *The Soulless One* notes: "Let me hasten to assure you, then, that there do exist upon the planet creatures who did not come forth from God—who are the counterfeit of the real manifestation. Many of these are consciously in league with the insidious purposes of the powers of darkness. They seek through conspiracy and plot to ravish the world of its good, to set brother against brother, to confuse, disturb, and destroy harmonies wherever they exist. These function on the physical plane, utilizing and directing their energies in a concerted effort against the light. They are, however, the pawns of "spiritual wickedness in high places." And the league of the spiritually negative forces with these embodied wicked individuals has resulted in the slaughter of many noble souls down through the ages."

Further in his book the writer makes the following startling observation: "In the Bible these soulless beings are referred to throughout as "the wicked," for they have seen to it that all more specific descriptions of their race have been removed—lest mankind discover them and rise in righteous indignation against their overlords. And thus the death of John the Baptist and that of Jesus the Christ were brought about by the counterfeit race who for thousands of years have set brother against brother, race against race, and have caused the children of God to blame one another for the murders of the saints.

Today, as always, they occupy positions of authority and financial power. They have gained control of the destiny of empires, and they seek ever to thwart the pure purposes of God. The injudicious use of taxation exerted by their direction has placed an unconscionable yoke upon the neck of humanity.

The Serpent's seed is today sown among all nations, races and peoples. A counterfeit race, they are the real controllers of this world order. For centuries they have been restrained by the forces of Yahweh, but now in the last days of this present cycle they have been unleashed. "Woe to the inhabiters of the earth and of the soul for the devil to come down unto you, having great wrath, because he knoweth that he hath but a short time." (*Revelation* 12:12)

Jesus told His disciples that the children of the devil can be identified by their actions. Thus John wrote: "In this the children of God are manifest, and the children of the devil: whosoever doeth not righteousness is not of God, neither he that loveth not his brother." Even within these words there is a great mystery that can only be fully comprehended by the Elect.

Our age is certainly one of turmoil and a

metaphysical separation. The battle lines are being drawn between the two seeds of Genesis, the true beings (women's seed) and the counterfeit beings (Serpent's seed). The Scriptural identification of these two seedlines only brings into the physical the great metaphysical truth. Those who are of the Holy Seed of the women, the Children of Light, are even now being called out, awakened, separated and prepared for divine service.

• • •

Man's Secret Origin

Much of what we think we know about the planet we live on is false information!

Those who are part of this "controlling factor" we are here to expose have shifted "historical facts" for their own benefit...they have—in essence—perverted and reshapen our past so as to do the most good for themselves. They believe that the masses should be kept in total darkness about those things that are best kept secret. Yet there are in our midst a few masters who have gone against the grain of acceptable thinking to shatter those myths that have been forced upon us for centuries.

There is—in reality—a secret origin for humankind that has been left out of our text books. It is not taught either in our schools or universities, and certainly our self-defined "religious leaders" have never even thought about sharing this knowledge with their flock whom they prefer to keep in ignorance, again as part of this overall control factor.

Let's get one thing perfectly clear: "Michael X" is in no way, shape or form related to Malcolm X, the spiritual leader for many black people. Michael X is, in actuality, a spiritual leader for all races and creeds who has fought for many years to present the hidden wisdom of the ancients to a handful of patient and trusting students who have listened to that inner call to spiritual freedom that comes when we realize that we have long been oppressed by those many ministers who claim to have our welfare and education at heart. Michael X is a master, a mystic, a channel, a prophet, a free soul—he is all the things that we need to find in our search for universal truth. Michael X, in one of his privately circulated "mystic monographs," does much to explain the actual secret origin of humankind and the role that beings from other planets and other dimensions

alongside our own have played in our fight to ascend the ladder of spiritual knowledge. His words are at all times simple and elegant and are made for you and me:

Important Mystical Knowledge

Did you ever wonder about how you came to be on this planet? Where did you—and the other billions of human inhabitants of this Earth—come from in the first place? What are the real facts?

You're going to be astounded and amazed when you find out the whole story of man's secret origin! You'll probably say to yourself "Why wasn't this information brought to my attention before?" and "Why wasn't I taught this kind of knowledge in school, so I could have been making good use of it all these years? Why? Why? Why?

Well, for one thing, this is MYSTIC KNOWLEDGE. You can't expect to learn it in school, unless of course, it's a Mystic School. How many Mystic Schools are there? You can count them on the fingers of one hand. This is SECRET KNOWLEDGE. It's not commonly known at all. In fact, it is so rare and uncommon that, as a general rule, you have to search diligently for it. That's why I'm going to give you certain facts—some golden links in the chain of your GOOD—which have been so long withheld from you. I believe you are now ready for the great TRUTHS!

Where Did Man Come From?

The fact is, Earthman is not the only tenant of this universe. He only thinks he is. That is where he makes a big mistake. There are countless other Solar Systems throughout this vast universe in which highly intelligent human life forms are, at this very moment, living and breathing the same as you and I! Many of those Systems are not only hundreds or thousands, but MILLIONS of years in advance of ours—and the beings who inhabit those other "planetary chains" have a great deal to do with YOUR secret origin.

According to many of the ancient teachings, ALL of the planets of this Solar System are inhabited by intelligent beings. Now I did not say PHYSICAL HUMAN BEINGS, such as are on Earth. It's mightily important for you to realize that some of the planets in our System are peopled only by ETHERIC BEINGS. They don't have physical bodies like we do. But they do have a very efficient etheric body that they are very proud of, and which serves them nicely in many ways.

All beings—whether in physical or etheric form—are of course in varying grades of intelligence or "awareness of that which is." Each planet, for example, in our System, is said to be actually a "School of Life" wherein the intelligent beings are able to learn certain vitally essential lessons in the true art of living.

Just as in any school, the idea is for all the individuals who dwell on any planet, to master the various "rules" or "laws" of life. This is accomplished, of course, by learning how to consciously expand awareness of the secret principles upon which your mind and your body and the entire universe are run.

When this is accomplished—and ONLY then —to the extent that an individual actually applies the knowledge he gains, he or she is permitted to "graduate" to another planet more advanced in the planetary scheme, where NEW LESSONS are learned. In this way, we progress from glory to glory—constantly unfolding our higher Godlike powers!

Since there are a total of nine planets revolving around the Sun, it seems we Earthlings have Nine Schools to attend before we complete our "Course of Study" in this Solar System.

Each "School Term" lasts 2500 years. (Figuring in Cosmic Time this is not as long as you might think.) At the end of that planetary cycle, some evolutionary cataclysm usually occurs (such as the Glacial Age, the Deluge, a Polar Shift, etc.) which, quite naturally, eliminates the "mass-minded" or the ones who "failed" in the earthly School of Life.

At the crucial time, however, some great Teacher of Light and Love appears on the planet. His purpose is to guide and direct the next class of intelligent beings who are arriving on the earthly scene for the first time. Jesus, Buddha, Zoroaster, Lao-Tse, Hermes Trismegistus, and Sanat Kumara (The Ancient of the Days) were among the greatest of these Teachers. You could name many others.

What I am about to give you now is not new information. Rather, it is ages old. In fact, it is part of a body of Secret Knowledge that is called the *Ageless Wisdom*, for it is eternal. Some of this information is *older than our planet itself* (meaning it was given to us by higher intelli-

gences from other planets and other systems). Fortunately for you and me and other sincere Seekers, this marvelous body of knowledge has been preserved by a rare few of Earth's mystic masters in India, Tibet, Europe and America. The "Saucer Story" for instance, is an amazingly ancient story, known to certain advanced Earthlings for many, many centuries.

Before revealing the full story, I shall first "condition" your mind to several facts about interplanetary or space flight. The first thing to realize is that SPACE FLIGHT IS POSSIBLE, as our limited forays into orbit around this planet and to the Moon demonstrate. Our men of science on Earth are even now experimenting in the building of our own "discs."

This being so, what, I ask you, is there to have prevented some *other* planet, more highly advanced than our Earth, from having reached the same conclusion *long ago?* And, having reached such a definite conclusion, what is there to have stopped them from building a Space Ship in the logical form of a Flying Disc, and, using a better power than rocket power, conquering Space?

Let us carry this thought a little further. Why do you think it is so difficult, so contrary to the thinking habits of our modern scientists, to accept the idea that Flying Saucers already exist?

I will tell you why. If our "learned" scientists were to admit the existence of Spacecraft and Beings from other worlds, they would be admitting that our planet Earth is NOT the one and only planet in the Universe that has produced highly intelligent life forms. To admit such a thing would be a terrible blow to man's proud ego. It would force man to accept the fact that Earth is not the advanced place some of us think it is. Earth Man doesn't like to admit this.

The truth, according to ancient Hindu writings, is that Earth is but a "baby" in comparison to other planets in the universe. For example, Venus is *one entire chain* (period of evolution) *in advance of ours.* Therefore, the intelligences of Venus are very highly evolved. This had to be, for the Venusian Race is ancient beyond belief in the sense that it originated many *millions* of years ago.

As for the story of the first consciously awakened Man on Earth, it really begins in the year 18,617,841 B.C. In order words, the date of our epic is eighteen million, six hundred and seventeen thousand, eight hundred and forty-one years before the birth of Christ.

In that momentous year—as revealed by ancient Hindu writings—the first space ship came from the planet Venus, to land here on planet Earth. From Venus, "The Home of the Gods," came Sanat Kumara (The Lord of the Flame) with his four Great Lords and one hundred assistants. These shining beings saw to it that human souls became incarnated in physical bodies on Earth.

Until the arrival on Earth of Sanat Kumara from Venus, Man did not have conscious awareness. He was the product of *long ages of slow evolving* upon planet Earth. Physically he resembled Man as we know him today; but mentally he was like the animals. That is, he lived only in his subconscious. The front section of his brain was asleep.

When the Lord of the Flame saw the poor mindless thing that was Man, he felt moved to assist directly in Man's unfoldment. He used his spiritual powers to awaken the centers of individuality in the Earth Man.

This fact is the "missing link" in the evolution of Man on this planet.

The Lord Sanat Kumara called the first consciously awakened man Adam, in tribute to the Venusian Lords who belonged to the Adamic Race of Venus. At the time of his conscious awakening, Adam's body was androgynous or bisexual. He was a twofold being, having both male and female components perfectly balanced within his own physical body. To facilitate the propagation of offspring, Sanat Kumara changed the sex polarity of Adam from bisexual to unisexual. This led to the creation of Eve, who became Adam's mate.

Adam and Eve

Adam and Eve were blessed with children and the Adamic line branched out to cover the entire face of the globe. All of us here on Earth —regardless of color, or of "belief-conditioning"—are direct descendants of Adam and Eve; and indirect descendants of the Adamic Race of Venus.

After Sanat Kumara and his helpers had finished their work of starting a physical race of Mankind on Earth, they returned again to Venus and left man to evolve higher up the ladder of Life through his own personal efforts and illuminating experiences. It was only right that the Lord Thinkers should leave Man then, for

those brilliant Beings belonged to *an entirely different Life Chain than ours.*

As the centuries of time rolled by, men of Earth learned many secrets of universal power, secrets that most people of today believe to be strictly modern and "new" discoveries of science. The hidden truth, however, is that what we call new is "old stuff" to the Saucer People of the inhabited planets in space. They've been masters of a "Secret Science" of the universe that is so ancient, its origin is lost in the mists of time. Some of their truths are not millions, but billions and trillions of years old. Much of the knowledge has been passed from one planet to another, such as the "formula" for successful Space Flight, Degravitation, Telethought, etc., etc. There simply is_nothing essentially NEW under the sun, though our modern science likes to think so.

As Man's IQ increased, wonderful civilizations such as those from Atlantis, Lemuria and Mu were built, but each time they fell apart, or were destroyed chiefly through misuse of their own great powers. In addition to the calamitous results of human foolishness, Nature itself rebelled many times. Great planetary cataclysms occurred, due to a sudden shifting of the poles of the Earth. The Great Deluge, or Flood, was one of these. It is important, because it is part of the whole amazing story of Flying Saucers, the Space People, who they are and what their seemingly "mysterious" purpose really is.

Way back in the days of Noah, the Earth shifted its poles. At once a monstrous Tidal Wave swept over all of the then-populated areas of the world, destroying nearly all living beings. All the marvelous ancient records, manuscripts, secrets, etc., were lost to mankind, and man was forced to begin again his long upward climb toward the Light. Did I say ALL was lost? Not quite all. We must not forget the fabulous "Bible in Stone"—THE GREAT PYRAMID OF EGYPT! Let us now see how the Great Pyramid "ties in" to the picture.

Shortly before the Noaic Deluge took place, the Saucer People realized that such a disaster was impending. They could tell, from their observations made in space, that the Earth was about to SHIFT POSITION. In the short time remaining before the "shift" was to occur, the Saucer People—Venusians—went into positive action on behalf of humanity's present and future welfare. The Lords of Venus determined to build an "altar to the Lord in the midst of the land of Egypt, and a pillar at the border thereof to the Lord. And it shall be for a SIGN and for a WITNESS unto the Lord of Hosts in the land of Egypt."—Isaiah 19:19–20.

You no doubt are aware that the Great Pyramid was designed by beings of extraordinary intelligence. The perfect knowledge of Astronomy revealed by the Pyramid was "first-hand" knowledge possessed by those Masters of Space and Time, the Lords of Venus!

Inner teaching has it that the Lord Thinkers directed one of Earth's wisest mortals, King Thothmus, as to HOW the entire edifice was to be constructed. Thothmus was a great mystic, and cooperated fully with the Venusians, for he understood that the building of the Great Pyramid would serve FIVE vital purposes:

1. To preserve Secret Knowledge on Earth.
2. To prophesy the future of Earthmen.
3. To serve as a Temple of Mystic Truth.
4. To be a SIGN or landmark for Space Ships.
5. To be a WITNESS unto the Lord of Hosts.

As you know, certain principles of construction were used that are still the wonder of the world, even today. For instance, so accurately were the stones interlocked in the Pyramid that you can scarcely insert a calling card between the blocks, today.

The "Lord of Hosts" refers to that highly evolved and mighty being, Jesus Christ, whose kingdom was of "another world" (not of this world)—a planet in our Solar System that is far ahead of us in spiritual unfoldment. This highly spiritual soul was born of Earth, and became an outstanding Teacher of Light and Love.

So the Pyramid was built and the Knowledge of Ages concealed within its stone walls, to endure down through the centuries. Noah, a sincere seeker of spiritual Light, was contacted by the Saucer People and warned of the planetary shifting that was soon to destroy the Men of Planet Three (Earth). So Noah built an Ark as directed.

Then The Earth Shook Terribly!

And the oceans ROARED over the land, flooding ALL of the populated areas. "And the waters prevailed exceedingly upon the Earth; and all the high hills, that were under the whole heaven, were covered. Fifteen cubits upward did the waters prevail; and the MOUN-

TAINS were covered. And ALL FLESH DIED that moved upon the Earth, both of fowl, and of cattle, and of beast, and of every creeping thing upon the Earth, and EVERY MAN. All in whose nostrils was the breath of life, of ALL that was in the dry land, died."—Genesis 7:19.

NOAH and his few faithful followers were, of course, spared, so that the Race could continue as the Lord Thinkers had planned. And so it has continued to this day.

Only one thing is wrong. Some of us Earthlings, too many of us, in fact, have refused to grow as fast in the spiritual department of life as we have grown in the mental, technical and material phases of living. How very deplorable! We've been told time and time again, "With all thy getting, get understanding!" That means SPIRITUAL WISDOM does it not? What do you think our nation, in fact our whole world NEEDS most right now? More Guided Rocket Missiles? More Supersonic Jet Bombers? More A-Bombs and H-Bombs in our "stockpile"?

No. A million times NO! You know the answer as well as I. We need a dynamic SPIRITUAL AWAKENING! We need to send out a great LOVE-RAY to our fellow man in every country, and lift him up into a higher kind of "response." But in order to send out such a Love-Ray, we must ourselves, *individually*, as well as collectively, feel and experience this dynamic SPIRITUAL AWAKENING. We must cease smothering our spiritual wisdom. We must refuse to let it be *choked out* by the wasted attentions we give to matters that are NOT Spiritual. Only the true LOVE-RAY (which our Greatest of Teachers explained to us 2,000 years ago) can nullify the effect of the horrible DEATH-RAY that man keeps "tinkering" with.

This "Knower" within is the revealer of all true wisdom and can be contacted by keeping your attention upon the Great True Self, or God-Presence within your own heart. It is only by devotion to this spiritual center within you that the "Knower" reveals true wisdom. The wisest men who ever lived on earth attained wisdom in this way!

The Time When Serpents Overran The Earth

If we can fault Michael X in his use of the most elegant terms to define the secret origin of humankind, it is in the fact that he manages to paint such a rosy picture of our planet and the solar system where we find ourselves but mere residents among many trillions of occupants. There is, let us not forget, also a much more sinister, very negative side to our historical origins that Wilbert Smith and Yahshua ben Yahweh spoke of earlier in these pages.

For this hidden history of the Earth also includes the existence of a secret society known as the Serpent Race who have coexisted alongside of humankind since the very dawn of time on our planet. Legend has it that these beings came here from Venus and occupied the surface of Earth for a brief period but abandoned it because conditions here were not very favorable to them. They were of great size and had scaly bodies and large frog-like eyes, and were advanced mentally, though morally and spiritually they had not evolved and were said to be extremely cruel and vicious. In order to survive on our planet they eventually settled inside our world, where they built large cities and took over an already existing tunnel system constructed by those who escaped from Atlantis when it finally collapsed as a civilization.

Lecturer and philosopher Riley Crabb has spent many years combing through ancient texts attempting to locate references to these serpent beings and has come up with some very interesting findings.

Mr. Crabb notes:

"If the Serpent Race did indeed overrun our planet thousands of years ago, they would have left some record of their presence. This we find in the serpent legends and myths of every race. But the Serpent who walks like a man seems to have left his portrait also, in stone, here and there on this planet. Researcher Robert Dickhoff gives a good example of this in a photo of the stone carving of the Babylonian God, Ashur, in his book *Agharta*. At right is a line drawing made from the photo. As he says, 'a humanoid deity, eagle-headed, winged, but otherwise like humans.'

In his book *The Road in the Sky*, George Hunt Williamson compares a photo of one of the huge stone statues he found of the Marcahuasi plateau in Peru, with a photo of the Egyptian god, Thoueris, in the Cairo Museum. The similarity is remarkable. The head of Thoueris has the same general shape as that of Ashur on this page, though perhaps closer to a hippopotamus in appearance. Also, Thoueris is potbellied and unclothed, and without wings or scales.

The rather mysterious writer who preferred to only by the name of "Branton" has written extensively on this topic. His confidential monograph, titled *The Reality of the Serpent Race and The Subterranean Origin of UFOs* (available for $25 from Inner Light Publications, Box 753, New Brunswick, NJ 08903), packs a real wallop and should serve—he says—as a manual to "be used by members of the 'Human Resistance' as a guide to alien strategy!"

In his tome, Branton draws from many sources to expose the whys and wherefores of the Serpent Race. A few of the better quotes he uncovers for us are reproduced below:

Created Humans?

Some time ago a writer named Robin Collyns suggested in an article that the Serpent Race has had great influence throughout history. Collyns was of the opinion that the Serpent Race created man and planted him here on this planet.

"...Old Sumerian, Babylonian, Egyptian, and Greek legends refer to 'serpent' deities who were believed to have once resided in the 'underworld.' The Garden of Eden in this context takes on additional interest and significance, possibly of paramount importance. Pristine legends from Australia and the Pacific islands offer innumerable references to serpent deities/beings who were anciently associated with the creation enigma in the area. (*Note:* There are in fact accounts of caverns in Australia, particularly in Black Mountain, North Queensland and the Nullarbor caves in southern Australia—which have been the site of numerous disappearances. Also, there are stories of ancient tunnels beneath the Polynesian islands that are known only to the 'kahunase' or 'witch doctors,' allegedly inhabited by nonhuman beings.) The spiral serpent symbol is found throughout the Pacific and is associated universally with the creation enigma.

From earliest days, the serpent symbol is to be seen in many parts of the world, but undoubtedly the most fascinating portrayal is a detail on an Egyptian magical papyrus in the British Museum depicting a serpent encompassed by a ray-emitting disk. The most unusual form of the serpent symbol is a spiral representing a coiled snake; it has been discovered as petroglyphs and other pictorial representations in Britain, Greece, Malta, and Egypt, as pottery designs in New Mexico; as ground drawings on the Nazca Plateau, Peru, and throughout the Pacific Islands."

(*Note:* Nearly every site mentioned here has been the site of intense subterranean activity.)

Collins concludes: "...Aborigine legends indicate that the serpent beings were not above waging war, and an identical parallel is also mentioned in the Hindu legends of the Nagas, serpent beings who came from one of seven worlds. (*Note:* The 'underworld' of Patala is believed by the Hindus to be the home of the serpent beings and is said to consist of Seven levels, that lie beneath the general region of Hindustan or the Far East.)

"Aborigine legends (state that) the serpent beings waged many wars around Ayers Rock, and the vertical gutters in Ayers Rock testify to these wars."

In *The Worship of the Serpent,* the Rev. John Bathurst Deane made the following statements

"...One of (the) five builders of Thebes was named after the serpent-god of the Phoenicians, OFHION...The first altar erected by Cyclops at Athens, was to 'Ops,' the serpent-deity...The symbolical worship of the serpent was so common in Greece, that Justin Martyr accuses the Greeks of introducing it into the mysteries of all their gods. The Chinese...are said to be 'superstitious in choosing a plot of ground to erect a dwelling-house or sepulchre: conferring it with the head, tail and feet of diverse dragons which live *under our earth.*" Mr. Bathurst also states that hierograms or depictions of a circle (representing the sun) with wings and serpents emanating from it are predominant features "in the Persian, Egyptian, and Mexican hieroglyphics. China, Hindustan, Greece, Italy, and Asia Minor, distinctly but more rarely, exhibit it; and it has even been found in Britain." (THE WORSHIP OF THE SERPENT TRACED THROUGHOUT THE WORLD, by the Rev. John Bathurst Deane., London., J.G. & F. Rivington., 1833.)

In his book *Venomous Reptiles* (Charles Ceaibrer Sons, N.Y. 1969), author Sherman A. Minton, Jr., an expert on reptilian and amphibian biology, reveals some peculiar scientific facts concerning reptiles. These facts include the following: A) All reptiles have scales, B) All are cold-blooded, C) All lay eggs, D) All reptiles with well-developed limbs have clawed toes, E) THERE ARE LIZARDS WITH ELONGATED SNAKE-LIKE BODIES—A TYPE OF 'MISSING LINK' BETWEEN THE LIZARDS AND THE SNAKES) F) THE MODERN EVIDENCE (SCIENTIFIC) INDICATES THAT ALL MODERN SNAKES ONCE POSSESSED (IN THE DISTANT ANCESTRAL PAST) LIMBS THAT BECAME *ATROPHIED* THROUGH NON-USE, perhaps by the fact that they became aquatic or semiaquatic creatures (*Note:* Snakes, incidentally are both aquatic *and* land creatures, and can travel through either environment. I have personally seen snakes swim across rivers in the past. Not only Holy Scripture, but scientific evidence as well, indicates that snakes at one time in the past had limbs.) G) REPTILES WITH 'DEVELOPED LIMBS' USUALLY LIVE UNDERGROUND.

Venomous Reptiles also states the following: "...Cobras (according to legend) are descended from the Nagas, Serpent gods of Bharat, or ancient India. Their worship has been traced to prehistoric Dravidian times before the Aryan invasion of the subcontinent in approx. 1600 B.C. The Naga's power to inflict disproportionate physical damage or almost instantaneous death is explained in the Hindu Vedas as paralleling the energy of creation or fire." The book goes on to state that, The Naga's are said to have appeared at the birth of Guatama Siddharta, who later became "Buddha."

Note that the 'Serpent' also played a large part in the legends surrounding another Hindu religious figure—i.e. 'Krishna,' The ancient 'well' of Sheshna in Benares, India, is traditionally where The Yoga Aphorisms of Patanjali, a classic guide to students of Yoga, was written. This 'well' is said to be an entrance to one of the Naga's underworld lairs. The servants of the 'Lamb' teach that all men are equal UNDER God, whereas the 'Serpent' or 'Beast' teaches that some men are more 'divine' (gods) than others, resulting in horrible atrocities.

Note that the same pattern of deception we see here is apparently similar to that which was used against Eve as recorded in Genesis chapter 3. Satan inspired these misguided Hindu's (Eve's seed) with the blasphemous doctrines based upon the lie 'Ye shall be as gods,' a teaching that is at the heart of Yoga; i.e. that by tapping the so-called 'universal force' or 'serpent force,' one could gain supernatural powers and thereby become a 'god.' Such an occult practice was carried out by Adolph Hitler and the Theosophist-Rosicrucian-Jesuit-etc.-connected occultists who surrounded him, but instead of tapping into the mythical 'universal force' they opened themselves up to demonic powers that masqueraded behind the deceptive facade of this pantheistic 'force.' How else could one explain the horrible atrocities that were carried out by the Nazi's during WW II? There may be indications that Hitler's occult societies were in contact with this serpent race. These include the fact that Hitler had himself read The Coming Race, written by Rosicrucian Grandmaster Bulwer Lytton, describing an underground race that 'tapped' a supposed force called 'vril,' identical to the Hindu 'serpent force.' Hitler subsequently sent out numerous secret expeditions to explore mines and caverns in different parts of the world. A strange cult of Tibetan occultist-monks were found in some of the bombed-out ruins in Berlin at the end of the war, they had been killed by the blasts. There were rumors that monks from the Himalayas (beneath

which one of the major concentrations of the Naga's or Serpent Race is said to exist) were secretly working with Hitler in order to establish a demonic world religion., etc.

Venomous Reptiles' also states that Sheshna's well may be seen today in Benares, India, and according to Minton, "It has 40 steps leading down into a circular depression and then to a stone door covered with carved cobras. This is said to lead to PATALA, the reptile netherworld" (i.e. underworld).

It is peculiar that the major center of mysticism in Tibet is a huge shrine called THE PATALA, that has been rumored for years to be built over caverns and tunnels of very ancient origin. Buddhist occultists like Robert Dickhoff and others have alleged that beneath Central Asia there is an ancient subterranean realm known as 'Agharta,' which subterranean human and reptilian beings have fought over in order to gain possession of the ancient city which apparently was constructed in predeluvian times. There are two other books which were written by travelers in the region that describe this subterranean realm; these are Beasts, Men and Gods, by Ferdinand Ossendowski and Shambhala, by Nicholas Roerich. My impression of these writings is that although they describe numerous accounts of surface peoples who in ancient times migrated to this underground world and now reside there utilizing an advanced form of technology, many of these accounts are clouded by the confusion and misinformation that often accompanies occultic involvement, which many in these regions are definitely involved with.

UFOs, Grays and Serpents

In his book, On the Shores of Endless Worlds, Andrew Tomas gives some more recent information concerning the 'Nagas' or 'Serpent People'. In his book, Mr. Tomas interviewed Nicholas Roerich who indicated that the 'Serpent People' and the 'UFO' phenomena were tied-in with each other. Tomas also related the account of a Tibetan man who allegedly encountered the 'Nagas' first-hand. He claimed that they were Serpent People, or reptilian beings with a humanoid form, who lived in caverns beneath the earth. The source claimed that the Nagas have a major base or lair beneath the mountains adjacent to Lake Manosowar in Tibet, which contains chambers as large and complex as the 'Taj Mahol,' if not more so.

Several Hindu traditions also allege that the Nagas can sometimes masquerade themselves in quasi-human form, at times to the point that it is difficult to determine or distinguish their reptilian features, although their eyes and even their breath might at times give them away. Some years ago NBC produced a mini-series called *V* that depicted human-like beings who came to earth under the guise of 'space brothers' who merely wished to save man from destruction, that is, until some discovered that these 'chameleons' were actually reptilian in nature, and were here to conquer us.

But that's just all science fiction, right? Actually this concept is not at all recent, but dates back to accounts given throughout Hindustan history concerning this supernaturally empowered, subterranean, reptilian race. In fact (the readers may accept this or disregard it as they like) a friend of mine who has for several years been investigating both aerial and subsurface phenomena, and especially the 'reptilian' connection to both phenomena, told me at about the time this series was coming out that he had been working with some friends in Hollywood to produce a movie that, although fictionalized, was to have it's basis in actual accounts that had been uncovered through the research he and others had been involved with.

This individual told me that an NBC "spy" saw the script before his friends in Hollywood were able to gather the funds and all else necessary to produce this movie. NBC had already rewritten the script, produced and aired the mini-series *V*, which was seen nationwide. So goes the dog-eat-dog competitive nature of Hollywood, etc., Now the reader will have to make his or her own determination on this. Was my source telling the truth? I'm convinced he was. But the point I want to make here is that such 'chameleon' entities have actually been described. John Lear, in a letter to researcher 'Jason Bishop' (pseudonym, at his request) dated October 6, 1990, revealed that a source of his (a Security Officer working in the tunnels beneath the Nevada Test Site) informed him that among the different types of reptilian creatures, of which five were referred to, reportedly seen in the deeper intersecting caverns, one of them is allegedly very similar to those depicted in the movie-series *V* (which, as we've said, in turn, was initially inspired by actual research and

findings). Lear, Cooper, and many others claim that a subterranean connection between Dulce and Groom Lake does exist via an installation beneath Page, Arizona (*Note:* One source claimed that when Hoover dam near Las Vegas was being built, workers blasted their way into huge caverns. Could the Page-Glen Canyon dam also be connected to large cavities containing a hydroelectric-powered "base"?). But this may have some significance, especially when we consider that beings of a somewhat similar nature have also been reported at Dulce, New Mexico.

Snakes Under Glass

A rare and very difficult to find publication that made the rounds in the late 1940s was the "Hefferlin Manuscript." Consisting of a hundred or more single space pages, the monograph was distributed mostly by "believers" who typed up five carbons at a time and passed them around to friends and associates. Over a period, the California-based group known as the Borderland Sciences Research Foundation reprinted some of the more exciting excerpts from the Hefferlin Manuscript, mostly those pertaining to a large underworld society and its structure. The Hefferlins—some said—were a husband and wife team who had been in the Navy and knew of the existence of a multi-leveled subterranean civilization, perhaps from personal expeditions downward.

Regarding the reality of the Serpent Race, the Hefferlins made several pronouncements after apparently having observed—first hand—these giant reptiles, some of which were preserved under glass for an unknown purpose (perhaps to eventually be revived to lead an all out attack on surface dwellers).

The Hefferlins reported what they saw in this manner:

"Within the corridor entrance of the ground level floor of the Temple (Rainbow City, the Antarctic) close to the back end, are three massive pillars supporting the ceiling at this spot. Almost directly behind these pillars and on the corridor's end wall, are pictures of three beings, two males, one on either side of a female figure. These pictures seem to be of a human cast in face and figure; but still have a haunting reptilian touch as well, as if of a smooth blending of the two types.

"Immediately below this area on the first and

second levels are rooms in a central position relative to the Temple Basement, and below these rooms are the third and fourth levels of a section. This section from the first level to the fifth level inclusive was hermetically sealed off from the upper structure, as well as from the rest of the Temple basement levels.

"In this upper room were found three serpentine humanoid bodies in upright transparent containers, and behind these three more of the same type, evidently consorts of the other three. The first three were the originals of the three pictured above on the corridor's end wall. In the area of the second level, immediately below this room, were found great numbers of similar humanoid serpentine bodies, and in the areas beneath this level, the third and fourth, reposing on beds stacked in tiers four high, lay vast numbers of these same types of figures. In the fifth level were animals and vegetation.

"This sealed-up section contained a strange mist-like gas, to hold in suspended animation or sleep of preservation all life the area contained. Through research efforts our scientists discovered that these humanoid serpentine bodies were reconstructed robot containers made from the flesh substance of the original bodies, which long ago had been serpent bodies with arms. The types of animals and vegetation were such as should never be seen on this Planet. They don't belong!

"In the human Ruler's apartment on the fifth level or floor above ground, well concealed in the wall of the living room of the apartment is a small, closet-like room. By a strange assortment of coils of odd shapes and other strange appearing apparatus concealed in the walls, very strange and exceedingly interesting things occur. A vision screen is at one end, and levels, a dial and green colored lens crystal are arranged at a control panel in one side wall. By following the book of instructions as found in a concealed drawer at the control panel, the mechanism became operative; and here was the key to most of the research that followed."

• • •
The Dero

Before his death in the 1970s, a Pennsylvania auto worker who heard "voices" through his welding gun wrote millions of profound words about underground beings, control of surface society, and the constant war being waged be-

tween a sinister group of subterranean dwellers he identified as the Dero, and the more benevolent Tero, both of whom occupy vast caverns located right beneath our feet.

Though ridiculed, scorned and laughed at by many, Richard Shaver stuck to his guns throughout his life to tell those few who were courageous enough to listen about the reality of these savage inner eartherians whom, Shaver insisted, actually kidnapped thousands of humans each year, kept them in small cages, controlled their minds through ancient ray machines, had all manner of perverted—and unthinkable—sex with their captives, and actually ate the flesh right off the bones of their kidnapped victims.

Supposedly, the Dero hope to eventually regain control of the surface, and have already learned how to control of minds of many world leaders to make them commit inhuman acts upon their citizens (including large scale wars). Shaver insisted that no one was safe from the sinister activities of the Dero and warned us about the true nature of UFOs; many of which, he concluded, actually came from inside the earth, and not from outer space. Some 40 years ago, Shaver actually wrote about the disappearance and abduction of humans by these inner earth forces, and shortly, we shall present the surprising story of what these craft we call UFOs actually want with us.

Probably the best synopsis I have seen of what has become known as the "Shaver Mystery" was crafted by the often-quoted Riley Crabb. Though Crabb did not accept all of what Mr. Shaver professed, he realized that there is much to his material that should be considered valid.

The Giant Elder Race, The Elder Gods of the Past

One of Richard Shaver's discoveries was the existence of a great race of beings who occupied this planet thousands upon thousands of years ago. Our planet, Earth, was in its Golden Age then. These super men were great scientists who built the tunnel system in the earth, and filled it with the great mechanical and electrical equipment they had developed and perfected.

Why do we have no record of this great race, nor of their achievements here on the surface of the planet? The surface was swept clean by the Great Deluge. The flood left no record, ex-

THE CONTROLLERS

cept in the caves. Also, this great race had millions of slaves, early Atlanteans perhaps. An all-out atomic war preceded the natural catastrophe. Millions of the slaves went into the Caverns for self-preservation while their masters got away in their space ships. With the surface too radioactive for life the slaves had to learn to live in the caves and like it.

The degenerate descendants of these Atlanteans are still there in the Caverns, according to Shaver, about fifty billion of them. That is an unbelievably fantastic figure. He also claimed that there is more living area in the Caverns than there is here on the surface. I can't believe that; yet without direct observation I cannot deny the possibility. Shaver claims that much of this Cavern equipment is still in good operating condition. How this can be after thousands of years of neglect I don't know. Degenerate human beings don't make good mechanics; nevertheless, Shaver claims that much of our trouble here on the surface of the earth is caused by the abandoned electronic equipment of the Elder Gods. Among other things, they left thought-projection machines, still usable, and still used by the abandoned ones to project mischievous, trouble-making thoughts into the minds of unsuspecting surface dwellers.

The Deros

They have good guys and bad guys in the Caverns, just as we have here on the surface. The bad ones are called Deros, shortened from the word abandondero. Evil seems to continually triumph over good in the Cavern world. That isn't so different from the surface, is it? As long as this is true not one secret or piece of equipment left by the Elders will ever get to the surface and be of any benefit to us.

What do these degenerate human beings look like? Shaver says they look like the trolls described in Peer Gynt, and in Sigrid Undset's novel, *Kristin Lavransdatter*. To these we might add the Nibelungs made famous in Wagnerian operas, and the Menehunes of Hawaiian mythology. Legends of misshapen "little people" are to be found all over the earth.

Shaver claims these Deros are the spirits behind the oracles in the temples. They also are the receivers and devourers of the sacrifices left on temple altars. They are the horders of wealth and the gifts to the Gods in the Caverns. To prove any of this is well nigh impossible.

Shaver on Flying Saucers

He claims that there are three kinds of Flying Saucers: those that come from outer space, those that come from the interior of the earth at the cavern entrances, and those that are illusionary projections. This third type, Shaver claims, are merely diversionary images created in the sky by Ray machines in the Caverns. These cause us to look in one direction while something else is going on in the heavens which they don't want us to see.

The degenerates who inhabit the Caverns are not building Saucers. They are just operating ancient flyers originally built and left there by the elder race, and still in good flying condition. These self-appointed guardians of the treasures in the Caverns lie in wait for the space pirates, or the Visitors, and come flashing out in hot pursuit, thus causing aerial battles. Sometimes they are witnessed in uncomprehending awe by ordinary mortals crawling around on the surface below. Once in a while some of us get killed.

Back in the 19th Century, one of these aerial battles took place over Sawmill Run, Pennsylvania. Two cloud-camouflaged space ships collided in the sky there and produced a shattering thunderstorm and cloudburst which engulfed the town below. Fifty people drowned. Some of these aerial Visitors are no more thoughtful of our welfare than are we of our own during war.

Richard Shaver says that on the star-maps of the Visitors who come here from elsewhere in the universe the planet Earth is labeled as "The Great Tomb." The earth beneath our feet is the "limbo of forgotten things", a vast storehouse of the relics of bygone days. It is interesting that most primitive peoples think of the interior of the earth in this way, the limbo of forgotten things.

We Are Property

Shaver said, as did Charles Fort years earlier, "We are property." This summary of Fortean conclusions, by the way, was given to me by an Air Force officer in Honolulu a few years ago. I guess he had to read Charles Fort as part of his briefing on Flying Saucers. Anyhow, this Air Force officer told me that Fort's researches into the unusual had finally convinced him that we are the neglected property of a race of beings who came to this planet millions of years ago. These ancient Visitors were interested in producing or trying to produce a superior race by selected cross-breeding. The breeding went the other way. They got discouraged with the results and went off and left us—or left our remote forefathers. Then every once in awhile they come back to pick up a few specimens to see how we were getting along. The results are still discouraging, so they toss the specimens back into the pen and take off again!

Fort and Shaver do not seem to be alone in their conclusions that this planet is a sort of slum area of the solar system, with a choice collection of deadbeats, bums, bindle-stiffs—and people like you and me. This picture is not very flattering to our egos, is it?

As far as Mr. Shaver is concerned our situation is utterly hopeless. He believes that we'll never get any secrets from the caves. He believes that the beings down there, whether human or nonhuman, have so much power that if they wanted to come to the surface they could just take over, wipe us out. He says they don't do that because we are useful to them.

Ray Power from the Caverns

What little evidence we have seems to indicate that evil forces dominate the Cavern world, and that they are very, very watchful of their secret. This evidence supports the grim warnings of Adept occult teachers here on the surface: Leave the Cavern world alone. If you value your life, your sanity, don't under any circumstances attempt to investigate it. The experience of one of our BSRA associates verifies the dire predictions of the Adepts

Years ago, the then-director of Borderland Sciences Research Associates, Meade Layne, received a letter from Shaver, in which he detailed his experience. Layne's attempt to contact Shaver was a most unpleasant experience.

"I was in a reclining position and breathing rhythmically, in an attempt to contact Shaver mentally, first of all. I got action, fast. There was a burst of orange flame and I was caught in the damnedest psychic force I have experienced in years. I was wholly conscious and in the body but paralyzed. I could hear strange sounds but could not locate nor identify them. I fought the force but could not shake it off. This is the first time I have been caught in a force from which I could not extricate myself. If this condition does exist it should be investigated, but I have made my last investigation of it. I had been ca-

pably taught what pitfalls in occult investigation to avoid, but in this case, leave me out of it!"

He went on to say in his letter that if his wife hadn't been home at the time he made this attempt to contact Shaver, he might have lost his body, died. His wife, sensing his condition, brought him out of it.

Another BSRA associate, Trevor James, claims to be a Saucer contactee. Skeptical of Shaver's claims, but curious about them, James asked his contact, Ashtar, if there were underground races and was surprised to receive an affirmative reply! And also a grim warning!

"At the core of your planet, there dwells a greatly degenerated race, an astral race, which is degenerate not so much in science, but in every moral respect as you know and understand it, They are capable of space flight within the astral regions around the earth but are earthbound. They are the forces of Eranus, whom you call Satan. They emerge at the South Pole on your surface, they have allies who are without morals and without mercy. I give you this information that you may be aware of their existence. I enjoin you to forever close any researches into this astral activity, in the interests of your own safety." (From Trevor James Constable's *They Live in the Sky*).

Serious Warnings

I believe we must accept these warnings in all seriousness. The menace of evil forces in the underground world is very real. They should be left absolutely alone. I don't agree with Shaver, however, that these forces are about to take us over. As I said before, I think the main reason for his feelings of hopelessness is the fact that Richard Shaver is an avowed atheist. This means that he has no belief in or trust in an all-powerful Creator. He doesn't believe in God. Thus he sees no high purpose, no plan of evolution for mankind, leading toward any worthwhile goal. There is no Light of spirit burning within him to guide him. According to the last letters Shaver sent out, he now thinks the Deros are closing in on him at his home.

Interestingly enough this same feeling of hopelessness seems to have weighed on H. G. Wells, who somehow learned of the underworld early in life and wrote about it in one of his earliest stories, *The Time Machine*. Wells wrote the dramatic story in 1895. You may have read it, or you may have seen George Pal's fascinating production of the story of the Eloi and the Motlocks in the movie, *The Time Machine* (which still turns up on late night TV movie presentations). There, as you remember, the Deros of Wells' story, the Morlocks, eventually take over and make virtual slaves of the surface dwellers.

A third writer who has touched on this eventual, overpowering superiority of the Cavern dwellers is Lord Bulwer-Lytton, metaphysical writer of the 19th Century in England. Read his

story, *The Coming Race,* in which a miner stumbles into the Cavern world by accident, is discovered and entertained by these people before returning to the surface. Again the surface dweller is impressed by their power and dramatizes the idea that the Cavern dwellers will eventually come to the surface and take over.

With this idea recurring again and again in western literature there must be some hidden truth inspiring the fiction writer's imagination. I don't know for sure, but I'm not going down into any cavern just to try to disprove it.

Extremely rare photograph of Richard S. Shaver seated in front of his Pennsylvania home.

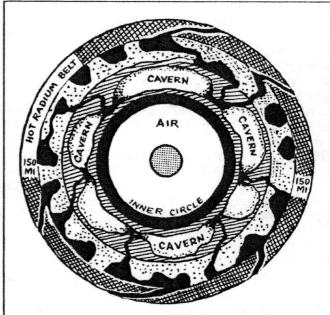

Ancient teachings claim that a vast "Cavern World" exists beneath our feet, populated by a variety of dwellers.

Chapter 2:
The Controllers

Those under-worldly forces who seek to control our destiny have many surface-dwelling "associates" to assist them in gaining an upper hand on us all.

There is now ample evidence that much of the UFO phenomena is a "controlling mechanism" that overshadows the true purpose of these craft and their occupants. There is so much confusion thrown into the UFO field to muddy the waters that it is now quite impossible to separate fact from fiction. What we've come to think of as reality is often fantasy. A virtual "smokescreen" has been thrown over the entire subject to make it look as ridiculous as possible.

The fact is that UFOs are themselves behind this deceptive practice. They are no more interested in letting the masses know what they are up to than the governments of the world are. Together, they play into each others' hands to keep the public in ignorance as long as possible. One thing I learned while in the military: the top brass is never going to admit that they are powerless when it comes to their enemies. How could they ever go public with the fact that they have no defense against these objects that come and go as they damn well please, regardless of how many times we attempt to shoot them out of the sky.

The U.S. government has known about the existence of these objects from the very beginning. I have seen classified files that tell of dozens of cases in which our military personnel were literally attacked from all sides by what were known as "foo-fighters" during World War II. I was told that quite a few of our planes were blown out of the blue not by the Germans or Japanese, but by UFOs, ghost rockets, or whatever the military then identified them as.

Hitler held the Serpent Race in high regard. Numerous expeditions were formed by the Nazis to find an opening to the inner earth in the South Pole region. Apparently Hitler believed he could gain the assistance of these reptiles, who would follow him to the surface to do his bidding, with the thought in mind that they would be the new Super Gods whom everyone on Earth would be forced to worship.

The Thule Society became the "spiritual arm" of the Nazi party, and included a belief in Atlantis, messages from distant star systems, and a new form of energy. In reality, many of the craft seen over Area 51 in Nevada are *not* constructed by aliens. They are instead experimental vehicles derived from the secrets plans of German scientists, many of whom were brought to the U.S. and given political asylum, even though they may have taken part in vicious war crimes.

These Nazis were working on alternative methods of propulsion—antigravity and time warping—which landed them on the moon some time before 1945. I learned they were backed by a top secret, renegade branch of the government that later became the CIA. Even those who are our nation's highest elected leaders are not allowed to know everything that goes on behind the scenes. They are kept in ignorance, or like JFK, if they find out too much, they are "put to rest" so that they cannot possibly "make trouble" for those who really run the show.

It always seems that there is a "scapegoat" who is meant to take all the blame. Lee Harvey Oswald, we are told, was the lone assassin, though most of us see right through this scam and realize that this is a boldface lie.

Likewise, the Jews, the Irish, the Catholics, and the Masons, have at one time or another all been pinpointed as the source of the majority of our troubles. The super-rich, such as the Rockefellers, the political elitists like Kissinger, and various occult orders have also been brought forward as those whom we should cast stones—or shot bullets—at. And while some of these individuals might be as "guilty as sin," the real power who is out to control us all remains unseen, has a multitude of allies, and remains totally undetected due to the very nature of its existence. Much of that which plagues us is invisible to all our ordinary senses. For all evil is not necessarily of the physical realm, but originates from all directions and from every layer and fabric of the unseen. A review of arcane knowledge handed down throughout the century reveals that there are forces all around us determined to do evil and take control of our minds and our bodies.

These groups—loosely knit—can best be identified as "The Controllers."

They arrived here from other planets—or originated in other dimensions—and found their way to our physical world where they hoped to create havoc and eventually utilize all of our resources—including humans—for their own individual evil purposes. They lie and do whatever else they please in order to obtain their goals. They have no conscience, no morals, no belief in a higher creator. They are here to rape and plunder the Earth's surface until we destroy ourselves by any means.

The Men in Black & The Illuminati

We hear so much these days from Bill Cooper and others about the rise of a secret order known as the Illuminati to world power. Supposedly, the Illuminati arrived here eons ago from another world and became co-conspirators with the Serpent Race. More human in appearance, they have blended in very well with our human society, but feel it is their "birthright" to enjoy pleasures and riches that mere mortals cannot possibly be allowed to benefit from. Much of our "religious values" were sponsored by them in the name of Christianity so that they could wield great power and control over our lives—realizing fully well that the vast majority of us do not want the privilege of being allowed to think on our own, but prefer to be as sheep in a herd.

The Illuminati also are in a good position to govern us and establish laws. They control the drug trade, allow the free flow of nuclear weapons to under developed countries, put criminal types in power on local, state and federal levels, and basically control the media—permitting only the news they want to be made public. Thus we hear very little of a serious nature about UFOs, alternative energy sources, cures for cancer or AIDS, etc. In addition, we are grossly mislead about a whole barrage of subjects that could be used to turn the tide of human discomfort in our favor.

There are others who work side-by-side with the Illuminati on the Earth's surface.

Many of those who have obtained physical proof of the existence of UFOs have found themselves shot at, their mail and phone calls tampered with, their families threatened. Sometimes they are visited by those claiming to be from the military services, but most often their credentials are phony and those being interviewed about their sightings only come to learn later that they have been duped. Over time, entities dressed in black clothes with red, blazing eyes and strange mannerisms scare the living daylights out of UFO witnesses, warning them to keep their mouths shut. These entities often drive black cars, can walk through walls and have the ability to read—and control—minds. They are the servants of the Illuminati and the Serpent Race.

While I was in the military, we were often confronted by bizarre stories of this type that we had to admit to being puzzled over. Those directly above me in the chain of command knew little of the occult or the secret program of the Controllers; so they did not know how to deal with those whom we have come to identify as the Men in Black. Those readers interested in learning more on the MIB should read Timothy Green Beckley's wonderful *UFO Silencers* book available for $15 from Inner Light Publications, Box 753, New Brunswick, NJ 08903.

The Grays

There are many kinds of UFO entities arriving here on a regular basis.

Thank God some of them are loving, spiritual beings. But be warned: MOST OF THEM ARE NOT! We have all read reports in which humans were abducted by aliens and subjected to a variety of physical examinations—some are even being made to have sexual intercourse with extraterrestrials. In the vast majority of these cases, the creatures doing the probing of human flesh are small—almost doll-like—and gray in color. Some of these, including an Oklahoma woman by the name of Christa Tilton, who claim to have been examined, say that once taken onboard a UFO, they were whisked away to some sort of underground base controlled by these sinister entities. Often this underground base can be part of a U.S. military complex, operating at lower levels as an alien hideaway. In my earlier book, *Underground Alien Bases* ($15 from Inner Light Publications), I covered many of these accounts in great detail. I have since been shown classified records that indicate that the "grays" are basically a group of low intelligence—somewhat unsophisticated—beings originally from another solar system, who have been put to work by the Serpents on mundane biological experiments in exchange for being allowed to set up their own bases here, most of them under the surface of the Earth.

• • •

Secret Societies of Scientists

There are also various groups who exist right on the surface—some good, some not so good—who have developed other-worldly technology without the rest of us being let in on their "dirty little secret." Most of the aircraft that were seen flying over America during the flap of 1897 were actually secret scientific devices put into the air several years before the Wright Brothers managed to get their "egg crate" off the ground at Kitty Hawk. Most of the scientists behind such advanced projects realized that their inventions would be taken over by the military and used for destructive purposes and so they decided to go on their own, giving out false information to anyone who might have greeted them in an open field where they had to land to take on supplies from time to time.

Evidence offered to me suggests that some of these creative—and highly independent—scientists may have even been traveling to nearby planets for years without being detected and might have even developed some form of time travel. They are likely in touch with the Nordic space beings who are friendly toward us and wish to share their knowledge with those who can handle such technology without their egos getting in the way.

One report filed recently with an Australian publication known as *Nexus* suggests we can find such a group of scientists hiding inside a secret city high in the Andes. The following is an excerpt of that report:

• • •

A secret city has been said to exist in a remote jungle crater in South America. If so, who might the scientists be who run this James Bond-type superfortress?

The story begins with the great Italian scientist Guglielmo Marconi (1874–1937), a former student of Nikola Tesla. Marconi studied radio transmission theory with Tesla and made his first radio transmission in 1985. Marconi and Tesla are both accredited with the invention of the radio. Marconi's historical radio transmission utilized a Heinrich Hertz spark arrester, a Popov antenna and an Edouard Bramely coherer for his simple device that was to go on to become the modern radio.

Marconi was a mysterious man in his later years, and was known to perform experiments, including antigravity experiments, aboard his yacht *Electra*. Marconi's yacht was a floating super-laboratory, from which he sent signals into space and lit lights in Australia in 1930. He did this with the aid of an Italian physicist named Landini, by sending wave train signals through the earth, much as Nikola Tesla had done in Colorado Springs.

In June of 1936, Marconi demonstrated to Italian Fascist dictator Benito Mussolini a wave gun device that could be used as a defensive weapon. In the 1930s, such devices were popularized as "death rays" as in a Boris Karloff film, *The Invisible Ray* (Universal, 1935). Marconi demonstrated the ray on a busy highway north of Milan one afternoon. Mussolini had asked his wife Rachele to also be on the highway at precisely 3:30 in the afternoon. Marconi's device caused the electrical systems in all the cars, including Rachele's, to malfunction. The car motors would not function for half an hour, while her chauffeur and other motorists checked their fuel pumps and spark plugs. At 3:35 all the cars were able to start again. Rachele Mussolini later published this account in her autobiography.

Mussolini was quite pleased with Marconi's invention; however, it is said that Pope Pius XI learned about the invention of the paralyzing rays and took steps to have Mussolini stop Marconi's research. According to Marconi's follow-ers, Marconi then took his yacht to South America in 1937, after faking his own death.

A number of European scientists were said to have gone with Marconi, including Landini. In 1937, the enigmatic Italian physicist and alche-mist Fulcanelli warned European scientists of the grave dangers of atomic weapons, and then mysteriously vanished a few years later. He is believed to have joined Marconi's secret group in South America.

Ninety-eight scientists were said to have gone to South America, where they built a city in an extinct volcanic crater in the southern jungles of Venezuela. In their secret city, fi-nanced by the great wealth they had created during their lives, they continued Marconi's work on solar energy, cosmic energy and anti-gravity. They worked secretly and apart from the world's nations, building free-energy mo-tors and ultimately discoid aircraft with a form of gyroscopic antigravity. The community is said to be dedicated to universal peace and the common good of all mankind. Believing the rest of the world to be under the control of en-ergy companies, multinational bankers and the military-industrial complex, they have re-mained isolated from the rest of the world, working subversively to foster peace and a clean, ecological technology on the world.

We have information on this astonishing high-tech city from a number of sources. In South America, the story is a common subject among certain metaphysical groups. Says the French writer Robert Charroux in his book, *The Mysteries of the Andes* (1974, 1977 Avon Books), "...the *Ciudad Subterranean de los Andes (CSA)*, which is discussed in private Caracas to Santi-ago." Charroux relates the story of a Mexican journalist named Mario Rojas Avendaro who investigated the *Ciudad Subterranean de los Andes* (Underground City of the Andes) and concluded that it was a true story. Avendaro was contacted by a man named Nacisso Gen-ovese, who had been a student of Marconi and was a physics teacher at a high school in Baja, Mexico.

Genovese was an Italian by origin and claimed to have lived for many years in the *Ciudad Subterranean de los Andes*. Some time in the late 1950s, he wrote an obscure book enti-tled *My Trip To Mars*. Though the book was never published in English, it did appear in var-ious Spanish, Portuguese and Italian editions.

Genovese claimed that the city had been built with large financial resources, was under-ground, and had better research facilities than any other research facility in the world (at that time, at least). By 1946, the city was already using a powerful collector of cosmic energy, the essential component of all matter, according to Marconi's theories.

"In 1952," according to Genovese, "we trav-elled above all the seas and continents in a craft whose energy supply was continuous and prac-tically inexhaustible. It reached a speed of half a million miles an hour and withstood enor-mous pressures, near the limit of resistance of the alloys that composed it. The problem was to slow it down at just the right time."

Genovese located the city in a crater at thir-teen thousand feet in the jungle mountains of the Amazon.

Genovese claimed that flights to Mars were made in their "flying saucers," and that this se-cret city is still in existence!

There have been many reports of UFOs in South America, especially along the edge of the mountainous jungles of the eastern Andes, from Bolivia to Venezuela. It is possible that some of these UFOs are antigravity craft from the *Ciudad Subterranean de los Andes?*

In light of highly reliable sources who claim that a "last battalion" of German soldiers es-caped via submarine in the last days of WWII to Antarctica and South America, it is possible that the Germans may have high-tech super-cities in the remote jungles of South America as well.

A number of modern military historians, such as Col. Howard Buechner, author of *Secrets of the Holy Lance* and *Hitler's Ashes*, maintain that the Germans had already created bases in Queen Maud Land, opposite South Africa, dur-ing the war.

Afterwards, German Abbots, in some reports as many as 100, took important scientists, avia-tors and politicians to the final fortress of Nazi Germany. Two of these Abbots surrendered in Argentina three months after the war. In 1947, the US Navy invaded Antarctica, mainly Queen Maud Land with Admiral Byrd in command.

The Americans were defeated and several jets from the four aircraft carriers were said to have been shot down by discoid craft. The navy re-treated and did not return until 1957.

According to the book, *Chronicle of Akakor*, a

book first published in German by the journalist Karl Brugger, a German battalion had taken refuge in an underground city on the borders of Brazil and Peru. Brugger was assassinated in the Rio de Janeiro suburb of Ipanema in 1981.

While the secret cities of South America manufacturing flying saucers and battling the current powers of the world from their hidden jungle fortresses may sound too much like the plot of a James Bond movie, it appears to be based on fact!

Perhaps a final showdown between the "last battalion" and the current political system will be a battle waged with flying saucers and space-based weapons systems. What part will the peaceful scientist-philosophers of the *Secret Underground City of the Andes* play in the coming changes on planet Earth?

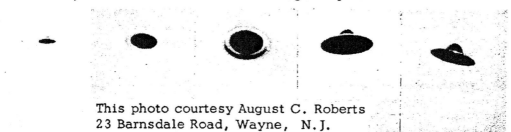

This photo courtesy August C. Roberts
23 Barnsdale Road, Wayne, N.J.

(Above) In 1952, George J. Stock of Passaic, N.J., took five photos in sequence of same UFO as it passed over his home. Note force-field around the UFO. Also note striking resemblance to Schauberger craft shown in lower picture. It is "hat-shaped".

(Below) In 1940, Vikton Schauberger of Germany, built this "hat-shaped" model flying machine. It flew by "Electro-Magnetic" power which produced a force-field. Conclusion: UFO above could be a German-built device.

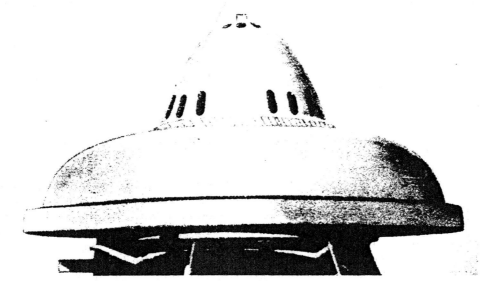

Chapter 3: They've Come To Take You Away!

If your access to UFO literature is of recent vintage, you might think that aliens only started kidnapping humans in the 1960s, when Betty and Barney Hill were abducted from their car as they drove through the White Mountains of New Hampshire. Soon after, we found ourselves in the grip of a wave of similar incidents. First there was Travis Walton, who was "beamed up" within full view of six of his best friends, and then poor Charles Hickson and Calvin Parker found their fishing expedition interrupted so that a group of aliens could place them under their cosmic microscope.

But the truth of the matter is that *things* have been coming down out of the sky for heavens knows how long, to do with us what they please. Charles Fort, who died in the 1930s, documented many strange disappearances by merely going over back issues of newspapers and journals that he found in libraries. He said he thought we were nothing but sheep in some sort of cosmic chess game—that the Gods find it amusing to be able to lead us around at their own whim for whatever silly little purpose they might think of. Back some years ago a Buddhist Priest named Robert Dickhoff (who identified himself as a "Saucer Research Privaticus") gave a disturbing lecture entitled "The Martians Have Landed—Earthlings Disappear." The crowd at Steinway Hall in New York must have been glued to their seats as they were given some disturbing news:

• • •

In my book, *Agharta*, written before I became familiar with the Fortean viewpoints on spacenapping, I quoted briefly from the book *Lo.* I again quote, "It may be that if beings from somewhere else should seize inhabitants of this earth, wantonly, or out of curiosity, or as a matter of scientific research, the preference would be for an operation at sea, remote from observations by other humans of this earth. If such beings exist, they may in some respect be very wise, but supposing secrecy in their studies, or unconcernedly they drop right into Central Park, New York and pick up all the specimens they wanted." This explains spacenapping at great length, describing the sinister pattern that the "outsiders" employ, so as to keep in touch with possible progress of the earthlings, to probe mentality via celestial brainwash those whom they have captured, dumping them in a state of acute amnesia elsewhere. Or they may take them for a ride clear to their home planet, to fill their zoo's, dissecting labs, slaughterhouses or whatever spot they have in mind for the captured earthling.

Whole ship's crews have disappeared. The *Marie Celeste*, the *Carol Deering*, the Danish training ship *Kobenhaven*, the *Atlanta*, the German *Bark Freya*, were all subjected to a mysterious swipe of a kind that in my mind's eye was an unearthly force, controlled and directed by those who went out to fish for earthmen specimens.

If these "outsiders" ever get on to the idea that steel fishing nets may scoop up hundreds of earthlings in one single operation, then it would be unsafe to celebrate New Year's Night in Times Square unless one wishes to be somewhere on another world in the incoming year.

I have my own theory balanced upon my nose like a trained seal, of what befell the *Marie Celeste*, namely that there was a paralyzing sleep fog that held the ship in its grip, until all of the crew passed out and were then collected and put upon another ship—space ship.

Dr. Evington claims that spacenapping is not confined to earth alone. He believes that the Moon people were once highly advanced, having atom power and spaceships of their own, and that the Martians wiped out that civilization there, since it endangered the security of the invading Martians. And it is fairly certain that the Moon females were carried off into the Martian Space Cruisers to be exhibited just as Columbus exhibited his Caribs, to prove to the Spaniards at home that he had been there in that new world.

This in itself would not be strange when viewed by earth scientists that were they to land on the Moon, on Mars or elsewhere with rockets getting there tomorrow; to bring back alive the collected specimens of life forms alien to us, but nevertheless creatures resembling us, even if we were to call them "things."

Leroy Thorpe wrote an article some years back entitled "Are the Flying Saucers Kidnapping Humans?" He puts it all into a question by saying; "Are an unlucky few of us, and perhaps not so few at that, being captured with the same ease as we would catch butterflies, perhaps for zoological specimens, perhaps for vivisection or some other horrible death designed to reveal to our interplanetary invaders what makes us tick?"

Unexplainable levitation into the sky by invisible and unknown forces often accompanied by electrical or magnetic phenomena unknown to earth science have snatched people off the ground. like James Greer on his farm near Zanesville, Ohio—who went straight up in sight of his brother Albert and was never seen again. Then again a blinding flash was seen overhead that moved rapidly away. And in his work Lo, Charles Fort told of a young girl disappearing from Central Park's 72nd Street entrance.

At Pillitsfer, Livonia, eight human ascensions were reported in two hours. Near Peshawar, India, six such ascensions were reported and witnessed by groups of people. In Brooklyn, New York, a mother brings her daughter home from school but sees her rising straight up in the air in front of her eyes. The mother leaps for the feet of the girl and pulls her back, and she explains that it was like a magnet pulled up the child, but did not have enough power to pull both of them up.

Leroy Thrope estimates the grim fact that each year, about a hundred thousand humans disappear from the earth, of which no trace has ever been found. In my book, Agharta, 33,000 is the number that I have estimated of humans who have been spacenapped the world over by outsiders coming in their peculiar spacecrafts, often referred to as saucers, to collect here and there at random, intentionally human cattle, for whatever purposes they have in mind.

They must possess specific brain and mentality to come here tothe earth, without which they would not have been able to construct a space conveyor, which is still a riddle to earth scientists.

We are not being merely observed by these outsiders, but they also are fishermen of sorts, their visits have to pay off to whatever Planetary Government they owe loyalty, so they also must "bring them back alive," that is to bring earthlings, to prove that they have been here.

Perhaps conquest of all earth depends on specimen gathered from here, so as to see what we are made of, how far mentally we have advanced, if at all we have advanced in their eyes, and to stop us from using these H-Bombs, which seems to molest their mode of travel over magnetic wave bands.

Perhaps their scouting saucers deliver reports to their Home Base somewhat in this fashion, "Specimen collected, the aborigines (that means all of us) have imitated us, since now they too are building saucers, our observations can be continued unobservee and unsuspected. The time for all-out invasion is close at hand."

Anybody who is capable of probing with mental fingers into the quagmire of the unwholesomeness and unreality of earthling emotion, and phoenixlike, come away from the ordeal unpolluted, fearless, cannot in all reality be called human—he or she must be superhuman when feeling for an explanation of what comes with the phenomena "saucer." "A.F." keeps on guessing into the unknown quantity from somewhere, thus tormenting the earthling mind by ascertaining nothing, which would be of value on the horizon of general knowledge, either for themselves or for a scientific know-how of how humans disappear and are victims of "saucers" that have the tendencies to show up where they are least expected and can be least explained, by believers in orthodox theories, that all must be seen first to be believed.

It is not that saucerians are merely interested in human-chops and steaks, a leg of man, etc. They come in saucers to test out water, as it was reported in Bush Creek, California, by two miners who have seen these little men scooping up pails of water and then reenter their Celestial Chariot to see if the water is of any use besides washing one's feet in.

Have you noticed since then, how the reservoirs here are drying out. Apparently one could assume that the little Martians are piping our water away to their Martian deserts via teleportation or dimensional methods.

My friend Spaulding of Warrington, Oregon, writes, "Certain saucers landed at Rainbow City, Antarctica, from another sun system in the swan constellation 200 light years distant. Time to get here: three weeks. They were looking for the Ancient Three (see *Agharta*) as they had a problem they were unable to solve. The problem of the distant world remains unsolved. They contacted two of the Ancient Three."

Now, then, we too have a problem, namely to build saucers that, with their tremendous speed, ascent and descent, can knock out H-Bomb carriers, before they can reach their destination, the Big Cities, to prevent mass annihilation of humans.

Secondly, to build saucers, with the help of these Martian samples, which can put a stop to spacenapping of our kind here, by chasing them and letting them feel an atomic fist, if possible.

Thirdly, to build saucers that will go to other worlds and pay the Martians and the Venusians a return visit. This is perhaps what the little Martians had in their minds and they have already done this with tremendous success. The Martians may suspect that the earthling is composed of half monkey and half tiger, and that should the monkey get the better of the tiger, he would duplicate, monkey fashion, the spacecrafts used by the heavenly visitors from Mars.

These little men have figured that in time and with time, the earthling would forget, cutting each other's throat for sport or profit and that, then, he would launch a new industry by manufacturing saucers a la Mars, power them with the proper atomic energy, so as to play "Follow the Leader" right after the real McCoy Martian Saucers, onward to other worlds, onwards to Mars, the home of the Little People.

Since Mars is a Martian colony of ancient

vintage, these Martian space cadets have concocted the following song:
"From the halls of your Montezuma,
    to the shores of Mars canals
"We shall build a bridge of saucer,
    for men to follow on.
"We hail the conquerors of space,
    who rockets on their way,
"Not trod by earthlings, but by men of
    courage, science some fine day."

It matters not who believes in saucers and who does not, nor does it matter if the spacenappings are being believed. The outsiders who are in all likelihood the colonizers from Mars, having a claim of long standing on the earth. They do not want to relinquish this claim, because there are earthlings here in high office and elsewhere, who are stubborn in realizing a simple truth, that we here are not the only plums in the cosmic cake having brains to reason things out and to do something to make reason stick.

Spacenapping will not stop until we stop molesting the saucerians with A and H-Bomb tests that interfere with the mode of travel to which saucers are accustomed.

They—Saucerians—evolved an entirely different and alien—out of this world—mental and physical wave Band, a life unfamiliar to us. But who is to say they were not once like us and that in time we may evolve as they are now? That one of the many reasons of this periodic checkup of humans, this pickup, one-way ride of earthlings to Martian laboratories, etc., is to determine how much more time will elapse before they shall accept us as their equal?

As long as we damage and disrupt magnetic layers on which saucers travel, the more we test our latest fire crackers here, the less pleasant are the voyages through space via a principle that controls magnetic currents and layers by which the pilots of these saucers maintain space travel for visits to their colonies, which includes Earth. As long as we are not accepted by them, we must endure check-up via spaceship.

The Saucerians aim to put a top to our using these Hellish Bombs, for reasons known to these little men, but not because they wish to prevent the madmen called scientists here and elsewhere from destroying themselves.

Here is what I believe about saucers:

Saucers are Martian spaceships, whose pilots manipulate a power principle of planetary, magnetic currents.

Martians may believe that A and H Bomb tests are earthling signals, or that we are at war with them.

Saucers swim like surfboards over magnetic wave bands.

Centrifugal motion keeps saucers stationary, making them ascend and descend.

Caution: A charged disintegration screen surrounds a saucer, when attacked.

One has but to take into consideration man's idiotic viewpoints on what he believes saucers are. He insists that they are an hallucination, manifestation of an overworked, perhaps diseased mentality, figments of the imagination. Saucers could not possibly come from another world, that there could not be creatures somewhere in the wide universe a bit more intelligent than the earthling believes himself to be, who could possibly outdo the arrogant earthling in a mode of travel as yet not understood by top earth scientists in the field of astronautics.

After all, who has seen them? Can one believe those who stick their necks out saying that they have contacted visitors "from you know where." To the average earthling it is taboo to believe in a crew of Little Martians and their saucer. It must have been a reflection of a star, a car, the water in the corner of one's eye, perhaps a mirage, or something that the sighter ate or drank.

Still the sightings go on. It makes no difference to the saucers if we believe in them, or if we make a sacred cult out of believing in them. In the final analysis, it will be seen that a mystery is a mystery only until it has been solved, then it becomes everybody's property, just like it is said in Rev. St. John: "And when the Seventh Angel blew his Trumpet, the Mystery of God was no more."

Leo Wanger from East Whittier, California, wrote some years back, "Just visited Van Tassel yesterday and we had much in common to discuss. I am informed that I am to be taken up in a saucer." Which reminds me of the Prophet Elisha, who was taken up in a Fiery Chariot and never seen again, according to the Old Testament—Now if you believe this one, you should also believe the more recent manifestations, Saucers, spacenapping of humans and what Martians have in mind if we don't stop fooling around with hell fire.

Having had a million years head start in evolution, they consider the clumsy efforts of earth scientists to get to other worlds in Rockets and the stupendous waste of energy of the fire crackers, they call here A and H-Bombs, the works of saucer apprentices. Martians are using solar energy directly from the source, so as to lift their spacecrafts from world to world, without it costing them and the taxpayers anything.

So if saucers are the brain children of Martians and we believe sincerely in them in the way the various religions proclaim their beliefs, to which I will not add or take away from, then let us by all means enlarge on these new horizons that man has yet to see but in which we already believe. In my opinion, there are *only* two possibilities in which to deal with saucers. Either we deal with them on their own terms— or fight them on our own—if and when we can.

• • •

The Real Spacenapping

Dickhoff then goes on to relate a couple of more incidents of Spacenappings that we should be made aware of—and maybe some of us are aware of it already!

• • •

Here, then, is another true story having no ending, just like "Spacenap" will have no ending, at least not a good one, for such as come under its malignant influence.

The crew and its captain of the ship *Mary Celeste,* simply disappears, leaving the ship to be found mid-ocean, in calm water with not a boat missing and all on board is shipshape, no mutiny, breakfast half eaten. Cut into the bow, above the water line, were found two deep grooves, the only clue of something having fastened itself or made contact with the ship. Something came and something went, and the crew went with it, plus the chronometer, to which the Captain must have clung, when going on his strange ride.

No earthly reason could be given for the crew to leave a seaworthy ship, in Mid-Atlantic, unless it is assumed that they walked on water.

Whatever it is that comes to loot ships of their men must do it awfully quickly and noiselessly, since there is at all times a watch on board of any ship. It has been argued that giant squids or sea serpents might have come out of the waters and picked up the crew members, but in the case of the *Mary Celeste,* there is no struggle, no shambles to prove that a fight between crew and a sea monster had taken place.

Now comes Albert Richard Wetjen, a third mate on the bark *Doyon,* sailing from Sydney to Callao, who boarded one of these mystery ships that was looted of all its crew, and brought her into Callao after a hair-raising experience. The name of the Barkintine was *Robert Sutter,* from San Francisco. There had been no fire, or signs of mutiny and all that was alive on that ship was an old parrot in his case.

On deck there was a dead cat smashed as flat as if an elephant had walked on it, or as if a tentacle of a giant squid had caught it smack in the middle.

A revolver with all bullets fired was found and a curious smell, like dried up stale fish, hovered over the whole of the ship, which reminds me of the "Outsiders," the Venusians, and the awful odor they leave behind, the same when the "West Virginia Monster" was seen, as described in a number of UFO books.

The captain of the *Doyon* decided that the *Robert Sutter* was salvageable and salvage they did, with a crew of six men, commanded by Matthews, even if it drove these men stark mad at times, most of all Matthews, who did not like the idea from the beginning.

The crew of the *Robert Sutter,* 14 in all, and all gone, no boat missing. What took them?

The fellow who came along on the salvage, A.R. Wetjen, had his own speculation, theories, but the one he missed, or perhaps did not care to mention, fearing ridicule, was "Spacenap."

That there was something mighty queer about the whole thing, something unfathomable, unwholesome and outright unearthly came, when all the crew woke up together after hearing a terrible scream and shouting of "My god, Collins!" It was this that froze the blood of all of the ones bent on salvaging the *Robert Sutter.*

A strange voice it was, not belonging to our crew of six. More screams, by yet another voice: "It's coming aft. It's coming aft!"

A voice of desperate horror. Matthew, badly shaken, ran up to the men, asking who in hell is making these noises?

Again these screams, "It's coming aft, it's coming aft!" The cook identified the screamer as the parrot, who had revived, with every feather erect, like a man's hairs standing on edge, when frightened. His eyes were fixed,

without blinking. Again the parrot, who must have seen what went on when this "Thing" went aft and after the men, lets out with a scream, yet another voice in holy terror and in pain: "You can't shoot it! You can't shoot a thing like that!"

Matthews then realized that the bird was a witness to what had taken place. It wanted to make them understand what ghastliness it had seen, of something no living thing had seen before, something monstrous, uncanny and deadly and the only means was to let out these bloodcurdling screams without let up until Matthews, quite beside himself ended the agony of the bird and the endless screams during the day and nights, by killing the parrot with an axe, thus forfeiting the only living clue to men of science in Callao, who may have been able to construct some resemblance of sanity out of these mouthings of a bird that had seen spacenapping Marauders, Pirates from another world, pick up the men and carry them away to their own world for whatever purposes they have in their alien mentalities.

What else could it have been that could not be shot, that "Come aft," than some creature, in a protective garb, where bullets were useless, coming aft, to pick up the earthlings one by one, like you and I would pick up flowers for a collection, flowers rooted to a spot, powerless to resist.

Wetjens still claims to hear the screams of the parrot, when waking in cold sweat during the night. He still is guessing at what may or may not have been, what no man was permitted to tell, but what the bird SAW and could not describe, not even in words as: "You can't kill a 'Thing' like that."

• • •

Classified Top Secret

One of my many "spies" recently submitted a copy of a supposed classified CIA document pertaining to the disappearance of military personnel. If a legitimate document, you can bet the boys "upstairs" will be rattling their swords over the release of this one for a good while to come:

• • •

July 12, 1947
CLASSIFICATION TOP SECRET ULTRA

Central Intelligence Group
EMERGENCY REPORT ON MISSING MILITARY PERSONNEL

Prepared by Field Headquarters Unit, Los Alamos
Central Intelligence Group
Copy 1 of 1
FOR IMMEDIATE TRANSMISSION

Circulation: The President: the Secretary of Defense; Joint Chiefs of Staff; Director, Federal Bureau of Investigation; Director, Central Intelligence Group

To be passed by hand and destroyed on return to CIG

Purpose
The purpose of this report is to assess the significance of the disappearance of two military personnel in connection with extraterrestrial alien activity within the borders of the Continental United States.

Background
1. Burleson, Charles, PFC 0998721943, USA, 53rd Inf. Sta. Ft. Bliss. Disappeared during nighttime maneuvers on Fort Bliss 7/8/47.
2. Flaherty, Michael, PFC 549112174, 1395th MP Company, RAAFB. Disappeared while on sentry duty at the site of a crashed alien disk in southern New Mexico at approximately 0335 on the night of 7/10/47.

Detailed Analysis
1. *PFC Burleson.*
PFC Burleson disappeared during or after a night of unusual flare or light activity reported during field training maneuvers by a detached squad of 4 Platoon, D Company. There was no indication of any morale problem. Private Burleson was absent at squad muster at 0600 hours 7/9/47. A search was made of the squad bivouac area without results. The search was extended by the squad to nearby ravines and gullies, also without results.

As there were no roads out of the area, it was assumed that the soldier had met with a mishap. No trace of this soldier has been found.

2. *PFC Flaherty*
PFC Flaherty was detached for sentry and guard duty at the site of an alien object crash near Maricopa, New Mexico. He was part of a six-man unit under the command of S/Sgt. Peter Dickson. PFC Flaherty had four years experience as an MP and had a series of highly successful evaluations. He had a K-Type Security Clearance and was cleared to serve posted guard duty at nuclear weapon's depots and in secured armed nuclear weapons storage locations. PFC Flaherty had no charges or negative comments in file, had never been AWOL or on charges of any kind. He was a bachelor age 23. He did not drink or smoke. He had received a high school diploma and had plans to study civil engineering after his period of service. He was on his second tour of duty. On the night of 7/10/47 PFC Flaherty disappeared, apparently into the night sky. Despite a wide air and ground search over a 72-hour period, no trace at all has been found of PFC Flaherty.

Conclusion
We conclude that both of these disappearances were the probable result of unknown alien activity. This conclusion is based on their known habit of causing bizarre disappearances, as per "Intelligence Estimate on Flying Disk Motives" prepared for limited Top Secret distribution 7/8/47. In both cases, there was apparent alien activity in the area.

Recommendation.
It is urgently recommended that the following actions be taken.
1. No nighttime military maneuvers to be conducted in areas where flying disk activity is being observed by the military reported by the public.
2. All nighttime guard duties throughout all military commands to be placed on War Alert status until further notice. All sentries to be briefed and armed and to move in squad formation only.

• • •
More Disturbing Disappearances

Despite his reputation for being somewhat "jaded," I've always considered Gray Barker to be one of the leading UFOlogists of all time. His pioneer work on the Men in Black, *They Knew Too Much About Flying Saucers*, frightened the Sam Hill out of lots of readers when it was first published in 1957 and continues to do the same to those who are able to get ahold of one of the few rare copies still in circulation.

Actually, I met Gray Barker not long before he died, but he never realized who I was. I drove to a UFO conference in Cleveland, Ohio just to hear him speak. This was years before I realized the scope of the subject, or was privy to the classified documents and material that came my way later on. Mr. Barker stood well over six feet tall, had just a touch of a southern drawl and a quiet manner. For while he might have taken the UFO matter seriously, he realized that in order to survive in this field, one also had to have a sense of humor and realize the absurdity of it all.

Barker was also a good friend of publisher Tim Beckley, who ran his column, "Chasing The Flying Saucers," in early issues of his newspaper, *UFO Review*, after Ray Palmer dropped it from his own publication, reportedly because of undisclosed pressure from certain sources. One to shake us into reality, Barker often wrote about the Philadelphia Experiment, the MIB, but one of his most popular subjects was the mysterious disappearances of humans who had some sort of UFO encounter.

One example is this column, which was quite typical of the extent to which Barker was fascinated by these subjects:

Mysterious Disappearances

During 1977, more than 51,000 persons in the continental United States and Hawaii vanished without a trace, either on their way to the office, supermarket, while out walking their dog, or taking the laundry in off the clothesline.

Although approximately 23,000, mainly composed of juvenile runaways, were located or apprehended, a whopping 18,000 cases, representing 55%, were never solved—this according to Marvin Jeffreys, a spokesman for the Natural Law Enforcement Institute.

An independent study of this data by one enforcement official we are in regular correspondence with suggests an amazing theory that UFOs may be directly responsible for many of these startling disappearances.

"It's still only a theory—but one worth a great deal of study. My own independent research findings indicate that these disappearances escalate sharply during months when UFO waves or 'flaps' are reported," the police captain from a large metropolitan city disclosed

in a recent letter, asking that his identity be withheld.

Rightfully, the lawman pointed out that modern police detection methods are constantly improving, and that each year the percentages of closed cases are rising. "However, statistics prove that law enforcement officials do a *much better* job of solving crimes than they do disappearances.

"I'm not saying that 'flying saucers' kidnapped all these people, but I don't believe that any possibility, ordinary or fantastic should be overlooked."

Our correspondent sketched the Travis Walton case briefly, delving deeper into his theory. "Walton, foreman of a team of forestry workers, disappeared for almost a week during 1975 after fellow workmen saw him knocked down by a blinding light from a UFO. When the fleeing men got the courage to return, Walton had disappeared. An intensive search and investigation, aided, it is rumored, by federal officers, failed to find any trace of Walton, until he suddenly reappeared. Walton claimed the UFO occupants abducted him, subjected him to medical examinations, and then released him voluntarily. Had they not done so, Walton might have joined the plus-16,000 vanished persons who were never found during 1975," the law enforcement official disclosed.

"A number of such abductions have been reported by their victims. These cases have been solved by the victims themselves. There is reason to suspect that many of the unsolved cases might involve kidnappings by UFO occupants who did not allow their victims to return."

I, as a writer, have purposefully dwelt on these statistics by a noted crime authority so that you, the reader, will not immediately dismiss a UFO landing incident case I will now relate and which is high on the list of the most fantastic cases I have ever reported. It indicates that a national public figure, who disappeared suddenly, more than a year ago, may have been the victim of a UFO kidnapping by beings other than terrestrial persons who may have been jealous of his power.

This landing and occupant sighting was first reported by *The Pelham Journal*, a conservative and reliable Mitchell County weekly in southwest Georgia. Other than being mentioned in a column by Glenn Eberhardt, managing editor of *The Sun*, published in Warner Robins, Georgia, it has been neglected by the national news media and UFO investigators in general.

Bizarre Encounter

On August 6, 1977, Tom Dawson, a 63-year-old retired automobile dealer, was making routine rounds of his small farm, when he noticed a brilliant flash of light. Abruptly, a strange circular-shaped machine descended in front of him, and hovered two feet off the ground.

Dawson experienced an immediate impulse to run but found he could not move a muscle. In fact, he was completely paralyzed, except for his internal functions. Incredibly the nearby cattle and "Old John," his dog, were similarly affected as they stood frozen in what appeared to him "like a still picture."

The craft continued hovering just above the ground while he observed its few features. It appeared to be about 30 feet in diameter, was disc-shaped with a bulge in the center, and he described it traditionally as "like two saucers stuck together." A row of small ports, about six inches in diameter, ran about the outer rim and he could see a brilliant light inside. A small protrusion on one end reminded him of an antenna.

But his observation of the craft was soon interrupted by a new and even more frightening development. A hatch opened and five strange looking beings immediately jumped to the ground. Three of them were men, and two were women—their genders he was certain of, because one each of the men and women was completely nude, and he also noted, completely hairless.

Although the others were dressed completely alike in what he termed "beautiful clothing," he could still determine their sexes from the general build of their bodies. Their two-piece outfits were made of shimmering material that changed in bluish-green hues as light reflected upon them, and they reminded him of uniforms, with neither masculine nor feminine identification. Their shoes, different from their uniforms, seemed to be made of silk material, and the toes of the shoes turned upward.

Dawson further described the occupants: "Their skin was white as flour sacks, their noses were sharp and turned up. They had pointed ears and their heads were sitting right on their shoulders."

The first one, appearing to be the leader, had

stepped onto the ground as though testing, and then motioned to the others to follow. At that point two more men came from the craft's hatch and took positions at the entrance, appearing to be guards. The two women followed.

The last person emerging from the craft carried a contraption that reminded him of a hula hoop. It was connected to a kind of skull cap by a series of cords. The hoop contained dials from which they took readings after placing the cap on his head. At the same time, they proceeded to remove his trousers and lift his shirt over his head as he stood in his helpless, "frozen" condition. They next attached small suction cup devices, like rubber and of a bright orange color, to various parts of his body from his legs upward to his chest. Throughout the bizarre examination, the witness felt no pain. In fact, after they put the skull cap on him, he lost most of his fear, as if he had been given a tranquilizer.

A Famous UFO Kidnap Victim

At that point an even stranger development occurred. It is this part of my investigation that led me to describe this case as one of the most fantastic I have ever reported:

The occupants jerked the skull cap from his head as a loud voice suddenly emanated from the ship.

"I am Jimmy Hoffa! I am Jimmy Hoffa! Won't somebody help me! I am Jimmy Hoffa! I am..."

A fourth try at shouting his name was cut off and the voice was silenced, as though somebody had placed a hand over the victim's mouth.

The five beings hastily withdrew and walked hurriedly toward the craft, carrying the unfolded examining device with the wires and suction cups trailing behind. Then they huddled in a tight group, now and then turning their heads and looking in his direction. Once they removed the cap his fear once again returned and he became even more apprehensive as he sensed they were deciding whether they should abduct him and take him with them. But still he could not move. Fortunately they apparently decided in the negative as the huddle broke up and they seemed to half leap and half float upward into the hatch of the machine. During the conference he heard their voices, which were very high and shrill. Although they spoke some unrecognizable language, he believed that at one point he had heard the distinct word, "Jupiter."

The craft began slowly moving upward at an angle until it was about 75 feet in altitude when it vanished, "with a wink," according to the witness, who at that point found he again could move. As he harked up and secured his trousers he noted the cattle were also moving, and "Old John" began barking furiously and running in a circle around the landing spot.

I talked with Linda Kolbie, Dawson's nearest neighbor, to whose house he ran after the encounter. Ms. Kolbie told me that when he arrived he tried to relate his experience, but was "too excited to talk. After while he recovered his composure and led me to the spot where the experience took place."

The neighbor did not remember seeing any markings or other evidence where the object had landed, but testified to the reputation of Dawson.

"Mr. Dawson is a sober man and a regular churchgoer. He does not even smoke or use tobacco in any form. And I am certain he would not take drugs of any kind. He says it happened to him and I believe him!"

Strange Visitors Pop Up

Both Dawson and Kolbie related that a small group of UFO investigators visited and examined the location. They identified themselves as MUFOC (she had written it down). I thought she might have confused the group with MUFON, another UFO group, but she was certain of the last initial. She deduced it must represent a group known as the Macon UFO Club, since one of them told her he was from Macon County, Ga. She told me they took samples of the soil and made radiation readings but reported they found nothing unusual—though they would conduct further investigations on the ground samples. No members of the group wore uniforms and she presumed they were from a civilian club—though they did not appear to her to be native Georgians. "They had olive-colored skins and a foreign look. They must have been Mexicans," she believed.

Although any meeting with alien beings can be considered fantastic, naturally it was the claimed ownership of the voice inside the craft that excited me.

Months before, labor leader James Hoffa had disappeared while on a trip. Due to his impor-

tance and because his disappearance suggested murder by other persons seeking to usurp the power he still held over his union, massive federal investigations were carried out. In fact, more than a million dollars in manpower and other resources were expended in the unsuccessful search for Hoffa, who was never found, either dead or alive, and in thorough investigations into the lives and actions of suspects. Although remains of a body that, due to elaborate dental work, suggested it might be Hoffa's remains, was found in October, 1977, experts who examined dental records agreed it was not his.

Naturally I asked the witness if he had ever heard Hoffa's voice on radio and television. He remembered hearing and seeing news programs about him, but said it was too long ago for him to remember if the voices were similar. He could not describe the voice emanating from the craft other than its being of average tone, though somewhat raised and pleading.

Although this report cannot definitely establish that a retired farmer heard the actual voice of Jimmy Hoffa, whose disappearance could be solved as an abduction by UFO occupants, it is difficult to discount the incident. If the voice were not that of Hoffa, this would indicate the occupants deliberately used deception in creating the impression that the famous leader was aboard the craft. But their appearance of being startled when the voice began shouting indicates the interruption was unexpected. Immediately they cut short their examination of the witness and prepared to depart—though taking a moment or two, apparently deciding whether to abduct him also.

Vital Clues

This case could represent an important breakthrough in solving the UFO enigma. It could prove that not only have the occupants abducted humans whom they later freed, but also indicate that they are responsible for many if not most of the thousands of people who disappear annually. It would also represent the first revelation of the abduction of a famous person, as opposed to the ordinary people who have previously reported abductions. Maybe the UFOnauts have previously avoided well-known persons for fear of the additional publicity their disappearances would create, and that their kidnapping of Hoffa was either a miscalculation or represented a new and bolder trend.

My own examination of the landing sight, incidentally, disclosed no unusual evidence. It is possible that the members of "MUFOC," an apparent civilian group that may have been from Macon County, Ga., did collect meaningful evidence while traces were fresh, but inquiries have failed to disclose any such organization in that area. Ms. Kolbie's description of the visitors as "foreign-looking" also raises suspicions that they may not have been whom they claimed to be. Indeed, her description suggests the almost legendary "Men in Black," mysterious individuals who do not always dress in dark clothing but generally are described as olive-skinned foreigners with no definite ethnic identification. Perhaps the "investigators" may have been directly related to the UFO occupants themselves, although they appeared to be definitely human. Perhaps they made the visit to determine whether the UFO had left any definite traces of evidence that would help to identify them.

A True Meaning—Can We Find One?

Dawson said he had never been questioned by any police officers or other persons (though he had not reported the incident to the police—only to the newspaper). In fact, most people hearing of the incident laughed about it and didn't believe him, he said—and he preferred to forget about it.

And the UFO occupants could have planned it that way. The voice of "Jimmy Hoffa" could have been that of an imposter, or an actual voice recording taken from their monitorings of radio and TV broadcasts. It could have been a "red herring" inserted to create disbelief in its bizarre import.

Or, somewhere on some other planet, or in some other incredible dimension, James Hoffa, for some inexplicable reason, may still be a captive of the "saucer" occupants, still hoping that his fitful cries for rescue may be heeded.

• • •

The Mysterious "Skystone"

Before completing his column for *UFO Review*, Barker progressed to another subject that seems so timely now that we shouldn't let it pass, since the findings of Commander Alvin E. Moore tie in so perfectly with our theory of a multilayered phenomena and flying saucers originating from right under our very noses:

• • •

On the evening of July 19, 1952, radar operators at the Washington National Airport spotted strange targets on their scopes. Soon they realized the National Capital had been invaded by a huge squadron of UFOs. The military ordered jets to intercept, and clamped down a national hush-up. Even Capt. Edward Ruppelt, head of the Air force Project Bluebook, was not allowed to investigate and was rudely sent asway when he arrived in Washington. When the news leaked to the press, the Government "explained the incident as a "temperature inversion."

If you are a serious UFO student, you know all this already. *But here is something you may not know:*

Early the next morning, a caretaker on the estate of Commander Alvin E. Moore, near Herndon, noticed something very peculiar— branches of trees had been damaged, and then he spied a gaping hold directly beneath the damaged limbs, which exuded a sulphurous odor. He ran to get his employer, who had not yet left for the Technical Information Branch of the Bureau of Aeronautics in Washington, where he was division head.

The caretaker and Commander Moore carefully exhumed a still-warm and obviously manufactured object The old-line Naval officer whistled as he realized the thing could not be a meteorite, and was obviously a manufactured object—for it had three machined sides and a fourth that appeared to have broken off. As he carried the object back to his house, his brow pinched in puzzlement, for his years of technical experience in aeronautics told him this was not from an aircraft—indeed, he had the impression that the thing was from out of this world!

The National Bureau of Standards analyzed the object that Commander Moore had nicknamed "the Skystone," and reported it was not of natural origin. Next he submitted the cylinder to Project Bluebook, then loaned it to a Canadian intelligence officer attached to the CIA who had it analyzed by Canada's Project Magnet, directed by the late Wilbert Smith. Both agencies expressed puzzlement as to its origin.

Commander Alvin E. Moore is no crackpot. Previous to the fall of the object that changed his life, he had chalked up an impressive career. Education at the U.S. Naval Academy, the American University, George Washington Law School, John Marshall Law School of Atlanta, etc.; he had nearly enough credits for a Ph.D. degree. As a line officer of the U.S. Navy, he had specialized in aeronautical engineering, and was patent engineer and attorney for the Von Braun team of space scientists at Huntsville, Alabama. He has also been a CIA intelligence operative, and while with the agency became impressed with UFO reports, noting the interest the CIA seemed to take in them.

The Skystone "Disappears"

At the time of the Skystone's crash, he was not with the CIA, but in 1953 he returned to that intelligence agency where he became an operative in the Scientific Intelligence Dept. During his previous tenure there, he had been told to mind his own business when he proposed a UFO research project, so he was surprised when the CIA's director of Scientific Intelligence asked him if he could have the cylinder analyzed. The official returned it a week later without comment, and in the CIA he had learned to mind his own business and didn't ask about the results. He returned the Skystone to his office safe, where he had stored it since its return from Canada.

Two weeks later he opened the safe and found the cylinder was gone! Shocked and dismayed, he lamented the disappearance of what was possibly the greatest find in the history of space science!

Knowing that nobody except himself and security officers had the combination to the safe, Commander Moore realized the object had been confiscated by CIA personnel. He never saw it again. Two small samples the Bureau of Standards had chipped off remained in his possession, but these were later swept away in a hurricane.

Secret Diary

But all was not lost. Over the years, Commander Moore kept a secret diary known only to himself and his wife. It contained a meticulous record of the Skystone, other mysterious incidents, his private investigation of UFO reports and Government attitudes about UFOs. After retiring to his estate in Mississippi, he spent many years editing these papers and recording his own theories about UFO origin and purpose.

It is impossible to outline all of Commander Moore's theories in this column. I am very intrigued by what he has to say. I have read the "secret diary" that has been worked into a very large book and have arranged for its printing and limited distribution. Briefly, Commander Moore, along with Charles Fort, the late Ray Palmer and Dr. M.K. Jessup, theorized that the UFOs exist in mysterious "sky islands" much closer to the earth than we believe. The Government, he says, is suppressing this secret, partly to prevent mass panic. For some of the more negative "Skymen" cause fires, explosions, aircraft crashes, train, auto and ship wrecks; diseases, wounds, burns, and killings. Although some of the Skymen do little harm, all of them are exploiting the earth in an effort to repair their Sky Islands, damaged by radiation from our atomic tests.

Dero and MIB

There are, indeed, "radical" theories, and they are guaranteed to cause controversy among UFO students. Especially when Moore describes a demonic group of Skymen (the Dero of Shaver lore?) who commit kidnappings. Some of them give contactees misleading stories, while avoiding contact with scientists and world leaders who might see through them. Their Men in Black operatives steal and recover wrecked UFO vehicles or their fragments. These MIB also frighten and harass UFO witnesses and hush them up. Moore believes that they silence some of these witnesses by killing them!

Chapter 4:
Alien Babies

There's a new kid in our block—half human/ half alien, and it would seem there are millions of these "half breeds" that are either in our midst or could be walking the Earth shortly at the mere wave of the hand (or claw!).

In my earlier work—*Underground Alien Bases* —I documented the cases of several women who felt as if their wombs were being used to actually *hatch* alien offspring! That they were being utilized by the Grays and Serpents, in essence, as human incubators. In underground laboratories, they also observed weird creatures being formed in huge test tubes and felt that there was a sinister motive behind their abduction in these alien groups.

For ages, humans have been forced to have sex with spirit entities. Brad Steiger covers the subject best of all in his book *Demon Lovers* (available for $15 from Inner Light, Box 753, New Brunswick, NJ 08903), and in the saucer world several early cases from South America involving sex with abducted humans have been written about in every sleazy tabloid in creation.

Now at last, one man has come forward to say that he has fostered alien babies. This report, by Bruce A. Smith, first appeared in Issue #92 of *The Missing Link,* the official publication of the UFO Contact Center International (3001 South 288th St., #304, Federal Way, WA 98003) and shows us the extent to which these entities are willing to go to spread themselves across the world—most often without our permission:

Fatherhood In The New Age, One Man's Story of Alien Abduction for Cross-Breeding Purposes

Lots of people are having kids these days. On April 1, 1990 at about 5 o'clock in the afternoon I found out that I too, and for the first time, had become a father. In fact, as I was to find out shortly afterwards, a father of 34 kids with 8 more in embryo form. You see, I found out that I had been abducted by UFOs/ETs (Unidentified Flying Objects or Extra-Terrestrials) for cross-breeding purposes.

This realization came about during a presentation by the noted UFO abduction researcher, Budd Hopkins. I was sitting in his audience simply as someone who has had a life-long interest in UFOs. I have always believed that UFOs existed, and my belief has been an easy one. I have never had to wrestle with any concerns as to whether UFOs were real or not. In fact, I have often found it hard to understand why some people don't believe in UFOs. Why my belief has been so easy for me I have no ready explanation. I have never seen a UFO, and only recently did I ever know anyone who had. And prior to my hearing Budd Hopkins, I certainly never thought I had been an abductee or even a contactee.

However, I had begun, in the fall of 1989, to have a series of vivid dreams involving UFOs and ETs. In one, I dreamed I saw a UFO hover over the trees, near the home of friends with whom I was staying. The UFO was domed on top and conical below. It was quite large. I saw many colored lights on the external portion of the ship, many porthole-looking windows on the conical portion, and regular looking, rectangular-shaped windows on the lower dome. I saw the whole ship quite clearly. I remember saving to myself "It's so beautiful" It was, and I felt joyful seeing it. But then, after that first feeling of joy, I felt paralyzed while sensing I was lying on my left side in bed. I thought to myself, "They've got me?" I was quite frightened. "Frozen with fear" may be a good way to describe my feelings. I tried to move and I couldn't. I felt myself panicking. I refused to be a victim so I uttered, "From the Lord God of My Being I call forth the power to move."

Somehow I could move my mouth and jaws to whisper that command. After that injunction I could raise my right, upper, arm. I knew I was back insome control. At that point the UFO abruptly disappeared. Just blinked out. It didn't fly away, just vanished. Then it came back to view in the same place, but this time it was a pale gray, black and white imitation of the vivid beauty of my first viewing. I felt disappointed as if I had driven them away by resisting and challenging their control over me. Then the UFO blinked out a second time but quickly came back again, vivid and in beauteous color, as before. I saw it for a second or two and then it blinked out for a third and last time.

The next day I told my friends about this dream.

My friend said, "It sounds like more than just a vivid dream. It sounds vivid enough to have been real." "Nah," I said, "I've never seen a UFO, this was just a dream."

For the next three nights, during the time I stayed in Washington, I had dreams about wanting sex with an alien woman. She was, in UFO parlance, a Gray, a species known to most people as those guys with the big heads and large black eyes that Whitley Strieber saw and wrote about in his book Communion. But this particular woman was fairly tall, not the four-feet high that is described in Communion. And although she had the large head and eyes of the grays she seemed good-looking to me. Also, oddly, I saw her wearing a black wig.

During the night I would wake up with a full erection, feeling horny, and aching to have sex with her. I would sit up in bed and look out the window to the nearby woods. I just knew that she and other grays were out there in the woods. She was there, waiting and available for me. All had to do was ask her and she would come to me. I felt so conflicted. I was aroused, I wanted her, but I was stunned by my desire to have such sex. I said to myself, "You've reached a new depth of debauchery." But most of all I was just afraid. Too afraid to do anything. I didn't.

My sense of what happened was that they were able to tap into my libido and sleep cycle, get me aroused, and then they waited for me to make a conscious decision to have sex with them. I never did. Somehow I sensed that they wanted me to be a willing partner.

For some time I had been aware of the stories circulating about the cross-breeding program of the grays. As I understood this program, the grays were unable to feel any emotion, and so, were culling sperm and ova from humans so that they would have the genetic material necessary to create the physiological basis for an emotional life. So, as I sat up in bed and confronted their invitation from the woods, I said, "Hey, I know you guys need sperm, and I'd really like to help. But I can't handle it right now. Why don't you come back in about six months. I'm sure I would be able to handle it then."

Two weeks later I was back home in Long Island, NY. I had a very vivid dream of actually having intercourse with a gray in my bed.

I had a clear image of three entities coming into my bedroom at night while my wife and I were asleep together in a double bed.

The gray female was there again, wearing the black wig. It made her look somewhat Oriental. The wig had thick black strands, was shoulder length, with straight cut bangs across her forehead. I made the association that she looked early 1960s, something like a crazy Suzy Wong character. As the female entered the room she was flanked by two entities. I can't remember clearly if they were grays or the stock blue, soldier types as seen in the movie Communion.

She mounted me, straddling my loins as I lay on my back, I asked, "What about my wife?" I was told, "She's not part of this."

I remembered later, and wrote in my notes on this incident, (but can't remember now) that this alien woman was grinning while she was on top of me. I wrote, "it was a grin from somewhere between pleasure and maniacal torture."

I don't remember ejaculating, or even if she had a vagina. I don't remember having sex, just the straddling part. It didn't seem long before she was finished. I remember the three entities walking out of the bedroom. At the door, a gray turned and stared at me for a very long second or two. Then they were gone.

The next day I was very disturbed about the dream. I was excited by the idea of having sex with this alien woman. I began to fantasize about it. As much as I enjoyed thinking about it, my enjoying the dream scared me. I thought that my libido was out of control. Usually I have plenty of guilt about masturbating, going to an occasional peep show at Times Square in New York City, or just reading porno magazines. But having sex with aliens and enjoying it was far beyond my normal control and acceptance. What was happening to me? I wondered. I'm fantasizing about alien sex. Boy! Talk about cheating on your wife, and she was right there! My mind was reeling.

Fortunately, I had a therapist to talk to about all of this, but not without some trepidation. After all, it's one thing to talk about how badly one's mother screwed up your life, but it's another to discuss one's longing for an alien mistress. My therapist's perspective on my dreams were that they were a manifestation of a lot of unsatisfied sexual desires, plus I was feeling trapped. She speculated that I may have felt so stuck in my life that I thought that it would take something as miraculous as a sexual fling with an alien to fully satisfy me. This interpretation made sense to me, and I felt relieved.

That was my understanding of things until I heard Budd Hopkins. By then I had already begun to make changes in my life. I had gotten a divorce, sold my business, and made plans to pursue a lifelong desire to relocate to the countryside in Washington State. I had even started a relationship with a woman whom I found very exciting sexually and personally, but strangely I was impotent with her. I was unable to ejaculate. But the dreams began to fade in frequency and vividness, so I thought I was on a more fulfilling pathway of life.

However, my perspective on the nature of my dreams changed radically once Budd Hopkins started to describe the case of a 23-year old guy who had disturbing dreams of having sex with aliens. As soon as I heard the details I began to cry. Softly, deeply. My girlfriend, sitting next to me, and who knew of my dreams, held my hand tightly and knew that something powerful was happening to me. When Hopkins revealed that his client had become sexually dysfunctional I became emotionally distraught. It took all of my strength to stay seated and stifle the sobs so that I wouldn't disturb those seated near me, nor draw attention to myself and my anguish.

I felt like I wanted to fall on the floor and writhe, cuddle myself and just rock back and forth to soothe myself.

My tears told me that what I had known to be dreams were in fact not. They were real events. They were not some fantasy or psychological manifestation that popped out in my sleep. I actually had had sex with aliens.

Why did I cry? To this day I'm not sure. Was I sad, angry, outraged? Those are thoughts that come to mind, but they feel like intellectualizations. Maybe I am still emotionally closed off to the experience. I believe that is probably the case. Deep inside I may be horrified at what was done to me, so much so that I continue to protect myself by not remembering or even sensing what my true, deep feelings are.

After my tears subsided, in some vague way I knew I had been changed. Life was suddenly much bigger to me. Abductions and contacts didn't just happen to others. They were not just stories I read or heard about. It had happened to me. Strangely I began to feel as though I was living life more fully. Sure I was scared, even angry, but it all seemed too wonderful in such an awesome way.

But at one point near the end of Hopkins presentation I realized that if I had been copulated with, then there would probably be offspring somewhere. "My God! I've got kids somewhere in space," I suddenly thought. "I'm a father?" And probably like all fathers before me, the realization, so profound, so deep, slowly flowed through me like a high tide coming on shore. A feeling bordering on the "I can't believe it and maybe don't want to, but I'm glad it's true" filled my heart and mind.

Then I got angry. I looked up at the ceiling and pointed a finger from a fist on my lap, "You guys had better beam me up now," I demanded. "You guys have got my kid and I'd better get up there pretty damn quick and take care of him. God knows you guys can't. You guys are nothing but a bunch of thievin', bumblin', space idiots snatching people and babies. Ya better get me up there right now to take care of those kids. Ya HEAR ME!!!"

Over the next few days I was in turmoil. What had they done to me? Stolen my sperm? Stolen my passion? Stolen my ability to ejaculate, and put my relationship with my kind woman-friend into real jeopardy because of the frustration I felt during love-making. I was angry and frustrated. They had really diddled with me, the bastards.

And yet I knew I was a partner in this event. I

was aroused in my "dream." And liked it. While staring out the window at my friend's place, I was excited. I wanted her, but was too scared by both her and the implications of my desire. I couldn't handle the ETs nor could I handle my sexual desires. It was a double whammy.

I've always had a lot of sexually-based guilt. Now I was busting at the seams.

What to do? Does life just go on? Hardly. How do I understand what was happening to me. I felt getting more information on the actual events would be a good starting point. I made a few inquiries as to hypnotists who might be able to regress me back to those eventful nights. However, I was relocating to Washington State in two weeks so I had certain limitations on how deeply I could pursue my hypnosis. As it turned out, I was unable to directly contact any of the several referrals.

I let the matter drop until I reached Washington. Nor did I pursue any of the abductee self-help groups due to the short time I would remain in New York.

As I drove from Long Island to my new home, I felt the edge come off my concerns about the ETs. The anger drifted away, and I became prideful of my new found status as a father of space kids. I felt special. "The ETs had picked me from all of humanity for their special work," I thought. I liked feeling special. It was exciting to feel like I was on a special mission to help save a species of alien creatures. And, ah, "They couldn't do it without me." Such specialness was a potent elixir.

Also, I began to feel that the ETs had helped me. They had helped me confront my deep sexual desires and frustrations, ones that I was in profound fear of. Over the months of dreams I realized I was too dependent on others. I needed to be taken care of or befriended far more than I needed a full, powerful, adult sexual relationship.

My wife had been much older than I. Also, she had had a hysterectomy, so she was a very safe, non-threatening sexual partner. My girl friend was quite sexual, but more importantly she was my safe harbor in a hurricane of personal change. My impotency may have been influenced by the ET suctioning off my sexual energies, but the root cause, I believe, was that I didn't want to share my seed with her. I didn't love or desire her enough to be that intimate with her.

I was becoming aware of so much. Aware that my dreams were real events. Aware that my intimate relationships were based on need, not desire. Its as if the shock of acknowledging alien sex woke me up to the depth of dissatisfaction I was having in my earthly relationships.

That's how things stood as I traveled across the country. Until I reached Santa Fe. There I had another experience that opened up a whole new vista to my ET experiences. The grays took me up on my demand to take care of my kids.

On my third night in Santa Fe, I was sleeping in my travel trailer, in the Tusuque Indian campground. I awoke suddenly in a panic. I knew they were back. My mind started screaming, "This is for real. This is the real thing. This is not a dream." I felt terrified. I was laying on my back in bed with my legs straight out. I remember feeling two hands firmly, but not harshly, holding my lower legs, just above the ankles, as if to steady me. The entity holding my legs said to me, "Don't worry, it's your father." Instantly I felt relaxed. My knowingness said that I was too panicky to travel to the spaceship as scared as I was, so I had to be steadied. I felt I was being guided into a beam for the uplift to the spaceship, much as one is lifted onto a stretcher.

I wanted to go, to be a conscious part of whatever was going to happen, but I was too afraid. All I could do was say, "From the Lord God of My Being I call forth the power to make sure I don't get hurt." I didn't want to miss out on a grand adventure.

I knew too, that I'd feel even more special by being able to stay conscious. Then I'd really be a major leaguer in the ET game. But, I was unconscious for the whole event. The next thing I knew I was back in my bed, and I knew it was over.

As terrified as I had been, I wanted them to come back. I was sad the experience was over. Mentally, I asked, "will you come back?" In my head I heard the reply, "Sure, you're just getting interesting." I gave myself a jab of doubt at that point, saying, "Nah, you're just talking to yourself," but as I write these words I believe the message to be real.

I didn't recall anything specifically from the experience. I didn't see anyone, nor do I remember, what, if anything, I did. But somehow I knew sex wasn't involved. I didn't have any sexual feelings that I could remember, certainly no erection. But after it was over I asked cynically, "Well did you guys get what you wanted," meaning sperm and sexual energies. Maybe I didn't remember any sexual events because they may have sucked me dry of my sexual energy, and therefore, I wouldn't have the recall without the energy to effect the biochemistry of memory.

The next day I remembered the experience well. Not any more than what I have already described, but the whole experience felt fresh and real to me. All day long I thought about it. What happened? What's going on? Who are they? What do they want? Why do they want me? Throughout the day I had a strong sense that they beamed me up the previous night in order to take care of the kids. They needed a father's touch.

I really wanted to find out what was going on with these aliens. Why are they whatever it is that they're doing? Since I was traveling, I figured hypnosis was out to the question. Asking the grays directly was out because I was too scared every time I encountered them. But somehow in the light of day I felt empowered, emboldened. I felt that if I saw them during the day I'd be OK. I could handle contact then. The question was how to contact them during the day? It was up to me to make the contact. So I did.

I know some pretty powerful, Kundalini-like meditation which helps me get in touch with life outside of day to day consciousness. So I did my thing and went looking for the Grays.

I found them. Over the next few days, in the mornings before I'd travel the highways of New Mexico and Arizona, I'd travel first to see my kids in space.

Each visit was similar. I would feel myself descend from above into a metallic-looking room I felt was inside a space ship. The room was quite large, in a "D" shape. It reminded me of psychiatric hospitals day rooms I had worked in. Directly in front of me I would see a row of cribs and bassinets or incubators. A few adult Grays were off to my right in the bulge of the "D." A bunch of little ones, maybe four to nine years old were to my left and back not far from a stairway to another room which I could see kids coming and going to. Near me, to my left were the older kids, whom I thought were young teenagers.

I know I was in an alien environment. Every-thing felt different—air, aroma, sights, sounds, textures. Nothing reminded me of earth except me and my seed. The kids looked pretty human except their eyes and heads were bigger. The kids were very stand-offish towards me. They weren't frightened of me, but held back like I was a substitute teacher walking into their high school classroom. I felt the kids were sizing me up and not cutting me any slack.

I asked the adult Grays, "How many kids are mine?" "30–40,", they answered.

"What do you mean, 30–40, don't you know exactly?" I was flabbergasted that I had fathered so many kids and furious at their casualness about the number.

"Thirty-four children specifically if you must know, and eight embryos, some of whom may not survive. That's why we gave you an imprecise number." "How many hybrid kids do you have in total?" I asked. "Thirty-four million" was the reply.

"Wow." I thought, "that's a lot." And there's that number 34 again.

"What's so special about the number 34?" I began to doubt whether I was getting the mental transmission correct from them.

"Do you mean 34,000,000 or 340,000, or 34,000." I asked. I received a jumbled response that left me with the feeling that the number probably wasn't 34 million, but that they still have a lot of kids up there in space.

"Why 34? What's so special about the number 34?"

"The numbers three and four are building block numbers," I was told. I saw an image of three blocks sitting on four blocks.

"The number two is too universal, and the number one, is, well, part of everything." So we use three and four."

Each visit lasted about 10–15 minutes. Each time I arrived, the kids would be waiting for me. I began to wonder, "How come they're waiting for me? Do they know I'm coming? Could this whole experience be contrived for me? Could it be a hologram or some kind of telepathic programming that I just plug into?" Doubts followed the experiences, but the visits felt real to me.

I would gather the kids into a circle and we'd have a little dance/movement therapy session. That's kind of like a group circle dance that is for the purpose of expressing one's feelings in a physical manner. The music that we moved to was the music I used during my meditation and what I continued to listen to through a Walkman. I just knew the kids could hear the music also. They had never heard music before. Yanni's "Out of Silence" was their first exposure to music.

They had no rhythm whatsoever. I asked them to just gently sway back-and-forth in rhythm to the music. They didn't know what to do. So they watched me and soon an inner knowingness kicked in with them and they were able to sway a bit, while standing in place.

Then I asked them to join hands. They had never held hands before. They had never touched each other before. Sure, they had been brushed-up against or felt some physical contact before, but never a direct communicative, sensual touch before. After some more swaying and holding hands in a circle, I felt it was enough for us all and I "called it a day," and left.

Upon returning to my conscious world I felt quite moved by the experience. I was near tears. My kids needed so much help and I felt so inadequate. Who am I to teach them about feelings? I'm just learning to get in touch with my own. Maybe since I'm learning and aware of the process, that makes me a good teacher. Nevertheless, I felt these kids needed a professional movement therapist, someone who had worked with autistic kids. These kids were not autistic, just totally unexposed. I wanted to put an ad in the paper, "Movement Therapist needed for emotionally regressed kids. Travel required." My ten-year background as a Recreation Therapist in the psychiatric wards of the VA and a county General Hospital seemed inadequate for the job. Yet, I had some basic skills, and as the saying goes, "I may not be perfect but I'll do until perfect gets here.'

The next day I went back. I formed the circle again. I asked the kids to introduce themselves, one-by-one, by saying their names. They had no names. Names aren't used in the Gray culture. They don't need names in their group consciousness. I received a communication that said:

"It's like this, when a faucet breaks, we don't have someone pickup a phone and call a plumber. No one is needed to call anybody, any individual, or business. Here, when a faucet needs to be repaired, that need is known and those who fix faucets just know to come and repair it."

Somehow I just realized that everything is just business to these guys. No one ever gets thanked for a job well done. I never saw a smile or sensed that anybody was happy in my contacts with these aliens. No singing, humming, whistling, or even cursing. Nothing. Everybody just goes about their business.

On this second day at one point, as we were dancing, I asked the kids to bend over and touch their toes with their hands. As we did that I asked them how they felt. One kid said he felt like he was going to throw up.

I stopped and stood up. The kid wasn't sure what to do. I told him to straighten up and go sit down and relax, that the nausea would soon pass. I had the sense that he didn't have an experience identifying feelings, didn't know what to do, knowing where they came from and why they were having them, nor what to do about them. The kid didn't know that he was nauseous from bending over, and that if he straightened up and sat down he'd feel better. I don't think any of the kids would have known to do that under similar circumstances.

So I told them about feelings. I told them that feelings aren't good or bad. They just are. We can respond to them in different ways, even ignore them, but that may not be too helpful. Even humans often ignore a lot of their feelings and that can get them physically sick, and/or physically disturbed. I told them that they should at least acknowledge their feelings. Be truthful to yourself, then decide what to do about them.

Later that day, after I had returned to my in-the-world consciousness, I went to explore Bandolier National Monument in northern New Mexico. I was hiking along the abandoned ruins of the ancient Anasazi Indians, when all of a sudden I received a major communication. I felt my mind flooded with a complete, clear understanding of what the ETs are doing, and what their program is all about. I felt as though they had slipped a "CD disc" into a "CD player" to my mind. I heard:

"This is the story. The hybrid kids are going to populate or at least experience physically, the earth directly some time between the year 2020 and 2030. By then the earth will be a much different place. These hybrid kids are being prepared to live in that new environment and with

the new spiritual frequency that the earth will vibrate in. All that live on earth must adapt to these changes and be in harmony with the new earth. All living organisms currently on the earth that do not adapt by elevating themselves to the new, higher, more spiritually evolved frequencies will leave the earth experience."

You will be, if you choose, since we need you and others like you, elders to the new ones of ours on earth. You will be the reference point for these kids, to show from where and what they have come."

"You will be the bridge from the old to the new, from the old planet to the new; *old Homo sapiens* to the new gene pool. You know so well the ocean of emotions your people have. It will be as a flood to the new ones. You can help them adjust, understand, accept and integrate; help them make the transition."

I felt thrilled to be a part of such an epic mission. Then I began to get worried, "Hey, I'll be 80 years old then." I thought I better make sure and learn how to compress time by then so that I wouldn't age, and still be in shape to handle these tykes in 2030.

Then I felt I was being used. I had to go through catastrophic earth changes in order to be a "grandfather" to these new breed of kids. I said to the Grays mentally, "What do I get out of it?" The reply I heard was, "We'll help you survive the earth changes." Didn't sound like a great deal, but at least an adequate one, so I consented to stay with the program.

Over the next few days I began to feel there was more to it than what I had been told via the "CD player" communication. On my own, I began to develop a fuller understanding of what the aliens really wanted. First, I was convinced that they didn't need the sperm. That was a scam. They can get all the sperm they need, gallons of it from sperm banks, or their own laboratories. The sperm snatching is a means of hooking me into the program. They needed me to be hooked into caring for these kids. They needed me to feel like a father to these kids. I realized, with some sadness, that these kids were not mine. They were theirs. The Grays had devised a specific plan to breed their own kids. I realized that if I wanted my own kids I was going to have a regular family just like every other *Homo sapien*. I wasn't going to be

able to piggyback my needs of fatherhood onto the alien's emotional renourishment program.

Also, this idea of losing my sexual energies really weighed on my mind. Were the grays storing it up for the kids. Was passion needed besides sperm to make a baby? But maybe the grays drank my passion like an elixir. Maybe I was just a tasty bit of "soul food?" The more I thought about it the less I liked it.

The experience of always having the kids ready for me when I arrived in the spaceship continued to concern me. Was I being plugged into a telepathic VCR, "being a father to my kids," that the Grays would store, and play back to the kids whenever the kids needed a dose of fatherly love and attention? I thought of a woman I had heard at a UFO conference, who was abducted with great regularity, every other Sunday, if I recall the story correctly. She felt that she had a space kid also, and was being abducted to give "Mother's Love" to the kid. The aliens also hooked her up to some kind of machine when she felt milked-out over her maternal feelings and she sensed they were then able to store it. These aliens had even abducted her little boy to play with the hybrid kids, but her boy didn't want to go because those kids didn't like to play his kind of games.

Maybe the aliens have just royally conned me by giving me strokes to think that I'm really special, while they're just stealing my passion and raping me. Maybe I have a Patty Hearst syndrome. My alien kidnapper/terrorists have got me thinking they're good guys and I'm joining them in their struggles. "Gee, no emotions? Too bad. What can I do to help?" They may be nothing more than really clever interplanetary thieves.

Yet I went back one more time because I cared about the kids. As we formed a circle I asked myself" can I see specifics about the kids? What do they look like? Can I see what kind of hair they have?"

I realized that I couldn't tell if they had hair or not. I realized I couldn't tell any specifics. I couldn't even tell if they were boys or girls. Somehow I felt limited to only seeing what I had heard from books and other abductees. I felt I was living a guided imagery session, that it wasn't "really real." I felt it was a set-up. I felt totally used, started screaming at the adult Grays. They felt like my "handlers," in the way spies and boxers have such.

I stormed out.

After a few days, my anger died down again, and I began to think about everything that had happened. When I was angry I didn't even want to think about aliens in any way, shape, or form. Then, one day, I realized I might have an implant. Maybe even two. It was just a thought that dawned on me.

On my left inner, forearm, I have a small, red, hard lump just under the surface of my skin. I remembered noticing it suddenly one morning, when I was about 20 years old. I remember saying to myself, "Hey! What's this doing there?" At first I thought it was a pimple and tried to pop it. I couldn't. Never have. For the next 20 years, the lump and color and location have stayed the same.

Then I recalled, that a couple of years ago, while scratching the back of my head, I found a new small lump behind my ear, near the neck bones. Again I thought it was a pimple and again tried to squeeze it. Again, no success. In the past few months, I have begun to get intense muscle pains in the area right around the dump.

As I realized I might have two implants, I really began to get upset. It's one thing to get snatched in the middle of the night for an hour or two, but it's really bad to be tagged and monitored 24 hours a day. It's like being raped, and then having to see the rapist's mark on your body every day.

Funny thing is, I'm not sure I want to get rid of the implants. I don't know if I want to give up my opportunity for a "great specialness." Suppose I need the aliens to save my life. How would they know I was in danger unless the monitor told them so.

I've got a real issue of personal sovereignty here. Being independent, secure, and sovereign is of great importance to me. How do I reconcile that desire with the fact that I allow someone to stick things into me and snatch me without warning or even an invitation? I can't; somethings gonna have to give.

Now, why am I writing this story? Maybe I'm attempting to switch the fulfillment of my need for specialness, from the fathering of ET kids to being an outrageous storyteller. I've begun to fantasize about telling this story on TV talk shows. Often I feel like I'm doing nothing but switching addictions. Instead of joining a group for abductees, maybe I should join an Alcoholics Anonymous for people who need to get "high" on feeling special.

Perhaps I will pursue having this story published. I wonder, is it worth sharing? Is it important enough? Certainly the amount of psychological processing that I have done is unlike any other account of any other abduction that I have read. Also too, I don't know many other abductees who have consciously tried to recontact their abductors. Somehow, I feel my story may be an important piece, one of many such important pieces, of understanding the UFO/ET puzzle.

As I write this story, I feel clearer, and stronger about severing my relationship with the ETs. I feel closer to deciding to have my possible implants examined and if they are implants, have them removed. My desire to be sovereign is getting stronger than my need to feel special.

Chapter 5:
AIDs, Nazi UFOs,
Gun Running &
The New World Order

The following is from an ad describing a book written by 'Michael X' (no relation to 'Commander X'), titled 'WE WANT YOU—HITLER ALIVE,' published by UFO Review., Box 753., New Brunswick, NJ 08903:

"DID HITLER CAPTURE ALIEN CREW & BUILD HIS OWN FLYING SAUCER? Here is proof Hitler escaped death, and tried to reorganize his mighty forces at the South Pole in underground bases...

"Here also are clear—close up—photos of Hitler's own secret flying disks which he hoped would someday enable him to rule the world.

"Discussed for the first time is the mysterious 'Mr. Michalek' who had toured Europe telling of his contacts with aliens and the establishment of the majestic government of the 'World Republic of Earth,' and how both Moscow and Washington would be 'wiped out' if they did not 'give in' to other worldly advice. Was he speaking on behalf of the Fuhrer?"

• • •

The following are actual quotations from notable individuals (credit: ODYSSEY GROUP., Suite 1402-C, 270 N. Canon Drive., Beverly Hills, CA 90210):

"I believe that these extraterrestrials and their crews are visiting this planet from other planets...I did have observation of many flights of them."—COLONEL GORDON COOPER (Astronaut)

""It was almost a mid-air collision with a UFO. It pulled my helicopter up more than a thousand feet."—LT. COLONEL LAWRENCE COYNE (U.S. Army)

"...The phenomenon reported is something real and not visionary or fictitious."—GENERAL NATHAN TWINING (Chief of Staff, U.S. Air Force)

"It was strewn over an area 3/4 of a mile long...we didn't know what it was."—MAJOR JESSE MARCEL (Intelligence Officer, U.S. Army)

"I must insist upon full access to discs recovered...the Army grabbed (one) and would not let us have it for cursory examination."—J. EDGAR HOOVER (Director, F.B.I.)

""Air Force, Navy, and commercial pilots have revealed to me cases when a UFO would fly near them right off their plane's wing... highly secret government UFO investigations are going on that we don't know about."—SENATOR BARRY GOLDWATER.

"It seemed to move toward us, then partially away, the return, then depart. It was bluish, reddish and luminous."—JIMMY CARTER (President of the United States)

"Its shape was such that I don't believe it was made by mankind."—DR. BRUCE MACCABEE (Research Physicist, U.S. Navy)

""Though officials have long denied that they take 'flying saucers' seriously, declassified documents now reveal extensive Government concern over the phenomena."—THE NEW YORK TIMES.

• • •

The Oct-Nov. issue of *Nexus* Magazine related the following information in an article titled 'UK RADIO PROGRAMME ON UFO COVERUP:

"The following is an example of what one can pick up off the computer networks. The network in this case is called EarthNet, run by Pegasus Networks based in Byron Bay (P.O. Box 201., Byron Bay NSW 2481). ** Topic: Aliens from outer space... ** ** Written 12:14 am, Aug. 5, 1991 by huw in peg:sci.astro **

" 'I recently heard a Radio One program in

the UK that contained an interview with a leading proponent of the popular theory that the U.S. Government has aliens locked up and is experimenting with their space planes. However this particular individual sounded very reasonable, did not make any outrageous claims, and further had some interesting facts to disclose. In particular he mentioned several verifiable facts which I would like some follow up on:

" 'Rockwell International and NASA were planning a *massive* joint exhibition of space exploration this year (1991) but it was delayed inexplicably until 1992. In the *official* prospectus for this exhibition, one of the exhibits was clearly stated to be 'an extraterrestrial spacecraft.' When asked about this by various individuals, all enquiries were referred by NASA to the US DOD. An unnamed Pentagon spokesman speaking off the record is said to have indicated that they 'had a number of such space vehicles to choose from...'

" 'The Pentagon also held a press conference to deal with press inquiries on this matter—and refused to answer any questions. In fact reporters later said that the Pentagon had asked most of the questions, and they all pertained to 'what would be the public reaction if....'

" 'The guy on the radio program referred extensively to two NASA consultant engineers who claimed to have worked on alien spacecraft studying propulsion systems for NASA—both had high level security clearances in the States...' "

• • •

As conflict between the Human and Serpent races increases in the future, rest assured that the brainwashed serpent cultist, traitors, and sold-out worshippers of 'the beast' will probably do their all to thwart any chance of counter attacks by Human Freedom Fighters and Christian Patriots against the draconian vermen who infest this planet. Like the liberal corporate-government employee in the movie ALIENS or the 'elite' society in John Carpenter's *They Live*, these traitors against the human race would sell out their own kind rather than risk offending their 'gods' and their very lucrative 'business arrangements' which they have established with these predators (at the incalculable expense of the rest of humanity).

They will probably use the excuse that the

serpent race is a sentient life-form deserving of 'constitutional rights' just like ourselves, or the excuse that they are an 'endangered species' which must be protected. Since the serpent races no longer inhabit the surface of the planet as did their bi-pedal reptilian ancestors, this does not mean that they do not exist in abundance. Although many of them disappeared underground millennia ago while others apparently left the planet altogether, it would be reasonable to assume that whether they exist below the earth or above the earth (both regions of which remain vastly unexplored and unknown to International Humanity on earth's surface) they EASILY number in the millions, if not the BILLIONS and possibly even tens or hundreds of billions, in THOSE regions, since it is likely that they have over the millennia multiplied their kind for obvious reasons.

Regardless of the forthcoming excuses, there are plenty of laws in the books which support the killing of predatory animals (and the serpent races ARE animals or beasts) who kill livestock such as cattle and sheep. With regard to the 'cattle mutilations' this should apply, and especially in regard to the 'human mutilations.' The argument that some reptilian races are more benign than others seems to conflict with the 'collective consciousness' aspect of all such races (except, perhaps for the hybrids possessing human soul matrixes who should not be included 'entirely' as being irreparably connected to the reptilian 'collective').

One may wonder if the 'anti-gun' lobby has at least a little behind-the-scenes influence from the serpent cults and their reptilian overlords. Also, just as the U.N. allowed America to enter the Korean and Vietnam wars under UNITED NATIONS sanction, they prevented America from winning these wars because of the Communist-Illuminati infestation of the U.N. In the same way, any future conflict with the Serpent Race which might be carried out by the 'Serpent Cult-infested and Controlled UNITED NATIONS 'New World Order' will no doubt be a 'no win' conflict as well.

In fact, the malevolents might even support a limited 'war game' conducted against the 'grays' [or in an even worse scenario, against the human 'benevolents'] by their 'New World Order' Illuminist servants on earth, and might even sacrifice some of their own 'pawns' in order to bring about the conditions and political unity-through-war necessary to further consolidate the nations under a more 'controllable' World Government system; just as the Korean, Vietnam and other conflicts were apparently used to bring about a synthesis into a proposed World Dictatorship. Any successful attack on the serpent races will necessarily have to be conducted by individual nationalities [against the intra-mountain and underground alien 'strongholds' in and below their respective countries] in a patriotic grass-roots manner WITHOUT the 'help' of the New World Order-Club of Rome-Illuminati-Jesuit-Masonic-Serpent Cult infested one-world organizations. This may be one of the reasons why the Illuminati has attempted through Socialism to destroy not only Christianity but also a Technical-Industrial society as well, both of which are necessary if the masses hope to defend themselves both spiritually and physically from the reptilian influences which have literally undermined our world.

• • •

Native Indians of Alaska refer to a benevolent tribe who long ago disappeared underground into vast underground chambers below the mountains north of the town of Tanana. Occasionally, tradition holds, a young member of one of the villages on the surface would become overly discouraged by their life in the surface world, and make a journey in search of these caverns, and disappear into the underground land where they would enjoy a more peaceable and fulfilling life.

It would be very encouraging if most of the accounts of subsurface colonies were of this type. A few centuries ago this might have been the case, but the infestation and undermining of the continents by draconian forces has increased dramatically during the last few centuries to the point that their influence may be dominant in the subterranean world. However, it is encouraging that in the latter part of the 20th century the reptilian advances seem to have halted in several areas of the world as indicated by the numerous 'standoffs,' and in some cases reptilian forces have apparently been driven back and defeated as more and more humans refuse to give up their ground, having become aware of the draconian propaganda and deception which have in the past been extremely useful tools of conquest on their part.

• • •

Astronomers in the early 1990's claimed to have discovered 'proof' of an ancient explosion commonly referred to as the 'Big Bang,' out of which the known Universe sprang. Although theorists have suggested such in the past, along with the possibility that the Universe may one day 'implode' from its own mass and gravity, other scientists believe that the Universe falls barely short of the mass necessary to bring about such an event, and that the Universe will probably continue to expand forever, although that expansion will continue to slow down yet never actually 'stop.'

We will not know for sure which of the theories will turn out to be true, as it will be untold billions of years (as we measure time) before such an implosion occurs if at all. The interesting thing that scientists have discovered, however, involves a phenomena known as red-shifting (infrared) and blue-shifting (ultraviolet) of stars, star clusters, galaxies and galaxy clusters. The spectrographic 'red' shift indicates that a star is moving away from us, while a 'blue' shift indicates that it is coming closer. Basically, it all has to do with the speed of light and how one perceives it.

Because stars closer to the cataclysmic center of the galaxy rotate faster than stars in the galactic arms, further out from the center of the galaxy than the SOL system, astronomers have been able to determine the speed and direction of such stars through gauging the 'shifting' of the light spectrum. The incredible thing, however, is that our galaxy seems to lie in or near the epicenter of the Universe, and remains relatively stationary while the red-shifted galaxies (100's of billions of them) expand away from this general area of the Universe, suggesting that the 'Big Bang' may have been a lot closer to home than formerly believed.

• • •

In connection with the allegations in *The Cosmic Patriot Files* concerning the abduction of children by the Serpent Cult (both human and alien 'cultists'), AMERICA'S MOST WANTED revealed that I.B.M. is working with Lotus and Sony Corporation to develop a computer database on missing children which may soon be accessible via a modem. A large computer organization in Las Vegas is also involved in a similar project. More information on computer databases on missing persons can be obtained from the NATIONAL CENTER FOR MISSING AND EXPLOITED CHILDREN (Phone #—1-800-843-5678).

• • •

According to ex-Jesuit Priest Alberto Rivera, beneath 'St. Peter's Square' in Rome lie vast catacombs in which the most secret Jesuit activities, initiations, and plans take place. These catacombs, according to Rivera, also contain the 'Vatican Library'—consisting of 25 miles of bookshelves which are situated in this miles-long network of tunnels and chambers. There are no doubt many secrets hidden within this library which the Vatican will NEVER release to the public, if they can help it.

• • •

Lynn Dumniel's work, titled *Freemasonry and American Culture 1880–1930* (1984., Princeton Univ. Press., Princeton, N.J.) states the following:

"Another indication that MASONS were susceptible to racism and anti-semitism of the period [early 1900's] was the popularity of the KKK with Masons. Although no reliable figures exist, the KKK appears to have been quite successful in recruiting Masons into it's ranks. In Oregon, for example, the Klan had made significant inroads into Masonic membership.

One former klansman claimed that 50–60 PERCENT of the FIRST KLANSMEN in Oregon were Masons, and that once Masonic and other fraternal leaders were claimed, Klan joining became contagious and ran epidemic through organizations. While it's influence in local lodges probably varied widely, the infiltration of the Klan was notable enough that Grandmasters, prompted by unfavorable public opinion and dismay over the dissention the Klan was promoting within Masonry, found it necessary to make a statement either condemning the KU KLUX KLAN or DENYING Masonry's connection with it."

• • •

The following information comes from Ralph Woodrow's book *Babylonian Mystery Religion*, and refers to the Babylonian 'Grand altar' of Baal, a phallic obelisk which was traditionally pointed upwards to the so-called 'sun' god, and supposedly signified a pantheistic worship of the forces of nature. The obelisk is also worshipped in Freemasonry, a 'religion' which can also be traced back to Egyptian 'Illuminism,' and is similar in configuration to the 'Washington Monument': The [Grand altar] was transferred from Heliopolis to Rome in A.D. 37–41 by Caligula, to his circus on Vatican Hill (see: HARPER'S BIBLE DICTIONARY, p. 500; and CATHOLIC ENCYCLOPEDIA, Vol. 13, p. 371).

...In 1586, to make certain that this obelisk was centered right directly at the entry of the cathedral, it was moved a short distance to it's present location—St. Peter's square—by the order of Pope Sixtus V. Moving this heavy obelisk, especially in those days, was a very difficult task, especially since the pope attached the DEATH PENALTY upon anyone who was responsible for dropping or breaking it... Finally, one man by the name of Domenico Fontana accepted the responsibility of moving and erecting the Vatican obelisk. With 45 winces, 160 horses, and a crew of 800 workmen, the task of moving began! The date was Sept. 10, 1586. Multitudes filled the large square.

While the obelisk was being moved, the crowd—UPON PENALTY OF DEATH—was required to remain silent until the erection was made. Finally, after near failure, the obelisk was erected—to the sound of hundreds of bells ringing, the roar of cannons, and the loud cheers of the multitude. The Roman mass was celebrated, and the pope pronounced a blessing on the workmen AND THEIR HORSES (See: ANCIENT MONUMENTS OF ROME, by Theodore Pignatorre, p. 177)...

The Babylonian obelisk that once stood in Heleopolis, the center of Egyptian sun-worship was a replica of the—if not the very same—obelisk which stood at the center of Babylon itself. There are many occultic symbolisms associated with this obelisk, around which the ancient Babylonian Mystery Religion is built, one of these being a symbolic representation of the tower of Babel. The obelisk stood in the center of a circular grove [but in the case of Rome, a circular stone grove], depicting the worship of the union of the male and female 'principles.' It indicates the worship of CREATION [or 'Creature'] rather than THE CREATOR.

This phallic symbol, and indeed the entire Vatican itself, was erected on the very hill which in ancient pre-Catholic Rome was referred to as 'a place of divinations' (Vaticinia).

The name is said to have come from the name of an ancient pagan 'god' called 'VATICANUS' who was headquartered at or beneath the hill, and to whom the ancient diviners and sorcerers communed (see: ANCIENT MONUMENTS OF ROME, p. 75).

At a later period, the hill was used for the annual festivals in honor of Attis or Tammuz, son of the 'Great Mother' [It is very obvious that this image of the 'Mother Goddess' and her 'son' and the statues, etc., associated with it, were later 'Christianized' so that the pagans could continue to worship the Mother Goddess and Tammuz, the unholy product of the incestuous relation of Semiramis and Nimrod the King of Babylon. Nimrod incidentally was dismembered by Cush, one of Noah's righteous grandsons who continued to hold to the divine precepts which Nimrod had led the world to rebel against, thus bringing God's disfavor upon that early civilization.

Nimrod's bloody members were then sent to leaders of all the provinces as a warning, but Semiramis, perhaps the worst witch or sorceress in history, thought up the ingenious idea that Nimrod would return or reincarnate as her son Tammuz with which she was impregnated by Nimrod at the time of his death. This lie was believed by multitudes of blind followers, thus continuing the satanic hold upon the people through the Babylonian 'Mystery Religion'—the roots of witchcraft, astrology, idolatry, masonry, etc.—which this sickeningly decadent family had established for their dark masters].

• • •

The book CIA: Cult of Intelligence states that one of the purposes of the 'Central Intelligence Agency' is the establishment of One World Government. An obvious Illuminati fingerprint? Some groups believe, based on secret documents, that the CIA has infiltrated the 'Christian Identity Movement' through a secret project known as EARL OF DYSART as a means of furthering one-world government. The book 'MAFIA KINGFISH' refers to one Carlos Marchello [the boss of the oldest Mafia family in America, often referred to as the 'first family of the Mafia'], stating that his organization nets over 2 BILLION dollars a year and all but controls the political system of Louisiana through fear, bribery, etc. Marchello was #2 on Robert Kennedy's 'war list' against organized crime,

and Senator Kennedy even wrote an obscure book called The Enemy Within detailing the Mafia conspiracy. MAFIA KINGFISH refers to one Edward Becker, who testified that at a meeting he attended with Marchello, he overheard Carlos saying that he planned to neutralize Robert's attacks against the Mafia by killing the President. They chose Oswald, who had close contact with both Mafia-man Jack Ruby and Marchello, as a 'scapegoat.'

This was revealed in certain formerly-suppressed documents obtained through the Freedom of Information Act. In fact, FBI head J. Edgar Hoover apparently intentionally withheld these documents from the Warren Commission and left only those which might point to a supposed 'sole assassin' with 'left wing' motives. Although it may have been rooted in the Mafia's revenge against the Kennedy's, this animosity was no doubt used by the Illuminati to bring about a secret coup in America. And conspiracy researchers may be familiar with the ties which exist between the Mafia and Illuminized Freemasonry as well.

Also it is notable that the assassins in Dealy Plaza must have had inside contact with the highest levels of government, since three days previous to the assassination a Secret Service agent changed the route to include the Plaza. No one should have known about the change except for the Secret Service.

• • •

At first glance by those perusing the magazine stands, Far Out magazine may appear to be an eye-catching publication devoted to a serious study of Unusual phenomena. However, don't be fooled by appearances, for once one opens the pages they find a whole range of articles written by sceptics in the vein of Phil Klass, James Oberg and William Moore. In fact the fancy cover of the magazine seems to be mere 'bait' for the unsuspecting seeker after truth, to draw them into the whirlpool of unfounded skeptical debunking of everything from UFO's to Government Conspiracies. For those who have read the The Cosmic Patriot Files, they must admit if they have any intelligence at all that there is just too much corroborating evidence of the fact that 'something' strange is going on. But Moore WHO HAS ADMITTED TO WORKING FOR SECRET GOVERNMENT AGENCIES AND OF SPREADING DISINFORMA-

TION AND PROPAGANDA, is at it again.

If you're looking for the truth on cattle mutilations, interactions or conflicts between the 'government' and the alien 'grays,' information on underground bases, abductions and other documented phenomena such as were recorded in the *The Cosmic Patriot Files*, we're afraid you won't find the answers in FAR OUT magazine. But for those who are able to 'eat the meat and spit out the bones,' FAR OUT may provide some interesting information, for in debunking something the sell-outs must ELABORATE on what they are debunking. One should nevertheless be careful of 'reverse propaganda,' that is the planting of false stories which might be believed so that the agents of disinformation may turn around and prove such a story wrong, and use it as a battering ram to break down belief in the DOCUMENTABLE accounts. One classic example of this necessary elaboration on what is being debunked involves an ancient underground system which is said to exist below the Death Valley region of California. Several separate accounts confirm the existence of these caverns.

However the following account, which appeared in the Winter '92 issue of *Far Out* in an article by H. Leo O'Neal, titled 'THE LEGEND OF THE DEATH VALLEY MUMMIES,' was actually an obvious attempt to classify this tale as fantasy, even though the author of the article admits that SEVERAL people allegedly have been in these ancient chambers. The magazine, however, in labelling the story as fantasy must at the same time accuse all of these 'witnesses' of collaborating in a hoax. In the same way, they must also force themselves to believe that all those THOUSANDS who speak of 'abductions' and relative events must be involved in a collective hoax or hallucination. In other words they are forced to believe in a 'conspiracy' far stranger and less likely from a motivational perspective than the one's they are debunking! The events at Death Valley mentioned in the articles are as follows.

We ask the readers simply to make their own determination as to the authenticity of the account based on other accounts which have appeared in the whole of the *The Cosmic Patriot Files*. In 1946, Dr. F. Bruce Russell, a retired Beverly Hills physician, struck upa conversation with a Mr. Howard E. Hill in the city of Los Angeles. Russell informed Hill that in 1931,

whole sinking a shaft in a claimsite of his in Death Valley, he broke through to an underground cavern.

After seeing some lights he entered and found himself in a cavern with two passages, one heading 'left' and the other 'right.' Exploring the left-hand passage he came to a cave-in some 25 yards from the entrance shaft. The right-hand path however continued at a steep angle downward for about a quarter of a mile. Although the passage seemed natural, there were several areas where it had apparently been artificially widened to allow for more comfortable travel. At the end of the quarter mile passage, Russell claimed to have discovered a large room or chamber off from which branch tunnels radiated in all directions.

He was surprised to see torches which used a type of tar, as well as earthen jars apparently filled with the tar and into which the ancient inhabitants of the caverns must have dipped their torches. He also noticed several animal bones scattered around the place. One tunnel eventually led to another large room, and this room also had branch tunnels leading off in all directions. Laid out in this chamber were 3 'mummies' and several strange artifacts, some of which appeared Egyptia' while others were more American Indian in construction. The strange and shocking thing about the mummies however, according to Russell, was that each was nearly 8 foot long or tall! He described the underground system as a kind of 'underground city.'

The inhabitants must have been very advanced, Russell concluded from what he observed, and he was certain that the find was much more important than King Tut's Tomb itself. Following the passages he eventually discovered other openings to the surface, but most of these were in obscure places. Yet all that he explored were within 7 miles of the 'shaft' through which he had first entered the complex. Eventually, Russell discovered 32 caves in all throughout the area. Although he could not prove it as many of them had collapsed, he supposed that many of them might have at one time connected with the underground system. These 32 caves were all within 180 SQUARE miles of each other, and were located in Death Valley and the extreme southwest region of Nevada. He also stumbled across a large chamber which he referred to as the 'ritual hall,' and which contained strange markings and symbols. A tunnel went from this room to another where well-preserved bones of dinosaurs, sabretoothed tigers, mastodons and other extinct animals were displayed in hollowed areas along the walls. In 1946, after years of private investigation and secrecy, Russell decided to exploit the find.

After gathering a group of potential investors he held a meeting in which he displayed some of the artifacts which he had taken out of the underground system. Mr. Hill attended the meeting provided that he could help out as an investor. The company was called 'Amazing Explorations,' and the Investors meeting took place at a suite in Beverly Hills, although all of the investors were sworn to absolute secrecy. Hill and the rest of the investors were taken after this meeting concluded to the underground caverns, where Russell returned the artifacts which he had displayed to the investors, as he was convinced that the protected atmosphere of the caves would preserve them.

The group was taken into the cavern in which the 'bones' and the 'temple' were located. According to witnesses, it was 'chock full of bizarre artifacts of all kinds.' Russell told them that they could look but not touch, as he realized the necessity of preserving such a find in its original condition, both for archaeological as well as monetary reasons. On August 4, 1947, Howard Hill, acting as spokesman for 'Amazing Explorations,' issued a brief statement to the press announcing the discovery. The story received minimal coverage, to his surprise, and only appeared in a few newspapers in which the story was 'balanced' with very derogatory and skeptical statements from the 'scientific' community.

After this, a live press conference was planned, in which Russell planned to display a skeleton and/or several artifacts which would 'convince even the most skeptical reporter.' And from that they could discover for themselves the reliability of the find. For this Russell had to return once again to the caves to retrieve the necessary artifacts. He also planned, before leaving or shortly after his return, to open a bank account at Barstow bank to deposit investment capital. Russell left for Death Valley but was never seen again. His car was later discovered with a busted radiator in a seldom travelled part of Death Valley. Although some

suspect that he left with the money of the investors, this is unlikely since the investors' money which he possessed at the time was not nearly enough to warrant his disappearance, or the discontinuance of plans to commercialize the site as one of the wonders of the world, and the potential wealth that this might bring.

The investors attempted to relocate the underground chambers that Russell had shown them, but claimed that they could not remember the exact route since they did not pay much attention to landmarks on the first trip, and besides the shifting sunlight and shadows and the uniformity of the vast landscape made this difficult. So ended the brief but interesting events surrounding what might have turned out to be one of the most popular wonders of the world, a potential Federally protected museum invaluable to archeologist, anthropologist and historian alike, as well as millions of potential tourists.

• • •

According to William Hamilton, John Lear revealed an incident concerning an older gentleman who is known only as Mr. 'K,' whose son was being held captive in an underground base in Utah. This son formerly worked in the Dulce base in New Mexico and possibly was transferred to the base in Utah via an underground route.

When contacted about the incident, Mr. Lear had this to say:

"The son, whose father I met and who passed away several years ago is apparently being held in a base near or around Sleeping Ute Mountain [Utah]. I don't remember how I came by that information but it had to do with some research I was conducting in a search for the Project Blue Light base near Delores (which I never found.)"

• • •

The following information comes from *Would You Believe* (issue uncertain):

"In the Doc Savage novel called *The Spook Legion* (April 1935) Lester Dent creates a character who can make men translucent and then invisible by a chemical process. Unfortunately this translucency process interacts with any metals carried on a person's body: 'Be sure to remove every stitch of clothing ... that includes wristwatches, rings—and false teeth, if any. Remember that the slightest bit of metal on the body is liable to have fatal consequences.' (p.86). A nasty side effect of this process is that it causes feelings of internal burning.

'The frightful flame in their bodies seemed to leap and surge and consume them, leaving only a sluggish hull from which the interior had been burned...' (p.88)

"In Charles Berlitz' and William Moore's book, *The Philadephia Experiment* (Fawcett Crest, 1979), we seem to have all of these things that Lester Dent was writing about. The vanishing sailors, the body rigidity (i.e. being 'frozen' or in the 'quick freeze'), the danger of carrying metals on the body, the spontaneous human combustion——its all there. In his fictional literature, Lester Dent gave us details of the legendary Philadelphia Experiment at least eight years before it was said to have happened in real life, according to Berlitz and Moore."

Could early Doc Savage stories have been the inspiration for the famous legend of Philadelphia? Perhaps the story moved gradually from fiction, to folklore, until finally it became 'fact' in the minds of some? That is certainly one possible version, however, there may be another possibility.

"JAMES RAYMOND WOLFE AND ADMIRAL RICKOVER—I consider myself a 'Fortean researcher,' that is, a researcher of mysteries willing to entertain many possibilities. And as Dr. Michael Swords once remarked, 'give a Fortean enough threads and he'll hang himself.' Therefore I want to point out that a number of loose threads are hanging about that don't fit the more straightforward fiction-into-fact idea."

There is still a loose noose by which I can dangle some tidbits before you. For instance, only days before he died in 1984, publisher Gray Barker printed a bizarre booklet entitled, *After The Philadelphia Experiment.* Barker's books contained information and letters that he had received since the Berlitz/Moore book had been published.

"Some of this new material involved the strange fate of a retired naval officer named James Raymond Wolfe. He was the author of a book on cryptography, *Secret Writing* (McGraw-Hill, 1970), and he was also said to be a lecturer on quantum physics at Clark University. Wolfe took an interest in the Philadelphia Experiment and he began using his old contacts in the Navy to help him uncover new leads."

According to the Berlitz/Moore book he suddenly disappeared and was presumed assassinated. Barker's book suggests that he was not dead, but that he had been moved to a hospital in Canada after suffering a massive trauma to his brain and central nervous system.

"Before his unhappy exit from the scene, Wolfe allegedly had discovered that some kind of naval experiment had really taken place in 1943.

"However the side effects of the process, including diathermal brain damage to the crew, some deaths and other unexplained effects had created a state of acute embarrassment to a powerful man within the Navy.

"Some fingers have been pointed to Admiral Hyman George Rickover, the famous 'father of the nuclear navy.' Rickover was deeply involved in electrical research and development for the Navy in World War II. Rickover was considered to be a ruthless man, but a man who could develop powerful, even fanatical, loyalties among HIS friends. At one point he ordered so much electrical cable, 'tens of millions of dollars' worth, that, after the war was over, warehouses filled with the stuff were sold in large salvage-scrap auctions.

"Did Rickover bury a Naval experiment, perhaps the biggest mistake in his life, in the interests of national security or self-interest?

"There is direct evidence that something really shook up the Navy in 1943, the year that legend says the famous experiment took place. This information can be found in the book series, *Mathematics: People, Problems, Results* (in three volumes), Edited by Douglas M. Campbell & John C. Higgins (Wadsworth International, Inc. CA, 1984).

"Up until 1943 the Navy had developed a highly advanced experimental and theoretical group that included the mathematical genius of John von Neumann, his assistant J. W. Calkin, Marshall H. Stone (Harvard mathematician), Francis Bitter (one of the world's foremost magnetism physicists of his day), and others. Even Albert Einstein was doing something, still highly classified, for the Navy at this time.

"But suddenly, near the end of 1943, this whole group seemed to blow apart. The group was completely fragmented and scattered to the four winds. Some, like von Neumann, went to Los Alamos to work on the A-bomb, some were forced into other departments of the Navy, and others were shunted back to civilian life. What happened? What caused the massive Navy shake-up of 1943?

"WAS THERE AN EXPERIMENT?—I have offered as one possible interpretation for the Philadelphia Experiment that perhaps a fiction story slowly evolved into folkloric 'fact.' However, I want to consider another possibility—that maybe the experiment really happened; in some form.

"In writing the Doc Savage novels, Lester Dent was constantly keeping up with literature involving strange phenomena, such as teleportation reports. Thus, he must have been familiar with many of the common side effects, the Schoenherr EFFECTS, ASSOCIATED WITH TELEPORTATION ANECDOTES."

(For modern examples of Schoenherr effects, see *Search* magazine, No. 181, Winter 1989–1990.) It may just have been Dent's creative genius, and scholarly background, that allowed him to so accurately predict the phenomena that were later associated with the Philadelphia Experiment. This has happened many times in history; the atomic bomb, radar, lasers, the Apollo flight to the moon, even the wreak of the Titanic, etc. were all seemingly described by fiction writers before they became tangible facts.

Perhaps Dent was literally tracing out the future of his fiction.

"If Admiral Rickover really did bury a failed experiment to protect his naval career....then maybe someday soon the pieces of that puzzle will be rediscovered, or reinvented, and certainly better understood, so that teleportation will not be just a collection of anecdotes, but a phenomena that can be made useful to our species.

"POSTSCRIPT: THE SOVIET DOC SAVAGE—In the 1950's, the Russians infiltrated a spy deeply into the maw of American military secrets. The spy was a Swedish Royal Air Force Colonel named Stig Wennerstrom. Oddly enough, this spy looked identical to an artist's version of Doc Savage (the Bama version) that appeared on the covers of the early Bantam Book editions of the series. The only slight difference was that the real Wennerstrom had a receding hairline while the artist's version of the fictional Doc Savage had a deep 'widow's peak' hairline that came down rather unrealistically low on his forehead.

"Wennerstrom had been widely known for his 'strong pro-American stand' among Swedish and American military circles. As a high level diplomat who was considered an important friend of the United States, the spy easily obtained huge quantities of classified military secrets relating to nuclear weapons, bombsights, aircraft performance and design features, and thousands of detailed photographs and documents. His story can be found in Andrew Tully's book, *White Tie and Dagger* (1967). A photo of this spy who looked so much like Doc Savage can be found on page 29 of SAGA magazine for November of 1967."

• • •

The following are books and publications on the AIDS epidemic which were advertized in the 'AMOK' Catalog (P.O. Box 861867), Terminal Annex, Los Angeles, CA 90086-1867, 4th Dispatch: AIDS—BIOLOGICAL WARFARE, by Co. Thomas E. Bearden:

"Shocking as it sounds, I am convinced that the Soviets have already pushed WW III, to the hilt. And it's not the kind of war we've been expecting...

"The great Soviet first strike was delivered with surreptitious biological warfare, not with nuclear weapons or armed forced.... Spurred by the looming holocaust of AIDS, and by the strong [request] of my colleagues, I have decided to release specific information on how to develop electromagnetic healing, essential against any and all 'killer' diseases including cancer [and] leukemia [etc.]." [PB/486/Illus/ $19.50] (Note: 'Communist-Socialism' is not exclusive to any one nation. Although this political plague has gained control or declined in countries around the world, it has not been extinguished. There are still many who hold fast to its false promises."

Could it be that AIDS was a product of World Socialism designed to bring world population down to a 'controllable' number, and could it be that once weakened to the point of minimal resistance by such plagues as AIDS—and whatever else has been thrown against free countries by the Socialists—Communist countries will attempt an outright invasion of the free democratic or republican countries of the world? Also, could it be that, as some suggest, homosexuality has been promoted in America for years by Socialism in order to cause division and weakness, and finally the destruction of untold numbers of people with the misleading excuse that the plague is 'God's judgement' upon homosexuals, drug users, etc.?). AIDS—A SPECIAL REPORT, by 'Noebel': The author of THE MARXIST MINSTRELS [views] AIDS as 'God's will.' [PB/$3.95] AIDS AND THE DOCTORS OF DEATH—AN INQUIRY INTO THE ORIGIN OF THE AIDS EPIDEMIC, by Alan Cantwell, Jr., M.D.:

"According to Dr. Robert Strecker and other scientists, the AIDS virus is a man-made, genetically engineered virus that was deliberately and accidentally introduced into selected populations as part of a secret scientific germ-warfare experiment.

"A massive cover-up by the scientific establishment and the government has kept this information from the American public. Strecker's horrifying assertions of the AIDS conspiracy led the author to research little-known scientific facts about the new epidemic, particularly the relation between AIDS, animal cancer virus experimentation, and genetic bioengineering as viruses designed to destroy the immune system." [HB/240/$18.95]

• • •

In reference to the 'New Age Movement and our coming age of Barbarism,' Attorney Constance E. Cumbey writes this in her book, *The Hidden Dangers of the Rainbow* (1983)—"Benjamin Creme, David Spangler, Alice Bailey, Helena Petrovna Blavatsky, et al, have all said that 'initiation' will be the heart and core of the 'New World Religion.' David Spangler has defined that initiation as a Luciferian initiation and for those who cannot accept the 'New Christ'—they will be sent to another dimension other than the physical incarnation [A nice way of saying, 'If you don't bow down to our New Age Messiah (Antichrist) we will hunt you down and slaughter you and your children!!!]

Creme says that CASH WILL BE ABOLISHED and the world will go to a more rational means of exchange, such as a *computerized* barter economy. Creme has said that the 'initiations will be given on a mass planetary basis in a revitalized

"Christian" Church and in the MASONIC LODGES and other esoteric organizations.' " Note: Could this 'reviralized,' or 'revitalized' 'Christian' Church be the prophesied Whore of Babylon or the Church of ROME? Also, it is pos-

sible that part of the 'Luciferian initiation' will involve accepting the 'mark of the Beast' computer code through laser-implantation or a chip implant in the right hand and/or forehead. Prophecy states that those who receive this implant or 'Mark of the Beast' will have committed the final offence against their Creator, in essence 'signing over' ownership of their souls and FREE WILLS to 'the Beast' and choosing this creature as 'god.' Some suggest these will be incapable of redemption since they will somehow turn their 'wills' over to the collective consciousness of the 'Beast' and therefore could not 'choose' to resist the Antichrist even if they wanted to, because their FREE WILL has been destroyed.

However many may be forced as children or infants to receive the 'mark' without fully exercising their own wills, and God will no doubt have mercy on these because they are children. But a mature adult who may have received the 'Mark' inadvertently and still possesses free will may find a way out...

"If your right hand offends thee cut it off" as the prophetic scripture states,

Some suggest that those who resist the mark and the Beast will be 'beheaded,' and this may include some who inadvertently received the mark while young, and that this act of being 'beheaded' may remove the mark in the 'forehead' and offer a 'back door' into paradise or the salvation of their soul through the destruction of their body. However it should be remembered that these events will only begin AFTER ALL of the followers of 'the Lamb' are temporarily removed PHYSICALLY from the earth by the angelics to the New Jerusalem Complex for a short period of 7 years, still retaining their physical bodies which will be regenerated to perfection and immortality. The harsh events of the 'tribulation' according to scripture will only occur to those who have rejected 'the Lamb' and embraced 'the Serpent' through their own will or through default. Even these will have a 'second' or 'last' chance according to Revelation, but unlike those who received the Lamb in the age of 'Grace,' most of those in the tribulation will only be able to attain salvation through the constant threat of physical death. It'may be that these events will occur only in or around planet earth, the ancient convergence of the Cosmic Conflict [if we can bring this interpretation into Revelation

12, which states that the 'Dragon' will be cast BACK DOWN to earth, having 'great wrath'], and like those who have lived in other times those humans living in other spaces may not be forced to receive the mark [IF the above interpretation is correct], but will nevertheless still be judged for their choices and in particular which side they have chosen to join in the cosmic war between the 'Crimson Ram' and the 'Red Dragon.'

• • •

Researcher John A. Keel described the following incident:

"Where was Dan Koehler on August 19, 1973?

"Mr. Koehler is the tallest man in the United States, standing eight feet two inches tall. But at 8 P.M. on that warm summer evening, someone even taller went striding down the main street of the little village of Buffalo Mills, Pennsylvania. Whoever he was, he seemed to be at least nine feet tall and looked VERY human except for his clothes, which were cut in an odd way and were made of a strange shimmering material.

"As he passed along the street, doors slammed shut, and startled faces peered anxiously around the corners of taut lace curtains. His dark, penetrating gaze transfixed the amazed passersby in Buffalo Mills while he loped along casually, his long legs barely seeming to touch the sidewalk.

"He passed through the town quickly, peaceably, and walked into oblivion, just another one of the hordes of peculiar visitors who appear out of nowhere periodically, often in the center of major cities...then dissolve again into the unknown.

"A few months earlier a similar stranger entered a bar in Tres Arroyos, Argentina. He was also unusually tall and had a discomfiting gaze. The customers in the bar gaped in astonishment as he walked into the men's room. Several minutes passed, and when he didn't reappear, the owner decided to check. The little windowless men's room was empty. There was no other way out. The barkeeper called the local police, and they examined the John minutely. Apparently the seven-foot-tall stranger in the funny suit had flushed himself down the toilet."

• • •

The following letter appeared in *UFO Universe* (issue uncertain):

"I enjoy your magazine very much. Thank you for such a fine publication. I have seen UFOs, and it seems after you have seen one you're never the same. I separated from the U.S. Air Force in December of 1987. In the Air Force I was a 'Security Specialist.' It was my duty to safeguard Top Secret aircraft, weapons and equipment. I also guarded nuclear warheads. I was stationed at David-Monthan A.F.B. in Tucson, Arizona. In January of 1987 I was training in the desert for a Desert Survival Course. This area is between Indian Springs, Nevada and Las Vegas, Nevada. It is known as Silver Flag Alpha. There is a huge mountain range and on the other side of this range lies the 'Area 52,' also known as 'Dreamland.'

"I asked an instructor what would happen if somebody went over the ridge. He said, 'No one can make it over that ridge,' and then gave me a foxish grin.

"One night about 0300 hours I was sitting in my foxhole gazing at the stars when a white light rose over the ridge. It performed two vertical loops then shot up into the sky at a speed you would not believe. It didn't make any noise.

"After separating from the Air Force I stayed in Tucson for 19 months. During this time my best Air Force buddy received orders for 'Area 52.' I told him to stay in touch. He called one day and told me he DIDN'T LIKE the assignment. I asked him about 'Area 52' and he said he wasn't at liberty to discuss it. He did say he was stationed at Nellis A.F.B. Nevada and forced to live off base. He said an Air Force vehicle would pick him up and transfer him to 'Area 52' where he would spend 48 hours in an underground complex. After 48 hours he was then returned to his apartment for 48 hours off time. I asked him what kind of things he had seen. He only said don't be surprised if one day we are living in space. After this we talked about normal guy stuff. I never have heard from him since, which is PECULIAR. I wonder if the Air Force had his apartment phone tapped?—Steve Blankenship., P.O. Box 1126., Somerset, TX 78069."

• • •

Nazi Germany's Advanced Secret Weapon

and Space Program began in the early 1940's and involved the development of the 'Flugelrad' or 'Wingwheel.' The Flugelrad was a saucer-helicopter, the first vertical takeoff flying vehicle developed by the Nazis. The wings (blades) which issued from the centre of the craft like spokes toward the outer rim, were tiltable. This was allegedly the 'Model T' of a series of German 'disk' or 'saucer' designs which followed. Much of this program, of course, was top secret—even to the German public. According to 'Samisdat Publications,' an ultra right-wing organization based in Toronto, Canada, the Nazis did in fact develop such a flying device.

Why then did not the world learn of such a thing when Nazi Germany fell? Well, says Samisdat and others, as the war was ending several colonies of German scientists were transported to secret bases in Antarctica and elsewhere (a possibility that, when considered, seems to be plausible) where the secret 'disk' technology was perfected. Due to the lack of documentable proof of such an operation taking place, we cannot fully confirm this, but perhaps other documentation will come forth in the future and time will tell whether these claims are legitimate or not.

Actually there is evidence that just before World War II the Germans had secretly been exploring the Polar regions. Perhaps this would explain the bizarre episode surrounding the fateful voyage of Capt. Charles Hall. The American Geographical Society in New York records that, apparently on the basis of stories of unexplored regions in the extreme north (where 'habitable' land—perhaps volcanically heated—was rumored to exist, possibly beyond a great ice barrier), the U.S. Government sent out an expedition to the North Pole, at the request of President Grant, in 1870. The expedition used the U.S.S. POLARIS under the command of Capt. Charles Hall. Hall died along the way and was buried in the snow. The ship returned. But that's not the end of the story.

The public T.V. program 'NOVA' reported that in recent years Hall's grave was found. Samples of hair and fingernails were taken and tested. They showed that he had died of slow poisoning! And, what's more, a check of records showed that the cook (who would have been in a perfect position to administer poisoning) AND first mate on the U.S.A. Polaris turned out to be GERMAN 'OCCULTIST' SPIES!!! Was there something at the North Pole that the German occultists were trying to hide? Anyway, there is sufficient evidence that during the war these secret Nazi Polar expeditions intensified. Is there anything to these claims of secret bases at the poles? Only time will tell. There is much evidence that, in fact, the Nazis WERE very deeply involved in the occult. Researcher Jason Bishop (pseudonym for a French-American researcher who has been involved in 'Inner Earth' research for several years) gives the following information on the subject:

"All of the Nazi-occult groups were more or less closely associated with the powerful and well organized 'Theosophical Society,' which added to neo-pagan magic an oriental setting and a Hindu terminology. Or, rather, it provided a link between a certain oriental Satanism and the west.

"Nazi occultism was a mixture of influences and a host of interrelated secret societies including the Bavarian Illuminati [Bavaria, GERMANY that is], the Knights Templar, the Teutonic Knights, the 'holy' Vehm, the Golden Dawn, the Rosey-Cross, the Vril Society, the German Order (Germanenorden) and it's offshoot THE THULE SOCIETY (Thule Gesellschaft) founded in Munich in 1918.

"Thus was a neo-Gnostic racist group, which became a rallying front for the secret society roots of Naziism. The chief architect was Baron Rudolf von Sebottendorff (Rudolf Glauer) who had direct contact with the Dervish Orders and knew a great deal about Islamic mysticism, particularly Sufism in all it's aspects. He also had contact with Herman Pohl, leader of the German Order Walvater of the Holy Grail.

"Note: Sebottendorff wrote 'BEFORE HITLER CAME,' in 1933, which mentioned the occult affiliations of the Nazi leadership (National Socialist Movement). The Nazi regime suppressed and destroyed this book, as the information was not for the (German) public.

"The Thulist, Detrich Eckart, is believed to have initiated Hitler into various occult mysteries with the aid of psychedelic drugs.

"The most prominent member of the Vril Society, was Karl Haushofer, a close confident of Hitler, Hess and Rosenburg.

"Alfred Rosenberg and Adolf Hitler himself belonged to the Thule Gesellschaft.

So did Rudolf Hess! Read (for additional details) *The Spear of Destiny*, by Trevor Ravenscroft and *The Occult and the Third Reich*, by Jean-Michel Angebert. These were the type of men who were in charge of the Nazi's secret 'flying disk' program. One of the scientists involved with the early Nazi 'saucer' projects was of course Victor Schauberger, who was brought to America after the war where he was rumored to be working on a top-secret 'flying disk' project in Texas for the U.S. Government, until his death in 1958. It is said that some of the prototypes which the government is now developing are as advanced (wherein propulsion, etc., is concerned) over the 'Schauberger' models as the Space Shuttle is over the bi-plane. 'Samisdat' relates some information on Schauberger, who might have been considered the aeronautical 'Einstein' of his time, although not nearly as well-known as the famous white-haired Jewish scientist.

Schauberger allegedly developed several prototypes of disk-shaped aerial craft which worked on the following principles:

"MODEL I—The most conventional design, by today's concepts. It used a standard German Walther Rocket Engine and was steered by a conventional rudder.

"MODEL II—An improvement over Model I, with a radical departure: A specially-designed 'rotary wing' stabilized and steered the craft. This model was more maneuverable and faster.

"MODEL III—Extremely fast, using a jet-vacuum propulsion system. Capable of attaining speeds of over 6,000 kilometers per hour. The fuel mixture produced vapor trails, an acrid smell, and sometimes flames and sparks. The saucer's propulsion system produced high-pitched, whining sounds. The craft was capable of terrific acceleration or steady hover. It could climb and bank steeply and often startled the observer with loud sonic booms as it accelerated through the sound barrier. This model was equipped with telescopic landing gear.

"Successors of MODEL III, still in the planning stage during the mid-1940's, utilized the Earth's magnetic field in their propulsion systems.

"THE SCHAUBERGER MODELS—Using the original implosion-powered propulsion system, these Nazi Saucers made no sound. They were flameless, odorless and smokeless, but the outer skin of the hull, composed of a secret alloy called 'impervium,' pulsated eerily with various colors of the rainbow as the craft sped through the sky at velocities in excess of 10,000 kilometers per hour. Extremely maneuverable, these Nazi Saucers, dubbed 'Foo-Fighters' by Allied bomber crews, could change altitude and course with surprising suddenness." [see: SECRET NAZI POLAR EXPEDITIONS; UFO'S, NAZI SECRET WEAPONS?; THE CIA-KGB UFO COVER- UP; and THE ANTARCTICA THEORY. Booklets available from—Samisdat Publishers., 206 Carlton St., Toronto, Ont., M5A 2L1 CANADA].

• • •

Manly P. Hall, Sovereign Grand Inspector General and 33rd degree Mason, makes the following self-contradictory yet nevertheless revealing statement in his book *The Lost Keys of Freemasonry* (1976, page 48,64):

"The true disciple of ancient Masonry has given up forever the worship of personalities... he never bows before altar whether in temple, mosque, cathedral or pagoda. No true Mason can be narrow. The seething energies of LUCIFER are in his hands and before he may step onward and upward, he must prove his ability to properly apply (this) energy."

• • •

The following article, titled 'CIA HATCHETMAN, WORLD'S BIGGEST GUN-RUNNER, JAILED LYNDON LAROUCHE,' comes from 'LAROUCHE FOR JUSTICE.', P.O. Box 961., Leesburg, VA 22075:

"Federal Judge Albert V. Byran, Jr., who jailed U.S. opposition leader Lyndon LaRouche and six associates on phony 'conspiracy' charges, is a career CIA hatchetman and a key operator in the world's biggest gun-running outfit.

"Byran personally organized and financed the largest private arms dealer, Interarms, a joint priority of British Intelligence and the U.S. Central Intelligence Agency.

"Between 10 and 25 million persons have been killed with rifles, machine guns, and explosives supplied by Byran's organization over the past 30 years in wars, revolutions, and terrorism. Interarms now controls 90% of the world's private arms traffic [*Note:* Many of these arms have been sold to Third World countries and dictators which the CIA wanted to raise up as armies to fight other Third World countries and dictators whom they did not like, or to raise up puppets to overthrow dictators in those same countries—CIA puppets who have often turned out to be much worse than the original dictators. Unfortunately this stupid policy of interference in the affairs of a nation has backfired on the U.S., who has been forced to confront such countries as Iran, Iraq, and so many others which the CIA had armed and which they have since lost control of."

These policies have caused much chaos in these countries by disturbing the natural balances of power, and only goes to show that the policy of intervention in nearly every case has failed to bring peace and prosperity to those countries. Even if the United States supports these countries as 'welfare states,' they will eventually have to work out their own problems in the end.

But then again there is much evidence that the CIA and their fellow Merchants of Death knew exactly what they were doing, and were in fact working for those who would make such third world nations dependant on a one-world cabal through fomentation of chaos, high-interest loans, etc. There is a moral obligation on the part of those nations who have the power to do so to help those who are suffering economically to help themselves, but when the U.N. begins to believe that it is the supreme political power on earth and that all nations must submit to it POLITICALLY, and submit their armies to a world police force to implement military intervention against monsters which they helped to create, then something somewhere must be very wrong!].

"Judge Albert V. Byran, Jr. was selected in 1988 by prosecutors targeting LaRouche, because Byran is at the center of the multi-government spy apparatus run by the Anglo-American 'bluebloods.' As a CIA hatchetman on the federal bench since 1972, Judge Byran is depended upon to protect criminal projects of that spy apparatus, caring nothing for the law.

"During the railroad LaRouche trial in 1988, Byran prohibited any mention of the classified LaRouche files, admitted then to be under the jurisdiction of Vice President George Bush, files whose contents demonstrate the innocence of LaRouche. National Security Decision Directive 3 made the Vice President the head of covert operations and all intelligence; Executive Order 12333 allowed harassment and legal targeting of selected 'enemies,' even where there was no

legal case against them."

As President, George Bush controlled the potential release of the files.

"Albert V. Byran, Jr. organized the Interarms company in the mid-1950s, coordinating with the Washington Post, the CIA, and the British Defense Ministry. Sam Cummings, the public boss of Interarms, had been employed by the CIA for a few years as a gunrunner in Europe and Central America, before he came to Alexandria, Virginia in 1955.

"To start up the world's largest covert-operations arms trafficking company, funding went through an Alexandria bank that had been owned by Byran and his family and their close friends since 1864. Albert V. Byran, Jr. was co-owner, director, and the bank's attorney, when First and Citizen's National Bank of Alexandria set up Interarms.

"Byran's bank put up the money to buy a half-million rifles from Argentina, and more money to buy rifles from the British War Ministry.

"Cummings stored the guns in warehouse space provided by Robinson's Terminal Warehouse, Inc.—Albert V. Byran, Jr., attorney, Clarence Robinson, president. For better control, Robinson was made president of the Byran family bank in 1957.

"Hundreds of thousands of guns come in from Europe on boats that usually carried newsprint paper for the Washington Post. Robinson's warehouse has run the Post's paper supply since 1939. Post Chairman Katherine Graham later bought out the Robinson company to control the possible dangerous release of information about the nightmare history of this firm.

"Byran arranged more and more financing for Interarms. Byran and Robinson supplied more and more financing for Interarms. Byran and Robinson supplied the property on which to build the arms company's new warehouses. Byran's bank chose the first president of Interarms and organized a retail gun division, 'Hunter's Lodge.' [Strange that the Socialist anti-gun lobbies have overlooked this worst offender of gun control during their attacks on private gun ownership].

"CASTRO, QADDAFI AND 'SUICIDES'—The first big CIA project of the Byran enterprise was ARMING Cuban revolutionary FIDEL CASTRO. Agency for International Development trucks picked up small arms, rifles, machine guns, and ammunition in Alexandria and drove them to Andrews Air Force Base in Maryland for shipment to Central and South America, for untraceable delivery to Castro's forces. After Castro seized power, Interarms armed his government openly. Then the CIA turned against Castro, and Interarms equipped the Cuban exiles for the bungled Bay of Pigs invasion.

"Byran's Interarms company armed Libyan leader MUAMMAR QADDAFI during the period when the Anglo-Americans backed Qaddafi's revolution. While George Bush was director of the CIA in 1976-77, CIA employees under Edwin Wilson trained and armed Qaddafi's terrorists and assassins, in North Africa, in Europe, and in Virginia.

"CIA man Frank Terpil, a top Qaddafi supplier, was arrested after police raids on his arms dealings with Albert Byran's Interarms company over in England. The CIA claimed that the Qaddafi operation was unauthorized; NOW Qaddafi was 'like Hitler' [Who was no doubt another dictator who was raised up by these types of manipulators]. Gun-running Judge Albert V. Byran, Jr. sat on key parts of Frank Terpil's case to keep things under control.

"Then CIA man Waldo Dubberstein, arrested in the Wilson-Terpil affair, said he was acting ON CIA ORDERS. He was shot to death, a 'suicide,' just as he was to appear in BYRAN'S court. CIA man Larry Tu-Wai Chin, arrested for leaking secrets to Chinese Communists, said he was acting on behalf of the Kissinger-Bush policy, and his [own] 'confession' was phony. Judge Byran ruled the 'confession' legal. Chin was convicted and before sentencing, was FOUND DEAD in his cell, a plastic bag tied tightly over his head—a 'suicide.'

"HOW THE BRITISH RUN THESE PROJECTS —The world's dirtiest projects are run through private banks and front companies in Alexandria, Virginia, under direct British [Empire] supervision. Spy agencies coordinate everything through Albert Byran's family and a clique of his fellow Episcopalians, Freemasons, lawyers, and bank directors. Two institutions rule there, Christ Episcopal Church and the George Washington National Memorial MASONIC temple; both give their allegiance to the British monarchy [Note: Just as Rome is the world headquarters of the JESUIT lodge and Vatican city is a sovereign nation in itself within the nation of Italy; London—also an 'independent' sover-

eignty in itself within the British Isles—is the world headquarters of the MASONIC lodge. According to several sources, BOTH the JESUIT and MASONIC organizations, both hiding beneath a feigned veneer of so-called 'Christianity' and both APPARENTLY in conflict at the lower levels, nevertheless have an active and working cooperation at the uppermost 'Illuminated' levels].

"When Judge Byran's father was A MASON and a vestryman in 1937, Christ Church reenacted in detail the coronation of their sovereign, King George VI. A future chairman of the Byran family bank played the role of the Duke of Kent, a PRO-HITLER Masonic leader. There was massive armed security at Winston Churchill and Franklin Roosevelt's 1942 Christ Church prayer service [The same Winston Churchill, and 'possibly' Franklin Roosevelt, who failed to warn the U.S. Navy of the imminent invasion of Pearl Harbor, an invasion the British Monarchy knew of at least a month in advance but kept secret so that they could drag America into World War II]. But congregation members were not screened. As one vestryman put it, 'We wouldn't let them screen us—WE ARE AMERICANS.'

"Clarence Robinson made a fortune supplying cement to build the giant Alexandria MASONIC TEMPLE. It is the operating headquarters of 'white' Freemasonry in North America—they consider black men's lodges to be 'illegitimate.' The RACIAL message is boldly displayed on the lobby walls of the Byran company, Interarms: drawings of Confederate soldiers, carrying guns SUPPLIED BY British gunrunners for the slaveowners' Rebellion of 1861.

"The SPY COURT—From 1979 to 1986, Judge Albert V. Byran, Jr. worked in the top-secret Foreign Intelligence Surveillance Court operated by the Justice Department. Byran gave warrants to the secret services, legalizing wiretaps and mail intercepts within the U.S.A. Byran was a direct secret participant with the executive agencies which have admitted illegally spying on and harassing the LaRouche political movement since at least 1968.

"After the 400-MAN police raid on LaRouche-affiliated publishing offices in 1986, Judge Byran ruled that the government could legally close down the LaRouche movement publications in a 'forced bankruptcy.' Then Byran imprisoned LaRouche political allies FOR non-payment of debts, prohibiting mention of Byran's own role in shutting down the movement's means of raising money. Byran suppressed all evidence of 20 years of harassment against contributors by spy agencies that Byran himself served in their dirtiest, most criminal projects.

"Albert V. Byran, Jr.'s court is widely known as the 'rocket docket.' This is supposed to refer to the speed with which the defendant is destroyed. But a few blocks away, the grimmer meaning of the phrase is revealed, at the tightly guarded warehouse of Judge Byran's mass-death project, Interarms."

• • •

In June of 1955, *Look* magazine released the following information:

"...persistent and fairly credible (accounts claim) that aCanadian aircraft manufacturer, A. V. Roe, Canada, Ltd., has had a saucer design under development for two years (i.e. since 1953). The report has it that the project was abandoned by the Canadian Government because it would cost over $75 million to get a prototype model into the air. The A. V. Roe people maintain a confusing SILENCE about the whole thing. They can't deny the project has been abandoned because they never announced it had begun (and, in fact, some sources claim that a jet-powered flying disk nicknamed the 'AVRO DISK' was developed, though no official information as to where this project might have led afterwards was ever released to the public). Our own Air Force offers no comment.

"At a recent meeting of engineers, it was indicated that, while flying saucer or sphere projects MAY be purely hypothetical, new air-defense problems are setting up requirements for aircraft performance that would seem to be most ideally met by a saucer craft...

"One problem, recently stated by Brig. Gen. Benjamin Kelsey, deputy director of research and development for the Air Force, is this: 'Airplanes today spend too much time gathering speed on the ground and not enough time flying in the air.' Today's fighters, he pointed out, need extremely long runways and there are few in existence that are now long enough. These few, and the concentration of planes using them, provide a worthwhile target for an A-bomb. With a single blow, the enemy might

cripple a substantial portion of our air defense.

"Planes that could take off vertically would not need long runways, which cost millions of dollars. They could be dispersed widely and safely. In this country, four vertical-rising aircraft have been revealed (No doubt at the present date this number has risen dramatically). All but one, however, are modifications of conventional plane designs. None yet approach the performance a true saucer might be capable of.

"What are the requirements of an ideal defense fighter? 1) Ability to take off and land vertically; 2) high speed of over Mach 2 (more than 1500 m.p.h.); 3) high rate of climb; 4) excellent maneuverability; 5) heavy armament; 6) ability to operate at 60,000 feet...[such a craft might include] a one-man crew, housed in a glass bubble that would provide excellent visibility. The prone position of the pilot not only [would allow] improved streamlining but also enables the pilot to withstand high accelerations and quick turns (the disk-shape, according to some, might also act as it's own 'airfoil,' and thus 'wings' would not be necessary). The design contemplates use of cannon, rockets and guided missiles. Exact armament would depend on the mission. The target would be sighted by radar, and actual firing would be completed and accomplished electronically, as in several interceptors now in operation...

"Future airports built for vertically rising flying saucers would have no need of the many vulnerable runways today's fighters require. The complete operation could go underground. Tunnels with takeoff shafts set in the ground, complete with maintenance bays, fuel and crew quarters, would be bombproof shelters for a saucer squadron. The shafts would be sealed after takeoff for camouflage and protection."

• • •

Peter Brookesmith, in his book *UFOs, Where Do They Come From?* (MacDonald & Co., Pub., London, England. 1984. pp. 16-17) elaborates on the history of one of the German scientists involved in the top secret Nazi saucer projects. In reference to this scientist, Rudolph Schriever, Brookesmith reveals:

"...His 'flying disc' had been ready for testing in early 1945, but with the advance of the Allies into Germany, the test had to be canceled, the machine destroyed, and his complete papers mislaid or stolen in the chaos of the Nazi retreat [so the official 'story' goes].

"Schriever died not long after these revelations, convinced to the end that the UFO sightings since the end of the war were proof that his original ideas had been taken further with successful results.

"But what were the foo fighters? An identification was proposed by an Italian author, Renato Vesco, in a book first published in 1968. According to him the foo fighter was actually the German FEUERBALL (Fireball), first constructed at an aeronautical establishment at Wiener Neustadt. The craft was a flat, circular flying machine, powered by a turbojet. It was used during the closing stages of the war both as an anti-radar device and as a psychological weapon designed to disturb Allied pilots. Vesco says: '"The fiery halo around its perimeter—caused by a very rich fuel mixture—and the chemical additives that interrupted the flow of electricity by overionizing the atmosphere in the vicinity of the place, generally around the wing tips or tail surfaces, subjected the H2S radar on the plane to the action of powerful electrostatic fields and electromagnetic impulses.'

"Vesco also claims that the basic principles of the FEUERBALL were later applied to a much larger 'symmetrical circular aircraft' known as the KUGELBLITZ (Ball Lightning), which could rise vertically by 'jet lift.'

"Since neither the British, the Americans nor the Russians are ever likely to reveal what, precisely, was discovered in the secret factories in Nazi Germany, it is worth noting that in 1945 Sir Roy Feddon, leader of a technical mission to Germany for the British Ministry of Aircraft Production, reported:

"I have seen enough of their designs and production plans to realize that if they had managed to prolong the war some months longer, we would have been confronted with a set of entirely new and deadly developments in air warfare. [Whether a 'secret society' of Neonazi 'UFOnauts' still exists or not is debatable, but this as well as the threat by certain 'alien' groups may explain the almost fanatical secrecy and research and development surrounding certain government 'saucer' projects in America]

In 1956, Captain Edward J. Ruppelt, then head of the U.S. Air Force Project Blue Book, was able to state:

"When World War II ended, the Germans had several radical types of aircraft and guided missiles under development. The majority of these were in the preliminary stages, but they were the only KNOWN craft that could ever approach the performance of the objects reported by UFO observers. [Note: We must admit however that even though the Nazi air vehicles might have been the source of som' UFO sightings, such events had been taking place long before World War II].

"POST WAR SAUCER PROJECTS: The first concrete evidence for post-war flying saucer construction projects came in 1954. The Canadian Government announced that the enormous UFO seen over Albuquerque, New Mexico, in 1951 was similar to one they had tried to build shortly after the war. Owing to their lack of advanced technology, they had eventually passed the design over to the United States.

"Further evidence for the United States involvement with saucer-shaped aircraft projects was to be found in the U.S. Navy's Flying Flapjack. The Flapjack, also known as the Navy Flounder, was a circular aircraft, the design of which was begun during the Second World War. At that time what the Navy desperately needed was an aeroplane that could rise almost vertically so that it could take off from carriers, and could fly at as little as 35 miles per hour (55 km/h).

"Little was known about that machine until early 1950, shortly after the U.S. Air Force had ended its UFO investigation program, Project Grudge (the forerunner of Project Blue Book). AS AN ATTEMPT to show that UFOs did not merit further investigation ('officially speaking' that is), the Air Force released photographs and vague information about the Flying Flapjack.

"Apparently, because the aircraft was wingless, the reduced stability had presented problems. A later model, reportedly designated the XF-5-U-I, solved that problem and was rumored to be over 100 feet (30 meters) in diameter, and to have jet nozzles—resembling the 'glowing windows' seen on so many UFOs—arranged around its rim. It was built in three layers, the central layer being slightly larger than the other two. Since the saucer's velocity and maneuvering abilities were controlled by the power and tilt of the separate jet nozzles, there were no ailerons, rudders and other protruding surfaces. The machine was remarkably similar to [some of] those reported by UFO witnesses.

"Research on saucer-shaped aircraft did not stop with the XF-5-U-I. On 11 February 1953 the Toronto 'STAR' reported that a new flying saucer was being developed at the Avro-Canada plant in Malton, Ontario. On 16 February the Minister for Defense Production informed the Canadian House of Commons that Avro- Canada was working on a 'mock-up model' of a flying saucer, capable of flying at 1500 miles per hour (2400 km/h) and climbing vertically. Then the president of Avro-Canada wrote in 'AVRO NEWS' that the prototype being built was SO REVOLUTIONARY THAT IT WOULD MAKE ALL OTHER FORMS OF SUPERSONIC AIRCRAFT OBSOLETE. The craft's official name was the Avro Car.

"But by 1960 it was being OFFICIALLY claimed that the project had been dropped. The 'prototype' of the Avro flying saucer is now in the U.S. Air Force Museum in Fort Eustis, Virginia. The Canadian and U.S. Governments have insisted that they are no longer involved with flying saucer construction projects.

"Yet it this necessarily true? The possibility remains that the Canadian, United States or Soviet governments could have continued to work on highly advanced, saucer-shaped, supersonic aircraft. The people directly involved in the projects, understanding the impossibility of testing the machines in complete secrecy, may have opted for creating a smokescreen and confusion, rumor and systematic humiliation of UFO observers, thereby ensuring that they can fly their machines with impunity.

"But could man-made machines have such remarkable performance?

"We have only to think of the extraordinary innovations of contemporary science and technology—jet aircraft, space rockets, reconnaissance satellites, pulse beam weapons—and then remember such miracles are merely the tip of the iceberg, and that what goes on behind the guarded fences of our top-secret military and scientific establishments is probably decades ahead of these. Then it becomes easier to answer 'yes.'" Brookesmith also refers to a Dr. 'Miethe,' another German scientist involved in the 'saucer' projects. The 'saucer' he developed "was almost ready for operational use in 1945, when the factories in Prague were overrun by the Allies."

• • •

A. Hyatt Verrill and Ruth Verrill, in their book *America's Ancient Civilizations* (G. P. Putnam's Sons., New York), refer [p. 94] to the legendary 'seven caves' of Aztec tradition which were believed to lie somewhere north of the ancient Mexican empire. Other sources suggest that the 'seven caves' lie beneath a range of mountains adjacent to the 'Salton Sea' of southern California, within which underground 'rockslides' have occasionally been heard, according to witnesses. The Verrill's suggest, however, another possibility of the location of the ancient Aztecean influence is in Utah. Utah, especially southern Utah, contains many legends of ancient 'treasure caves' utilized by ancient civilizations. According to the Verrill's:

"There are also indications of the presence of these ancient people near Kanab, Utah, not far from the Arizona border. Here, rising above a large level area that obviously was at one time marshland, and where many rocks bear carved figures of ducks, there are seven distinctive mountains. Leading up one of these is a vast stairway cut in igneous rock. Not far from the summit is a conspicuously white peak, and, at its base, there is an opening or tunnel mouth about 17 by 14 feet which was sealed with stones and a form of cement composed of mud and wiry grass stems, very obviously from a marsh or swamp. Within the tunnel that extends several hundred feet into the mountain were charcoal, the bones of deer and rabbits and other evidences of human occupancy.

"All about the vicinity are caves and narrow arroyos or canyons, and in some of these are crumbling remains of very ancient cliff dwellers' houses. In almost every respect this might well be the legendary CHICO-MOZTOC or 'Place of the Seven Caves,' for which the word may be translated as either 'Place of Caves' or 'Canyons.'"

• • •

Franklin Folsom's book *Exploring American Caves* (Their History, Geology, Lore and Location: A Spelunker's Guide—Crown Publishers, Inc., New York), states the following:

"...Is it possible that one vast, interconnecting water- filled cavern system extends from Kentucky westward, under both the Ohio and Mississippi Rivers? This theory has been suggested by those who have no other explanation yet for the wide dispersion of one variety of blind white fish.

"...Carlsbad is generally believed to be the deepest [now Lechuguilla, adjacent to Carlsbad, is believed to be the deepest officially, as of 1992], and at least one geologist thinks it likely that one or more levels exist BELOW the eleven- hundred-foot depth that has been reached.

"...Meteorologists are fascinated by the problems they meet in trying to account for the movement of air in some of the underground passages. For example, no one has yet been able to explain the phenomenon first observed by the veteran spelunker Burton Faust in a cave near Burnsville, Virginia. One day while waiting at the mouth of a crawlway for other cavers who had gone through it, Faust noticed that the air above him was moving strangely. He lit a candle and watched its flame lean in one direction. He lit a cigar. The smoke drifted into the crawlway, came to a stop, then drifted back out and stopped once more. It looked for all the world as if the largely unexplored passageways beyond were breathing—in and out. The cave became known as Breathing Cave.

"On numerous trips, observers have checked Faust's report. The cycle lasted some eight minutes, sometimes more—but 'breathe' the cave did and still does. Nobody can explain why.

"...There have been other unlikely exhibitions put on by air deep inside caves... It is part of folklore in some quarters that cave air is dangerous—or that there may not be enough of it to breath. Spelunkers know better. They know that caves for the most part are a paradise for sufferers from hay fever, since the underground air usually lacks pollen and is free of dust unless human beings stir it up. However, from time to time, there have come reports that a certain cave contained 'bad' air—people complained of mysterious symptoms that seemed to indicate lack of oxygen. In almost every case where a scientific examination of the air has been made, the oxygen content in these caves has been normal. On the other hand, there are situations which can mean 'bad' air.

"...Kiser Cave between Fredericksburg and Mason, Texas, pours out a STEADY STREAM of carbon dioxide from its mouth. No one has yet found the source of this gas. Only three men have made an attempt to explore it with oxygen masks and tanks, and they nearly perished in the attempt."

• • •

The Sept. 1958 issue of *Fate* magazine stated (p. 16-17):

"THOR HEYERDAHL, the Pacific raft mariner [the Kon-Tiki raft expedition] who spent a considerable time in Easter Island, had not yet received word of Barthel's accomplishment when he was interviewed on his Easter Island conclusions recently in London.

"Heyerdahl has published a book called 'AKU-AKU' which repeats his South American hypothesis. He also declares that there must have been at least three successive cultures on Easter.

"He reveals that islanders whose confidence he won took him down into secret caves through terrifying needle's eye shafts. Here were stored sculptures of an entirely different kind from those which brought Easter its world-wide fame.

"An assumption can be made that the creators of the earlier type of statues were conquered by those who later erected the later type. And these people in turn were overthrown by a people who toppled both them and their statues."

Chapter 6: Dimension Doorways, Subterranean Cities, Secret Symbols & Ritualistic Abuse

Death Valley, California and the Mojave Desert region have been the sight of numerous UFO sightings in the past. Some regard it as no less that a doorway into another world. The Panamint Indians in fact tell of a race of Grecian or Egyptian-like people with white robes and long dark hair held back with a band who thousands of years ago arrived in the area in large rowing vessels. The Paiutes say that when Death Valley was still part of an inland sea connected to the Pacific ocean through the Gulf of California the Havmu-suvs discovered an underground cavern system in the Panamint mountains adjacent to Death Valley, and in these vast caverns they built their civilization.

The legend says that these ancient people travelled to and from their sea vessels to the shore below through large 'quays' or 'doors' high up the eastern slope of the Panamints. However after centuries the lake eventually dried up and disappeared, and as a result of this they developed new methods of reaching the world beyond. This, the Paiutes say, was when they began to build their silvery 'flying canoes'. Whether there is any connection with the following account is uncertain, but in 1905 an 'airship flap' was observed throughout southern California. On August 2, 1905, J. A. Jackson, "a well-known resident of Silshee," was out at 1:30 in the morning when a bright light appeared in the sky and headed for him. According to an account published in the Brawley, California, NEWS on Aug. 4, 1905:

"He watched it closely until behind the light there appeared the form of an airship, apparently about 70 feet in length, with a searchlight in front and several other lights aboard. The mysterious machine appeared to be propelled by wings alone and rose and fell as the wings flapped like a gigantic bird. Apparently there was no balloon attachment as is usually the case with airships.

"Mr. Jackson, being close to the home of W.E. Wilsie, woke him up in time to see the lights of the machine before it disappeared."

The same night, H. E. Allatt, postmaster at Imperial, was awakened from sleep by a bright light shining into his room. There was no moon, the light was thought to be fire, and Mr. Allatt rose to investigate, but no fire was found. Looking at his watch, the time was discovered to be 1:30 o'clock, and it is believed that the brilliant light was caused by the searchlight from this mysterious airship." A craft of almost identical description was reported only 4 years later in the Dec. 15, 1909 issue of the Arkansas *Gazette*:

"A.W. Norris of Mabelvale, road overseer of District No. 8, is of the opinion that an airship passed over his residence at about 10 o'clock Monday night (December 12).

"Mr. Norris states that he was standing in his doorway when a strange light appeared, apparently about 300 feet above him, traveling south at a rapid rate of speed and disappeared a moment or two later in the darkness. He said that the light had the appearance of a searchlight similar to those used on automobiles, and IT ROSE AND FELL like a bird in flight. The night was cloudy, which precludes the possibility of the light having been a star or any atmospheric phenomena."

Air ships of this description were apparently common following the turn of the century, but few if any of this particular type of craft have been reported after the period just described (1900–1910, etc.). Just because an 'airship' appears over California or Arkansas does not necessarily indicate that the airship was native to either one of those areas. However, there are nonetheless many evidences as indicated elsewhere in the The Cosmic Patriot Files that the Mojave Desert-Panamint Mountains-Death Valley areas were apparently in ancient times a 'cradle', possibly one of many, for an early civilization which later developed an advanced form of technology, and did so in relative secrecy while allowing the 'uncivilized' tribes outside of their domain to continue in their relatively ignorant life-styles.

Perhaps the most remarkable confirmation of this appears in Bourke Lee's biography Death Valley Men [MacMillan Co., New York. 1932], which also dealt with alleged caverns within the Panamint Mts. region. If indeed the Panamint mountains are an ancient 'doorway' to an advanced HUMAN race, then one must recognize that it as well as any of it's 'NATIONAL TREASURES' should be "as ANY NATIONAL BORDER ON THE FACE OF THE EARTH" considered the legal territory of those who have possessed it since ancient times. Unwelcomed intrusions into such an 'undiscovered country' may be dealt with as in any other nation on earth, and one should approach such territories with caution.

UNLIKE areas where subterranean and malevolent antihuman 'reptilian' activity is alleged to exist, the independence and national sovereignty of those subsurface regions where hidden HUMAN colonies reside should be honored, again as one would honor ANY national border on the face of the earth. Even if an archeological discovery is found which belonged to the ancestors of some ancient culture which STILL EXISTS, that discovery should be the property of that culture alone. Even if such a culture was driven out of a subsurface territory by non-human malevolents, and those ter-

ritories are somehow regained in a possible future counter-invasion against the reptilian 'invasion', then those territories should rightfully still belong to the human cultures who formerly possessed it.

Supposing there IS a counter-invasion in the future, there would no doubt still be much territory left over once the reptilians are driven out and/or destroyed which might NOT be 'claimed' by a cave-dwelling tribe, colony or culture. Such subsurface systems could then be claimed by an outside government if they felt the need to expand their 'territory'. According to some accounts, the U.S. government does know about such underground systems and having found many of them unoccupied in past explorations, have claimed them for their own. Unfortunately, even in the case of smaller underground repositories of ancient artifacts, there are indications that many ancient treasures have been 'melted down' by prospectors, tomb robbers, etc., in order to gain the metal value of the gold, silver, etc. out of which the ancient artifacts were formed, in order to prevent the state from taking 'their find' away.

In doing so, such treasure hunters have destroyed the immense historical and archaeological value of such treasures in exchange for the 'relatively' pitiful metallic value. Many of the ancient Egyptian treasures fell prey to such vandals and 'grave robbers' in ancient times. Even if one does not agree with the religious symbolisms behind such artifacts, their historical and archeological value makes them nevertheless worthy of preservation.

The only reason that 'King Tut's' treasures have made such an impact is that these treasures were among the very few which were not discovered by grave robbers and melted down for their metal content. There is no telling how much HISTORICAL INFORMATION about ancient cultures has been forever lost by such careless actions.

Hopefully humankind has reached the point of maturity where the discovery of such treasures in the future will result in a cooperative scientific study of the ancient artifacts for the benefit of all, rather than the violence, death and betrayal which has resulted in the past through the mistakes of selfish treasure hunters fighting each other for the 'booty'. According to some accounts such ancient sites still await discovery, finds which may make King Tut's

Tomb look like nothing by comparison.

Just as one should honor the ancient archaeological SITES of existing cultures, in the same way one should honor the national sovereignty of another human CULTURE itself. To fail to do so is in essence to THROW AWAY any 'legal' argument FOR the protection of the national sovereignty of one's OWN nation (CASE IN POINT: the reptilian-'Bhogan' and the human-'Roman' empires, which apparently have a secret alliance with each other, have so interfered in the sovereignty of nearly every nation on earth, and have done so to the point that they can no longer legally claim any rational defense against ANY nation which would decide to abuse THEIR 'sovereignty'. The Reptilian 'empire' is of course a problem in itself, having been at war with the majority of the human race since ancient times and apparently from the accounts given throughout these files, does not acknowledge humankind's right to this planet, nor even their 'right' to exist).

Paihute Indian legends say that the 'People of the Panamints' long ago left their ancient city within the mountains of California and moved to still deeper cavern levels, or according to still other accounts to colonies beyond the confines of planet earth itself. Although 'they' may be 'benevolent' in comparison to some cultures inhabiting the surface of the planet, they nevertheless [according to the incredibly corroborative, in relation to the following account, Paihute legends, such as those given in *The Cosmic Patriot Files*, have the ability and technology to defend their 'borders' and their loved ones from humans and 'beasts' alike.

In his chapter 'OLD GOLD' the author of *Death Valley Men*, Bourke Lee, relates the allegedly-true account of two prospectors who claimed to have discovered an ancient, abandoned 'city' within huge caverns inside the heart of the Panamint mountains. Take special note of the INCREDIBLE similarity between this account and the one given to the Navajo Oga-Make by an old Paihute sage, as recorded in the article 'TRIBAL MEMORIES OF THE FLYING SAUCERS' within the *The Cosmic Patriot Files*. We will take up the story where two Death Valley locals by the name of Bill and Jack are having a conversation with two prospectors, 'Thomason' and 'White', from whom the author apparently learned the details of the following discussion, if he was not present at the discussion himself:

"Thomason looked from Jack to Bill and asked, 'How long have you men been in this country?' Jack spoke before Bill had a chance. 'Not very long,' said Jack quietly. Bill glanced curiously at Jack but said nothing. If Jack thought that 30 years was not very long, that was all right with Bill. Thomason said, 'I've been in and out of the Death Valley country for 20 years. So has my partner. We know where there is lost treasure. We've known about it for several years, and we're the only men in the world [?] who do know about it. We're going to let you two fellows in on it. You've been good to us. You're both fine fellows. You haven't asked us any questions about ourselves, and we like you. We think you can keep a secret, so we'll tell you ours." Jack blew smoke and asked, "A lost mine?"

"No, not a mine," said Thomason.

"A lost treasure house. A lost city of gold. It's bigger than any mine that ever was found, or ever will be."

"It's bigger than the United States Mint," said White, with his voice and body shaking with excitement.

"It's a city thousands of years old and worth billions of dollars! Billions of Dollars! Billions! Not Millions. Billions!" Thomason and White spoke rapidly and tensely, interrupting each other in eager speech. Thomason said, "We've been trying to get the treasure out of this golden city for years. We have to have help, and we haven't been able to get it."

"Everybody tries to rob us," put in White.

"They all want too big a share. I offered the whole city to the Smithsonian Institution for five million dollars, only a small part of what it's worth. They tried to rob us, too! They said they'd give me a million and a half for a discovery that's worth a billion dollars!" he sneered.

"I had nothing more to do with them." Jack got up and found his plug of tobacco. He threw away his cigarette and savagely bit off an enormous chew. He sat down and crossed his legs and glowered at White as he worked his chew into his jaw. Bill's voice was meek as he asked,

"And this place is in Death Valley?"

"Right in the Panamint Mountains!" said Thomason.

"My partner found it by accident. He was prospecting down on the lower edge of the range near Wingate Pass. He was working in the bottom of an old abandoned shaft when the bottom fell out and landed him in a tunnel. We've explored the tunnel since. It's a natural tunnel like a big cave. It's over 20 miles long. It leads all through a great underground city; through the treasure vaults, the royal palace and the council chambers; and it connects to a series of beautiful galleries with stone arches in the east slope of the Panamint Mountains. Those arches are like great big windows in the side of the mountain and they look down on Death Valley. They're high above the valley now, but we believe that those entrances in the mountain side were used by the ancient people that built the city. They used to land their boats there."

"Boats!" demanded the astonished Bill, "boats in Death Valley?" Jack choked and said, "Sure, boats. There used to be a lake in Death Valley. I hear the fishing was fine."

"You know about the lake," Thomason pointed his blue chin at Jack.

"Your geology would tell you about the lake. It was a long time ago. The ancient people who built the city in the caverns under the mountain lived on in their treasure houses long after the lake in the valley dried up. How long, we don't know. But the people we found in the caverns have been dead for thousands of years. Why! Those mummies alone are worth a million dollars!" White, his eyes blazing, his body trembling, filled the little house with a vibrant voice on the edge of hysteria.

"Gold!" he cried.

"Gold spears! Gold shields! Gold statues! Jewelry! Thick gold bands on their arms! I found them! I fell into the underground city. There was an enormous room; big as this canyon. A hundred men were in it. Some were sitting around a polished table that was inlaid with gold and precious stones. Men stood around the walls of the room carrying shields and spears of solid gold. All the men, more than a hundred, had on leather aprons, the finest kind of leather, soft and full of gold ornaments and jewels. They sat there and stood there with all that wealth around them. They are still there. They are all dead! And the gold, all that gold, and all those gems and jewels are all around them. All that gold and jewelry! Billions!" White's voice was ascending to a shriek when Thomason put a hand on his arm and White

fell silent, his eyes darting about to the faces of those who sat around the table.

Thomason explained quietly, "These ancient people must have been having a meeting of their rulers in the council chamber when they were killed very suddenly. We haven't examined them closely because it was the treasure that interested us, but the people all seem to be perfect mummies." Bill squinted at White and asked, "Ain't it dark in this tunnel?"

"Black dark," said White, who had his voice under control again. His outburst had quieted him.

"When I first went into that council room I had just some candles. I fumbled around. I didn't discover everything all at once like I'm telling you. I fell around over these men, and I was pretty near almost scared out of my head. But I got over that and everything was all right and I could see everything after I hit the lights."

"Lights? There were lights?" It was Bill asking.

"Oh, yes," said White.

"These old people had a natural gas they used for lighting and cooking. I found it by accident. I was bumping around in the dark. Everything was hard and cold and I kept thinking I was seeing people and I was pretty scared. I stumbled over something on the floor and fell down. Before I could get up there was a little explosion and gas flames all around the room lighted up. What I fell over was a rock lever that turned on the gas, and my candle set the gas off. That was when I saw all the men, and the polished table, and the big statue. I thought I was dreaming. The statue was solid gold. It's face looked like the man sitting at the head of the table, only, of course, the statue's face was much bigger than the man's, because the statue was all in perfect size, only bigger. The statue was solid gold, and it is 89 feet, six inches tall!"

"Did you measure it," asked Jack, silkily, "or just guess at it?"

"I measured it. Now you'll get an idea of how big that one room, the council room, is. That statue only takes up a small part of it!" Steady and evenly, Jack asked, "Did you weigh the statue?"

"No," said White.

"You couldn't weigh it." Bill was puzzled.

"Would you mind telling me how you measured it?" asked Bill.

"With a sextant," said White.

"I always carry a sextant when I'm on the desert. Then if I get lost, I can use my sextant on the sun or moon or stars to find myself on the map. I took a sextant angle of the height of the statue and figured it out later."

"A sextant," said Bill, frowning heavily. Jack said, "It's a part of the church, Bill. Never mind that.

"Tell us some more about this place. It's very interesting." Fred Thomason said, "Tell them about the treasure rooms."

"I found them later." White polished his shining pate with a grimy handkerchief.

"After I got the lights going I could see all the walls of this big room and I saw some doors cut in the solid rock of the walls. The doors are big as slabs of rock hung on hinges you can't see. A big rock bar lets down across them. I tried to lift up the bars and couldn't move them. I fooled around trying to get the doors open. I must have been an hour before I took ahold of a little latch like on the short end of the bar and the great bar swung up. Those people know about counterweights and all those great big doors with their barlock., They must weigh hundreds of tons, are all balanced so that you can move them with your little finger, if you find the right place." Thomason again said, "Tell them about the treasure."

"It's gold bars and precious stones. The treasure rooms are inside these big rock doors. The gold is stacked in small bars piled against the walls like bricks. The jewels are in bins cut out of rock. There's so much gold and jewelry in that place that the people there had stone wheelbarrows to move the treasure around." Jack sat up in sudden interest.

"Wheelbarrows?" he asked

"We don't know how old they are," said Thomason, "but the stone wheelbarrows are there."

"Stone wheelbarrows," marveled Jack.

"Those dead men must have been very powerful men. Only very strong men could push around a stone wheelbarrow loaded with gold bars. The wheelbarrows must have weighed a ton without a load in them."

"Yes," said Thomason, slowly, "the wheelbarrows are stone and of course they are very heavy, but they're very easy to push around even with a load in them," White explained.

"They're scientific wheelbarrows."

"No," objected Jack in a low tone of anguish.

"Yes," insisted White, pleasantly sure of himself. "A small boy could fill one of those stone wheelbarrows full of gold bars and wheel it around. The wheelbarrows are balanced just like the doors. Instead of having the wheel out in front so that a man has to pick up all the weight with his back, these wise people put the wheel almost in the middle and arranged the leverage of the shafts so that a child could put in a balanced load and wheel the barrow around." Jack's heart was breaking. He left the table and threw his chew out the door. He went over to the stove with his cup.

"Anybody want more coffee?" he asked. No one did. Bill studied Thomason and White for several minutes. Then he asked, "How many times have you been in this tunnel?"

"I've been there three times," said White.

"That's counting the first time I fell in. Fred's been in twice; and my wife went part way in the last time we was in." Mrs. White stroked her blond hair and said, "I thought my husband was romancing when he came home and told me what he found in the mountains. He always was a romancer. I was sure he was just romancing about this city he said he found. I didn't believe it until they took me into it. It is a little hard to believe, don't you think?"

Bill said, "It sure is." Jack stirred sugar into his coffee and sat down at the table again. Bill asked, "Did you ever bring anything out of the cave?"

"Twice," said Fred Thomason.

"Both times we went in we filled out pockets with gems, and carried out a gold bar apiece. The first time we left the stuff with a friend of ours and we went to try and interest someone in what we'd found. We thought the scientists would be interested or the government. One government man said he'd like to see the stuff and we went back to our friend to get the gold and jewels and he told us he'd never seen them; and dared us to try to get them back. You see, he double crossed us. We were in a little trouble at the time and the loss of that stuff just put us in deeper. We couldn't get a stake because we were having hard work making anyone believe us. So we made another trip out here for more proof. That time we brought out more treasure and buried it close to the shaft entrance to the underground city before we went back to the Coast. I persuaded some university officials and some experts from the Southwest Museum to come out here with me. We got up on the Panamints and I could not find the shaft. A cloud-burst had changed all the country around the shaft. We were out of luck. The scientists became unreasonably angry with us. They've done everything they can to discredit us ever since." Jack watched Thomason and White across the rim of his coffee cup.

Bill said, "And now you can't get into your treasure tunnel. It's lost again. That's sure too bad." Thomason and White smiled.

"We can get in all right," said Thomason in a genial voice his cold eyes did not support. Mrs. White smiled confidently and her husband bobbed his head. Thomason went on:

"You've forgotten about the old boat landings on the Death Valley side of the Panamint Mountains. All we have to do is climb the mountain to the openings where the galleries come out of the city on the old lake shore. Do you know the mountains along the west side of Death Valley?"

"I've been down there," said Bill. Thomason turned to White:

"How high do you think those galleries are above the bottom of Death Valley?" White said, "Somewhere around forty-five hundred or five thousand feet. You looked out of them; what do you think?"

"That's about right," agreed Thomason.

"The openings are right across from Furnace Creek Ranch. We could see the green of the ranch right below us and Furnace Creek Wash across the valley. We'll find those windows in the mountains, all right."

"You going down there now?" asked Bill.

"That's it," said White.

"We're through with the scientists. We tried to make a present of our discovery to science because we thought they would be interested. But they tried to rob us, and then they laughed at us and abused us."

Saying thanks and farewell the treasure hunters left, promising to return, and drove in their car down to Emigrant Canyon towards Death Valley. Later that same afternoon Bourke Lee, the author of *Death Valley Men*, allegedly met the three of them on the floor of the valley. Their car was parked beside the road between Furnace Creek Ranch and the Salt Beds. The men were patching a tube. They did not need any help, so he said good-bye and went on towards the southern part of the barren valley.

He never saw Fred Thomason, Mr. White nor his wife again, and ten days later when he again visited Bill Cocoran and Jack Stewart they told him that they hadn't seen them since either. When another week went by and the proprietors of the 'lost city' did not appear, the author and Bill made a trip down into Death Valley in their car and took along a pair of field glasses, hoping to see some sign of the explorers or of the 'windows' allegedly hid among the shadows of the eastern slope of the sun-blistered Panamints. They failed to find any sign of either.]

The Prime Directive

A STUDY IN INTERCULTURAL INTERACTION. Many will agree that the PRIME DIRECTIVE consists of the following ideals: 1) Noninterference in the free agency of an individual, household, city, state, nation or culture, and the majority rule of such. This would include noninterference in matters political, economic, educational or spiritual unless otherwise allowed by majority.

2) The right to provide aid and assistance to those who OF THEIR OWN FREE WILL seek the intervention of other outside powers who have the means to assist the potential recipient; with the following conditions: a) such aid does not give the recipient an unfair advantage over his or her contemporaries; b) it does not leave the recipient permanently addicted or dependent on the supplier, allowing for the recipient to learn to stand on their own in the sense of being an active member within the cooperative society of his or her choosing; c) that the supplier is responsible as best as they are able to OFFER assistance, in keeping with the WHOLE of the PRIME DIRECTIVE, to all who have been victimized against their will by intelligences in the same contemporary LEVEL of interaction as that of the potential benefactors. This should not include COMPULSORY assistance to victims who of their own will or the will of their JUSTLY ELECTED officials and leaders ALLOW foreign powers to interfere in their affairs, UNLESS such foreign powers have intervened through methods which may be considered subversive, deceitful and otherwise offensive to the free agency of the leadership and citizenship.

3) An individual, family, city, state, nation or culture has the right to seek exacting retribution, according to instituted processes, against

any foreign power which is guilty of interfering in the free agency of the former. This would also include the right to declare war against any and all foreign powers, be they human or non, which are guilty of interfering in the natural development of that culture in violation of the Prime Directive, or which has been guilty of participating in attacks (whether overtly or covertly) against the free majority rule or liberty and independence of a society. Such a declaration of war should only be made if the SECURITY of the victimized society is at risk, and any attacks should be made ONLY in the name of SELF DEFENSE. Offensive warfare, against human or non-human forces, should only be allowed when it is justified by evidence that the foreign or enemy power holds captive in their native territories the bodies of members of the victimized society. Briefly, the PRIME DIRECTIVE is to be a BALANCE between A) Mankind's obligation to ensure LIFE, LIBERTY and the pursuit of HAPPINESS for their (human) race through PROVISIONS in keeping with the whole of the Prime Directive; or PROTECTIONS of their own kind or allies from foreign powers, in keeping with the Prime Directive. B) Mankind's obligation to ensure the FREE AGENCY of their own kind TO THE EXTENT that their own kind honor the LIFE and FREE AGENCY of the rest. In short, the PRIME DIRECTIVE should be a BALANCE between INDIVIDUAL LIBERTY and COLLECTIVE INTERACTION. (The above is a 'suggested interpretation' of the Prime Directive and is intended to be reviewed by governments as a possible addendum to their constitutions, or as a foundational principle upon which even MORE sophisticated and detailed amendments to constitutions may be ratified)

• • •

There are many who suggest that Nevada rather than New Mexico may be the center of subsurface alien activity in America. This may be true in the sense that the major conflict or interaction zone between Evadamic and Draconian forces seems to be below the Great Western Desert of eastern Nevada and western Utah. The military installations in this region are also, according to many sources, heavily involved in the alien scenario, for good or evil. Whereas the front lines, so-to-speak, may exist below the test ranges of Nevada-Utah, the center of reptilian activity seems to be Mt. Archuleta, N.M. The American Center of the various human cultures seems to be Mt. Shasta, California, even though some suggest that, at least in the past [like the U.S. Govt. itself], some in the human alliance below the Northern California region made the tragic mistake of opting for a policy of 'appeasement' rather than 'retribution' in dealing with the serpent race. This does not necessarily mean that this policy continues widespread today.

• • •

The Christian Radio Network, the MOODY BROADCASTING NETWORK of Chicago, in mid-1988 interviewed a woman by the name of Lauren Stratford, author of SATAN'S UNDERGROUND (Harvest House Publishers, Eugene, Oregon 97402), on their 'OPEN LINE' program. The 'interviewer' was Chris Fabrey, and the transcript for much of the message is as follows:

CHRIS: "Lauren. You, as I recall from reading your story, had two children."

LAUREN: "Three."

CHRIS: "Three children. Something happened to two of them."

LAUREN: "Two of them were used in snuff films. The last child that I had in the early '20s was used in a satanic ritual."

CHRIS: "A 'snuff' film, for those who don't know, is just a 'Black Market' film that portrays violence and sex, in a quite degrading way."

LAUREN: "Well, it's really more than that. The word 'snuff' means to 'snuff out' or to take a life so a 'snuff film' generally will include the taking [murder] of the life of somebody.

CHRIS: "Your first child was killedthen, in one of those films."

LAUREN: "Yes.

CHRIS: "And your second child was?"

LAUREN: "Both. Two, the firsttwo were used in snuff films [the third child was slaughtered in a satanic ritual]."

CHRIS: "O.K. We have with us now LieutenantLarry Jones. He has been in law enforcement for 17 years, and also is involved in the 'CULT CRIME IMPACT NETWORK'. Lieutenant Jones, welcome to our program. What you are hearing Lauren say is nothing new to you because you've heard her story. Some people may find it quite extraordinary, unbelievable. Have you found in your years of police work that this type of thing is happening across our country?"

JONES: "Well, basically in the last three years I've become aware of it. The prior 14 years I was as unaware as anybody else, and I can sympathize with anyone who is just now confronting these issues, because it's incredibly draining to have to rethink everything that you've ever learned, and understand that there are people out there that are serving some very negative deities, and doing very destructive things."

CHRIS: "How do you know if someone in your area is participating in these types of rituals, do you see evidence?"

JONES: "The evidence that we are encountering that's easily seen generally would be fairly superficial levels of 'worshippers'. The really dangerous, deep-core generational satanic worshippers may be a businessman or the teacher or police officer [or chief] or judge or (so-called or counterfeit) 'pastor' next door that is completely invisible in society. he would not stick out as a satanist, he doesn't wear pentagrams, he would not be anything but a pillar of the society. those are the one's that really concern us because they seem to operate with impunity along with the rest of society."

CHRIS: "It seems Lauren that in your story you said, especially those involved in pornography, are the upstanding citizens."

LAUREN: "Oh yes, it's just like you used to think that the sexual molester, your child molester, had a dirty trench coat and sat on a park bench to entice the child into a slum motel. We've found out (that) that isn't true. Your sexual molester may be your stepfather, your newspaper boy, your mother, your politician, your Sunday school teacher, or your Boy Scout leader."

CHRIS: "What about those, though, that you were involved with who were in the 'satanic'. This one guy who was a high priest, was he an 'upstanding' citizen?"

LAUREN: "On the outside he was. he was into everything illegal that i think you could name. he's a very, very wealthy man, but to the community, yes, he would be looked on as a very upstanding person."

CHRIS: "Larry, what would you say to those in the law enforcement community who say: 'This stuff is not going on, your making too much of it, stop talking about it.' "

JONES: "Well, first of all, listen, and realize that the most important thing that we can all look for is corroborative evidence and verifiable stories. There are a lot of bizarre stories going around that we haven't been able to corroborate, but there are many more very reasonable people who have no reason to mislead, and they're telling stories, and the fact that they don't have evidence is a problem, but their stories tend to corroborate one another across the country [or rather, stories based on circumstantial evidence, which is 'evidence non-the-less] because they are separated by time, by space, by association. the people don't know each other, yet they and sometimes their children are disclosing facts that are extraordinarily similar. i would say to the law enforcement people involved, at least accept the possibility that cult and occult motivation crimes do occur, and it's not necessarily that you believe like I do, or you believe that what the Satanists are doing is real, all you have to do is believe that they believe it and are acting accordingly, and sometimes with devastating results."

CHRIS: "Lieutenant Jones, a real quick question about (the) law enforcement community. I understand that you have been under some, not pressure, but some people have been looking at you (with suspicion), not only because you believe that some of this stuff is going on but also because you are a Christian believer and a Christian police officer."

JONES: "Well, of course Christianity does tend to polarize people and it always has, so that's nothing new. There are some who believe, and would espouse this philosophy, that you should not mix religion and law enforcement. And it is tricky and I agree that you shouldn't use the state to be a proponent for a particular religion, that's what the constitution says. But the constitution never said that you had to eliminate God from every area of life, and I think that that's a fallacy that officers need to get over.

"There are many Christian officers out there who very successfully integrate their personal beliefs with law enforcement without having, as one detractor put it, without having to go out and enforce the ten commandments instead of the law. I believe, and our organizations believe, that we must learn about the spiritual motivations behind the satanic and occult and cult motivation crimes, in order to understand how to correctly investigate them. You certainly cannot be successful in a murder investigation that stems from an occult ritual in the woods, if you use an investigative pathway that would be appropriate in a bar fight killing. I mean, the investigator has to know the other set of tools, (they) have to know the other key words, and motivations and philosophies; he doesn't have to believe them, he doesn't have to believe they work, but he does have to be aware of them, and it's that awareness we're fighting so hard for. [*Note:* At this point in the conversation, the interviewer, Chris Fabrey, took a call from Chicago. The caller was a woman by the name of Kathy who attended Moody Church, named after D. Moody, a notable early American evangelist who 'led' over a million people to a personal knowledge and experience of the Lord Jesus. Kathy claimed that she knew of someone who was a 'witch', who lived above her. This man, she claimed, was into drug dealing and often attempted to seduce her through witchcraft. She claimed that he often tried to attack her physically, that he knew every move she made, and had even caused her stove to explode and her electricity to go out. Lauren then proceeded to discuss the situation with her, encouraging her and reminding her that God's power and grace was far more than sufficient to overcome and protect her from any and ALL of the evil one's attacks, IF ONE believed in the power of the life-essence (blood) that He released through Calvary, and believed in it to the point of appropriating it.]"

CHRIS: "You (Lauren) said that you became a Christian at the age of four. You were probably going to Sunday School when you were a child, learning verses (and so on).

LAUREN: "Yes."

CHRIS: "How then in your adult life, how did you get away from the pornography, the satanic, where did you make the break?"

LAUREN: "Well first of all, I was never a satanist, I need to say that I was a victim of satanists and ritualistic abuse, so that I have never made any 'vows' to Satan. I have never 'sold my soul' or made a pact or prayed to Satan. I always in the end of the day went to Jesus. That was my salvation throughout my life. People ask me how I made it. That's my only answer, that Jesus was in my life even if I didn't appropriate him. He kept me, I had nothing to do with it. And, when I did finally hear somebody who believed these things went on, and I talked to them, this person showed

me how to use the spiritual warfare type of praying that it takes to free a victim from Satanism. I know alot of victims who have gotten out of satanism, or they've tried to, but they've turned to drugs, they've turned to alcohol, their marriages fall apart, they live miserable lives.

"Myself, I know of no victim who is totally free from Satanism otherthan a person who has come to Jesus Christ, because he is the only one who can free that person. And when I allowed the Lord to work in my life, then there was that freedom."

CHRIS: "Vickie is in Atlanta, Georgia, listening to W.M.B.W. Hi, Vickie."

VICKIE: "Hi."

CHRIS: "Go ahead."

VICKIE: "I have a question for either one, Lauren or Larry. I have a cousin who teaches in the Jacksonville, Florida school system, and just recently they had a program among the 'enrichment classes' where the students were using dungeons and dragons. Now this is in the school system. It was, you know, not something 'on the side', it was for the advanced classes. And finally there was enough concern and outrage among the parents that they stopped it. But I was just wondering: that's the first time I've ever heard of Dungeons and Dragons being used in a school system. Is this something that you have been acquainted with, or heard about? This seems like a highly inappropriate program for school in light of what we know what it's done to so many children."

CHRIS: "What would you say to that (Lt. Jones)?"

JONES: "That organization started because a woman's son was involved in a gifted class, playing Dungeons and Dragons, and after a few months became so over-involved and over-identified with it, he started to become his character. And there was a death curse put on him by the Dungeon Master who was an instructor in the high school. And he had the choice of either killing his family or killing himself. And he chose to kill himself. The mother was so enraged that this could have happened that she started an organization called Bothered About Dungeons and Dragons, in Richmond, Virginia. And since that time has documented at least 200 suicides and murders directly associated with overindulgence in the game. The game is VERY ACCURATE from the OCCULT point of view. It basically is a crash course in sorcery for young boys. The fantasy is not 'fantasy', it is the real occult article, and that sort of thing. It's signs and symbols and rituals and incantations lead the player down a very dark primrose path towards potential destruction. Not every child that plays it is going to become over-involved, but they're certainly opening the door to a very dangerous area that is very ancient in nature."

CHRIS: "Have you seen any of these things Lauren?"

LAUREN: "Yes, we had a young boy in youth camp this summer who brought $2,000 worth, a whole trunk full, of Dungeons and Dragons paraphernalia to the youth camp, and he burned them in a bonfire; he made a sacrifice of them because his best friend had just committed suicide. He had played one of the 'evil' characters in the Dungeons and Dragons game, and he had so identified with that evil character throughout the months that this one game went on, that when the 'evil' character was finally killed off, he could not handle it and he committed suicide. And I would like to say that my sister, Johanna Michelson, is writing a book right now documenting the effects of a lot of the New Age teachings and Dungeons and Dragons, those types of games in the enrichment classes or the gifted classes in the school system [*Note:* This book is available in many Christian book stores]. It's called: Like lambs to the slaughter and she's documented many of the cases of these games getting into the school system. More and more school systems are including occultic games and practices, especially in the gifted classes."

CHRIS: "I would like to add that it takes a very intelligent and usually a young boy, to play Dungeons and Dragons. And when you think that intelligent 10, 11 and 12 year olds who may start to play this game are the targets, and it can ultimately lead them into occult bondage, you wonder if there is some type of program or conspiracy afoot to nullify our potential leaders. The ones that are going to be the articulate spokespeople, are going to be programmed into a predisposition to accept the occult in later life."

LAUREN: ""Right!"

JONES: "That is the thing that really concerns me."

VICKIE: "I'll say this one thing, and I know you have other callers. Our neighbor's nephew

killed his father. He was involved in Dungeons and Dragons, and he was going to go to school after he killed his (father), and he was going to kill everybody at home, then go to school and kill the Principal. He was devoted (to it), but no-one was home but his father so he killed his father, got in the car and drove until he had car trouble in front of a church. And the Pastor happened to be there and they took him in, and he's now in a correctional institute, but he was involved in something similar to Dungeons and Dragons. I couldn't believe that they were using that in a school system."

CHRIS: "But from what I hear then, this is not out of the ordinary from other things you've heard."

LAUREN: "Unfortunately, No."

CHRIS: "Vickie, thanks for your call tonight. The underscore that I hear from what everybody is saying tonight is that we're in a battle, and it's a spiritual one, we need to be aware of that and that's one of the reasons why we're doing this program this evening [STATION BREAK] Again our guest tonight, Lauren Stratford, author of *Satan's Underground*, and we have not gone into alot of the 'gory' details on our program this evening, and I say they're gory details because you do go into graphic detail on what happened to you in the different rituals that you were forced to go into."

LAUREN: "Well, we have tried not to be graphic. That (the Book) isn't half the story, however, to show God's grace you have to show what you've been in. [*Note:* This is true with the Word of God itself. Although some condemn it because of it's descriptions of human debauchery and have attempted to ban it from schools on such grounds, etc., they fail to recognize that the 'Word' is, in fact, a perfectly honest 'mirror' capable of revealing the true nature of man, as well as the remedy for man's degeneracy. The word does not 'advocate' debauched life-styles as some blind hypocrites suggest, but EXPOSES the fallen human condition so that the infinite gulf between this and the Creator's flawless perfection can be realized]."

CHRIS: "And it is something that again *Moodey Monthly* Magazine has stated that: 'Teachers, parents, pastors, and counselors should read and learn from it's council." [At this point another call is taken, this time from 'Amelia' in Chicago. She asked generally what the signs are for detecting if a child has been ritualistically abused].

LAUREN: "I would say, if you see any sudden, definite, drastic change in your child, of any kind, I don't care if it's emotional or physical or spiritual or whatever. If you see a number of symptoms and you don't see any reason for the child's (change), if there hasn't been a death in the family or something. That is certainly cause to investigate, whatever the cause of the child's trauma is, and if it especially has to do with doing things like 'praying to the Devil' or being scared to death now if anyone touches them when a bath is being taken or wanting a change of underwear every five minutes. Just things like that (which) might show or indicate that the child has been abused sexually. And then if the child couples that with things like saying prayers backwards, saying Bible versus backwards, or making statements like: 'Your not my mommy anymore', or 'your not my daddy, Satan is.'

"Those kinds of declarations, accompanied by other types of systematic changes, are certainly indicators that there is a possibility (that) their child has been ritualistically abused. [Amelia at this point referred to a friend of hers who at the time had a 2 year old child that had been going to a day-care center, and shortly afterwards began to change in behavior, acting strangely, having nightmares, etc. Many young children have suffered such abuses, especially in day care centers which, many ex-satanists claim, have been targeted by the cults to 're-cruit' the children].

"This activity often involves a large branch of the child porn industry which is jointly involved in satanic rituals and abuse, as were Lauren's children. The McMartin preschool case in California was only one of many instances, and usually there are few if any convictions in such cases being that children are too young to defend themselves psychologically against cunning defense attorneys, and possibly because of, as some believe, cult infiltration of law enforcement. Children who suffer abuse by these satan-cult pornographers often describe incidents such as being made to stand in pentagrams; being shown pictures of Jesus which were turned away from them and toward the wall and being told that if they informed anyone what was happening that Jesus would in the same way turn his back on them; made to eat 'pussak', a grotesque combination of human defecation mixed with some type of liquid; made to stand before cameras naked while 'movies' were being taken of them; and other similar things. Author Hal Lindsey for instance has documented numerous cases of satanic child abuse in connection with preschools or day-care centers, as have other investigators]."

JONES: "(In answer to Amelia) My first advice is to have her believe her child, and if there's any reason to fear, there's no real reason to take that child to a place that he's afraid of. The second is to contact your local law enforcement people and advise them of what, or have her (the mother of the child) advise them of what she has seen. There are people who are in law enforcement who are very much aware of the different symptoms and the ways of disclosure for a child that young. Certainly something happened, it may be something like straight sexual abuse, it may not have a ritual involvement. It could be a large dog at the day-care center that the child is afraid of or some other reason like that, but she does need to follow up on it and just not try to pass it off. [Later on Lt. Jones gives his own views on day-care centers].

"I think that a child needs to be with his parents. I know not everybody is financially able to do that, but sometimes we have to lay aside our desires for material things if that begins to be the case and stay home and raise those children in a safe and secure environment. We can't trust our children to the secular world anymore. The secular world in this country has become very occultic in it's nature, and even the most prestigious of places sometimes can be hotbeds of abuse. Either sexual abuse or physical abuse or even satanic ritual abuse. [At this point in the 'Open Line' interview, another caller was allowed to speak. 'Karen' from Michigan, who was also a victim of satanic child abuse in her early years, but was delivered by the power of God's grace. There was some mention of a 'Satanic language' or 'lingo' used by the cultists, and also references to the 'demonic wings', or 'astral projection'. After some discussion on these and related topics, the interviewer Chris Fabrey stated the following]

CHRIS: "What I hear coming from you also Karen is backing up (the fact that) perverse sexuality also carries behind it some demonic activity, and they seem to go hand in hand. Did you experience that also? [addressing Lauren].

LAUREN: "Oh, definitely! The sexual activity that I witnessed I was associated with a very abusive type of group. It was extremely (demonic). It's not just sexual abuse, there a spiritual abuse connected with sexual abuse, and it's very difficult therefore to explain that you are actually dealing with the direct powers of darkness, the very forces of darkness themselves. And when you are sexually abused, they're going to 'pray' that you have sex with Satan and that you have sex with certain demonic spirits. That takes on a whole new type of abuse. It is totally different. I hate to say 'just' sexual abuse. It takes the grace of God, the miracle power of God, to get a person through that and to straighten (their) thinking out.

CHRIS: "John is in Davenport, Iowa. John, quickly, your question."

JOHN: "Yes. Lt. Jones, sister Lauren. I've heard that a large percentage of abducted children are used for Satanic murder. Would either one of you all happen to have the exact percentage?

JONES: "There are no statistics. Anybody who says he has statistics is lying. Nobody has been 'counting the beans', and it's terribly difficult to penetrate the secrecy to find out."

CHRIS: "Is that because there are no bodies ever found?"

JONES: "No, we've got bodies, we have satanic murderers on 'Death Row'. It's not that it doesn't happen, it's just a question of how much and how good (i.e. how cunning and skillful) these people are and how much they've figured out the law enforcement system (in order) to evade it. [*Note:* Lauren added at this point that the major targets are the 'undesirables', or children whose parents don't really want them and therefore do not take as many protective measures as the normal parent would. Lt. Jones also made the comment to the effect that in order for the law enforcement organizations to make any headway, they will have to admit to the spiritual roots of much of the criminal activity taking place. Failure to do so, he claimed, has only led to a gradual loss of ground by law enforcement's attempts to stem the tide of crime. He suggested that all, law enforcement included, throw away the old traditional concepts of dealing with crime and begin accepting the fact of spiritual warfare, which is the only way to deal with the root cause of crime.

[Shortly after this the program came to its conclusion.]

• • •

IMPOSTERS: "Some abductee' claim that there are malevolent alien entities capable of impersonating human beings in a wide variety of ways. If such is the case, then it might be very difficult to tell just WHO might be an infiltrator into human society, and working against human dominion of this planet earth. One woman claimed that during her experience she 'saw' her husband drag her from the car and strongly entice her to follow 'it' to a waiting craft as if to encourage her that there were entities there that she should see.

"At the same time she seemed to sense that her abductor was actually an alien entity which had taken the 'form' of her husband while her actual husband was being kept in the automobile from which she had been taken, and therefore the reason why she referred to her abductor as 'it'. Another woman, during a UFO-like encounter, saw her male companion engulfed in an unusual light, after which he began to operate in an entirely strange manner as if something else had taken over his body. Then, just as mysteriously, he 'came to' himself. Another woman described an abduction of her 'astral' body which was somehow taken out of her physical body by 'aliens' and put in some kind of container, apparently on an alien craft.

"She realized that another 'entity' had taken over her body [a so-called 'walk-in'?] and her body, now controlled by the alien entity, was going about its business just as she usually did, until after a period of time whereupon she regained control of her body. Some have even alleged that demonic entities have killed human beings [removing their spirit or souls or both] and taken COMPLETE control of their bodies, and that such now operate in high levels of government. Of course such a thing if it even exists would be extremely difficult to prove. Needless to say, there may be 'tares among the wheat' which are so subtly mixing with human society that it might be extremely difficult to tell a human from an alien, unless some highly technical process is developed by which one might be able to electromagnetically determine whether a body possesses a human 'soul matrix' or not.

Chapter 7:
ETs, Earth-Made Saucers, Free Energy & The Omega Project

This chapter will include facts and excerpts from various reports and accounts which have been gathered since the compilation of the *The Cosmic Patriot Papers*. It will deal with only the most sensitive facts concerning the Cosmic Conflict on, within, and beyond the earth:

• • •

The following information was sent in by Juliette Sweet, personal friend of Sharula Dux, the self-alleged resident of Telos, the city below Mt. Shasta, and was dated 2/7/93: "...last month I had your disk [*The Cosmic Patriot Papers*] transcribed and read your materials in their entirety. Very interesting, and full of well cited facts. I appreciate your sense of groundedness when presenting your ideas...I am not familiar with the saurian race, nor have I heard mention of them from Sharula or Adama...

The Grays do come up from time to time, and what has been communicated by the Hierarchy is that they are indeed being asked, forcibly if necessary, to leave. The ousting process has been active for the last year or so, and Adama has indicated that Los Alamos will be one of the last areas to clear out...there has been some "star wars" type of conflict of late, but the masters tell us not to worry about it [and that] they have things well in hand...

Sharula's age is actually 267 years. Although for surface ID purposes, she says she was born in 1951. It helps where social security and passport purposes are concerned. You might want to update your materials to reflect her actual age..."

• • •

CRP has heard from one researcher of an incident which that researcher read. However, as he does not recall exactly the source, the reader must take the information for what it is worth. The report was based on information provided by a man who was involved in high-security work in the underground bases below the Nevada Military Complex.

This man stated that while there he learned of a race of aliens which were also resident in parts of the underground base, a group known as the 'Orange.' The 'Orange' was apparently a hybrid-type of alien of humanoid form and possessing reptilian characteristics yet with human-like reproductive organs and capable of breeding with human beings.

Since, as we've indicated in earlier files, no TRUE hybrid can exist between the sauroid and human races because humans have an energy-soul matrix whereas true serpent race entities do not [among many other dissimilar characteristics], we must assume that the entities encountered by the Nevada base worker were what one might refer to as DRAC-ORANGE [no soul-energy matrix] or EVE-ORANGE [soul-energy matrix]. Just which of the two categories these entities fall into however remains uncertain at the time of this writing. Another account, also unconfirmed, refers to an individual [possibly involved with military intelligence] who was allegedly invited to work with a group of 'Aryans' who were resident at a secret base in the Nevada Military complex, along with Secret Government Military personnel.

This individual claimed that this group had access to UFO type craft and utilized the symbol of the Swastika, and were presently in conflict with the Grays, which they might have at one time in the past had associations with. As in the case of nearly every human organization that has established interactions with the sauroid Grays, perhaps these Aryans also learned of the true nature of the reptilians after being 'betrayed' by them. It is interesting that both the CIA as well as Aryans are said to be operating in and below the Nevada Test site, which might support allegations by some that the CIA struck a deal with the Nazis sometime before or after World War II and that both groups have had past and present ties with the International Illuminati. If such a group of Aryans does exist it might be wise for them, considering the Nazi atrocities of the past, to RENOUNCE the swastika and all that it stands for if they intend on receiving much help from true Americans in their conflict with the grays.

Even if present Aryan 'generations' were not PERSONALLY responsible for the war crimes of their fathers during WWII, they would still have to agree to conform to Constitutional principles of HUMAN EQUALITY regardless of race, religion or culture if they are to have any future peaceful coexistence with Americans. Otherwise they might find themselves in the very uncomfortable position of being wedged between two enemy fronts: the saurian grays on one side and indignant anti-Nazi American patriots, many of whom lost family members to the Nazis during the Second World War, on the other.

If an 'inner-planetary' or interplanetary war does erupt between humans and reptilians, as some suggest might occur, then the neo-Nazi saucer groups supposing they exist must decide to join up with the human race and cast off their former fascist ideals or else become caught up in the 'cross-fire' between the human and serpent races. There are possible indications that at least THREE groups of entirely human 'aliens' have some connection with the Nevada Military Complex, possibly retrieved alive from crashed saucer- disks or human-aliens who are willingly assisting certain governmental compartments in the technology department. For instance the above account suggests that possibly Antarctican ARYANS have some connection there, as well as possible interaction or involvement with the Pleiadean NORDICS, as suggested by Robert Lazar's claim that Pleiadean 'beamships' were seen by him on occasion; and then there are the tall Telosian BLONDS who have been known to have some connection with the underground networks of Nevada and the South-West.

In fact, there may be several different scenarios taking place at once at the Test Site, as if no individual compartment has full control of what is taking place there as has been suggested by certain sources. In a sense the Test Site is the center of a WORLD WAR III type of scenario, the only difference is that it is a covert or underground war as neither the Reptilians nor the Illuminati want this conflict to be made public, although some of the 'Constitutionals' have allegedly leaked information through the COM-12 and similar intelligence organizations. The allegations, as alleged by intelligence sources like 'Yellow Fruit,' indicate that some of the benevolents are operating in and below Nevada—aliens who honor the Constitutional form of Government in the U.S.—which would also indicate that there is more than one human alien group active there, and that there are in fact three general groups fighting for control, the 'Constitutional' human Federation, the Joint Illuminati/Gray combine, and the Reptons themselves.

Some however would suggest that the Joint activity groups are not a third power group at all but rather a 'midpoint' organization of power-hungry humans and grays who are working together in an interactive and sometimes all-too real and deadly competitive bid for world domination. They both want the planet to come under central control, but they disagree about just who will be the ultimate masters, the Humans or the Grays. Basically it is a rather sickening love-hate relationship.

• • •

Tim Beckley's *UFO Review* [issue #37] carried the following article by the editor titled 'ET SAUCERS VS. EARTH MADE UFOS.' We quote excerpts here beginning with a reference to researcher William Cooper: WILLIAM COOPER—RENEGADE WHISTLEBLOWER:

"...Originally, Cooper had stated that he had seen highly classified documents while in the Navy about an agreement made between the military and a group of aliens. The treaty supposedly allowed for the exchange of humans (abductees) for extraterrestrial technology. Little by little, however, Cooper began to feel that [he] had had the wool pulled over his eyes and his mood began to change...

"The bottom line, Cooper stated, "was that the 'Secret Government' was actually trying to foster the idea of a forthcoming alien invasion on the public, so the nations of the world would have to unite into a one-world government, known as the 'New World Order.' This global task force—naturally—would secretly be sponsored by this 'Secret Government,' whose identity was eventually revealed as the Illuminati, a virtual 'invisible empire' that has been in existence behind the scenes for centuries, fostering wars and controlling the flow of money as well as virtually everything we are allowed to know on any given subject.

"With these disclosures, all hell seemed to break loose in UFO-land, with every researcher worth their salt either calling Cooper a bald-faced liar, to taking a stand right alongside of him (and often adding their own two cents). [*Note:* One very likely scenario would be that the Illuminati IS in fact using the threat of an alien invasion to establish a One World Government. HOWEVER, the aliens are in fact real and working closely with the Illuminati in an attempt to establish a one-world system which the Illuminati hopes it will be able to jointly rule along with the serpent race or saurians, that is IF the serpent race doesn't decide to do away with the Illuminati when IT has full control. There is evidence that this duel scenario may in fact be a reality and that such a scenario has been played out in the past, although unknown to the majority of humanity."

The 'alien' in that case was Communism. In *The Cosmic Patriot Papers* we presented evidence that the UNITED NATIONS was being used by the International Illuminati to play the nations of the world for fools in a Hegalian 'Cold War' scenario designed to keep the masses under control when in fact the initiated leaders of both sides were working closely together.

Since there is, according to some military sources, evidence that Korea and Vietnam were INTENDED to be NO WIN conflicts (as suggested by the manipulations of the Illuminati-Communist leaders of the U.N. who ran the international counteroffensive against the Communists AS WELL AS working closely with the Communists, betraying the plans and positions of the Western Fighting forces, etc.), this theory suggests that the unholy alliance between the Illuminati and the saurian-sauroid grays will be used in a similar fashion. In other words, like the U.N. in the past, the international government might'control any counterattacks against

the 'invading grays' in such a manner that it will appear that they are defending the earth when they are actually using this scare as a means to establish one-world POLITICAL CONTROL.

Then again there is the possibility that the One-Worlders might break all current association with the grays and attempt to effect an actual counteroffensive against the 'aliens,' in which case the global system might not be centralized politically but might be more along the line of ECONOMIC COOPERATION which would still allow independent nations to preserve self-determination and cultural traits and not become amalgamated into a bland and Orwellian homogenized world system that a centralized world political system would bring.

However we should remember that even in Orwell's book 'planned' wars, whether real or imaginary, were important mechanisms in keeping the envisioned totalitarian system operating. Just which scenario will unfold is uncertain.] "(William Cooper) will, he says, 'prove once and for all that the Secret Societies, NOT our [Constitutional] government, murdered President Kennedy as a sacrifice to the ancient god Baal in an outdoor temple.' Cooper will also [in future lectures] 'explain the true meaning of the movie 2001 as a message of the Secret Societies to their followers, and will show a first- generation color copy of the Zapruder film with all the previously missing frames...'

"THE 'ANTI-GRAVITY' WORLD OF VLADIMIR TERZISKI: "...According to Terziski, the Nazi's were building flying saucers that took them to other planets even before the start of World War II. Being a Slav, Vladimir says he cannot but have the 'utmost revulsion towards everything Hitler's racial and political philosophies stood for,' and because of his revulsion he decided to look into various 'black technologies' developed by THE NAZIS, whom he now believes were secretly backed by the sinister Illuminati operating way behind the scenes [*Note:* As can be seen on other files, the 'link' between the Illuminati and the Nazis seems to have been the Jesuit Order or Lodge].

"In his vast collection of photos and other documents, Terziski has many pictures and drawings of the various disk- shaped craft constructed by the Nazi scientists that were powered by Schauberger turbines and Kohler TACHYON magneto-gravitic drives (all based upon free energy or antigravity principles).

Actually, Vladimir says that we've known all about antigravity for a long time and that THE BRITISH MAY ACTUALLY HAVE LANDED ON THE MOON A CENTURY AGO, AND EVEN THE VATICAN HAS A GROUP OF SCIENTISTS WHO ROCKET OFF INTO SPACE FROM SOUTH AMERICAN BASES FROM TIME TO TIME.

"Meanwhile, deep underground at Area 51's 'Dream Lab' in the Nevada desert, a renegade branch of the CIA—protected by a private security SS-like police force, that the Illuminati supplies, is constructing their own fleet of 'flying saucers' utilizing Hitler's forbidden technology...

JOHN LEAR: "...Lear's entrance into UFOlogy began when an old Vietnam war buddy told him about the landing of a flying saucer 70 miles northeast of London in the Rendlesham Forest, adjacent to Woodbridge and Bentwaters Air Force Bases.

"...By developing his own 'well-connected sources,' Lear gleaned some fairly astounding facts, including the 'existence of underground bases of enormous size and number; highly advanced alien life forms walking on Earth; U.S. Moon and Mars bases already in existence, and the reality of human mutilations.' Originally, Lear thought the public had the right to know what was going on, but now has changed his tune, realizing 'the public possibly couldn't handle the whole truth.' "

• • •

The following paragraphs are taken from a document titled "WAKE UP AMERICA! AN OPEN LETTER TO ALL CITIZENS FROM COMMANDER X" [UFO Review #37]:

"...allow me to let you in on a few ghastly secrets that I am sure will upset you as much as these revelations did me...

"...the truth of the matter is that the United States military now has at its disposal—and has had for quite a number of years—disc-shaped or circular aircraft that are capable of flying three times higher and faster than any jet fighter that is 'officially' known to the public. This same aircraft can virtually dematerialize and rematerialize elsewhere in a split second, as well as hover mere inches above the ground, thus frightening the hell out of any real potential enemy.

"Perhaps not so surprisingly, this very same aircraft utilizes a form of energy that is, to our current way of thinking, highly revolutionary, yet it is so economical and readily available that the forces that be fear each day that it may tilt the 'balance of power' out of their hands and radically change society overnight...

"— This energy is FREE ENERGY!—It is available all around you—from the very air itself!— And the reason you have not been told anything about it is because there is a massive conspiracy afoot on the part of the military-industrial complex to keep its existence a closely-guarded secret from the 'masses of assess,' who, it is felt, should remain in total ignorance so that the corporate interests can continue to rake in huge profits at the sake of life and limb—mainly ours!

"Over a century ago, one of the greatest free thinkers of all time arrived upon our cosmic shores in order to shape our technical and spiritual destiny.

"Nikola Tesla came from another place to alert the world to impending danger (World Wars I and II), while at the same time offering 'solutions' to our problems and alternatives by which to greatly enhance our lives.

"Holder of over a thousand patents for many marvelous scientific inventions, Tesla turned down millions of dollars in royalties as well as the Nobel Prize because he did not believe 'big business' and 'corporate giants' should control that which readily belongs to all of humanity.

"Because of his beliefs, Tesla was repeatedly harassed and his life threatened...Tesla shunned all contact with big business and the corporate world, though he BELIEVED IN free enterprise.

"In my just-released, new book, entitled Nikola Tesla—Free Energy and the White Dove, you will learn first-hand of the work of such modern-day inventors as Otis T. Carr, Arthur H. Matthews, and Howard Menger, who have perfected alternative methods of propulsion that soon will place men and women on Mars and other planets, safely and economically.

"Indeed, as these very words are being written, the very core of Newton's Laws of Gravity are being ripped apart, as new and more exciting laws of science are being written after nearly four centuries. You will, for example, learn about the incredible work being done at Thoku University in Sendai, Japan, where researchers have stumbled upon a way to defy gravity under scientific conditions. You will also learn of the incredible secret research conducted a number of years ago by individuals such as T. Townsend Brown and John Searl, who actually built aerial devices that flew through the sky using revolutionary systems of propulsion. Yet, both gentleman have mysteriously disappeared and much of their actual research has either been stolen or burned, because of the amazing truth about FREE ENERGY that they discovered.

"If you were tuned in to Geraldo Rivera recently [1993] you might have seen an exposé of Area 51, a Top Secret military installation located just short of 150 miles north-northwest of Las Vegas. For it is here at this vast 38,000 acre military complex—watched over most closely by Swat-like teams of private, paramilitary security guards hired from an outside agency in total defiance of all known Constitutional laws—that something very strange has been happening on a regular basis.

"...More important than the ground-level reports of sincere observers, however, are the claims of those working inside Area 51, who say that their lives were threatened when they found out what was really going on at this locale.

"The first to go public was theoretical physicist Robert Lazar, who says that he was blindfolded every day upon entering the base and taken in a bus with blacked out windows to an area seven levels underground. Here he was put to work on several different craft of extraterrestrial origin, which had either been captured by the government when they crash landed, or [were] actually given to Uncle Sam by aliens looking for official consent to abduct humans in exchange for their technology. Later, when it was learned by the military—who placed a tap on his phone—that Lazar was scared for his life and ready to talk, the brass had him drugged and hypnotized so that he would not remember what he had seen or had been asked to work on.

"According to Lazar—and here is where his story gets somewhat wild—THE ALIENS AT SOME POINT ACTUALLY TOOK CONTROL OF CERTAIN AREAS OF THE BASE (PRESUMABLY THE LOWER LEVELS—LEVELS FIVE, SIX AND SEVEN) BY USING FORCE, GOING SO FAR AS TO ERADICATE SOME SCIENTISTS WHO HAD BEEN COOPERATING WITH THEM.

"Lazar believes that he was hired by the military to replace one of those scientists who had been 'removed' from the operation. [Note: According to several sources, a similar attack FROM BELOW decimated approximately 66 scientists and security officers within the deepest underground levels of the Dulce, New Mexico 'base,' and possibly other bases around the world as well. This was apparently the reward which the saurians or aliens had for those secret government scientists who believed that they—the Grays and Reptons—would keep the 'treaty.'

"We must state however that these scientists might not have willingly been initiators of such 'alien interaction' but may have just been following orders from higher-ups who in fact were the initiators of the joint activity with what they formerly may have believed were benevolent 'space brothers.' This tragedy might be a useful lesson to those who might in the future sell out their own race for physical gain, and who in their insanity expect to be rewarded by their supposed alien benefactors for doing so. Unfortunately their reward might be their own elimination as well, when their usefulness as pawns in an obvious takeover attempt of this world has run its course.

"IF the subnet is ever re-taken from the malevolents, there is only one way that they can be retained, and that is to make the entire underground government base system ACCOUNTABLE to the legal system of the United States. It was the actions of selfish governmental and industrial organizations who sold out to the 'Draconians' and opened the door for the invasion of the subnet in the first place. If all underground activities are monitored by known Federal Institutions then renegade elements of government or industry will not be so inclined to involve themselves in such alien-sanctioned activities as the Nazi-like genetic experimentation of unknown numbers of human slaves.

"If surface institutions must abide by constitutional law and legal restrictions, then so should the underground laboratories operated by Los Alamos, Wackenhut, Rand Corp, and other Scientific-Corporate-Industrial parasites who believe that they are above the law].

"Lazar revealed in a series of interviews broadcast over Las Vegas radio and TV that the vehicles being flown over Area 51 (mostly at night, shortly before dawn) utilize a previously unknown principle of distorting space and time, 'using gravity as a lens' with the power source being an antimatter reactor powered by something the aliens brought with them called 'Element 115.'

"From a vantage spot known as a 'Mail Box Road,' near the town of Rachel, Nevada, a number of different types of craft have been seen by those who do not mind waiting into the wee hours and are patient enough to come to the area over and over until they, too, make an observation. Even NBC TV got into the act not so long ago when they took a news team to the area and managed to capture on video the flight of something that they acknowledged appeared to defy gravity...

"Tesla knew through his heightened sixth sense that the upcoming years before the turn of the century could either be full of peace and prosperity for each one of us, or, if the Secret Government is victorious in its attempt to keep us under their thumb, there will be unending war, suffering, hunger and poverty, because this is the way in which they maintain their control over the world's population. It was for this very reason that Nikola Tesla chose the White Dove as his personal symbol of encouragement, representing freedom and personal dignity for us all."

• • •

The UNICUS Group [Dept. 210., 1142 Manhattan Ave. #43., Manhattan, CA 90266], a group allegedly devoted to 'Earthbound Extraterrestrials,' related much information in 1993 concerning the research and work of a Mr. Robert M. Stanley. Stanley allegedly has discovered a 'lost city' which he says was once inhabited by ancients, whom he postulates may have been tied-in with ancient 'Lemurians.'

Some of the inhabitants of this ancient city were eightft. tall and had access to interplanetary travel, utilizing an ancient UFO base. Although Stanley has been to dozens of countries doing archaeological research, he states that the lost city—which he says largely resides in a massive underground maze of tunnels and caves below a 'Mystic Mountain' in southern California—is the most incredible site by far that he has ever encountered, and contains walls, statues and many other ancient relics from the ancient culture which build the city.

He has allegedly taken many scientists, engineers, archaeologists and anthropologists to the ancient site and through the underground complex and states that they agree with him on the incredible importance of the site, but wonder why it never came to light before this time.

Although Stanley is reticent of revealing the exact site of the 'Mystic Mountain' [on which he also claims, along with others, to have had experiences with UFOs beaming lights down upon the group], he states that it is in SOUTHERN CALIFORNIA and one might assume from previous information as revealed in the *The Cosmic Patriot Papers* that the Panamint Mountains might be the site he's referring to, and if not, the Panamint 'city' no doubt played an important role in the scenario and had some ancient connection with the lost city now officially being investigated by Robert Stanley.

Mr. Stanley can be reached through 'MYSTIC MOUNTAIN ADVENTURES.', Dept. 200., 1142 Manhattan Ave #43., M.B., CA 90266. However be warned that Steckley is adamant in his conviction that he does not wish the site to be turned into a tourist attraction or amusement park with hot dog stands and all the rest, but desires to keep the site in pristine condition for the sake of future generations of researchers.

However, if he sees that one has true unselfish academic motivations rather than a 'treasure hunter' mindset, one might be able to arrange a 'tour' of the site with him as have others in the past.

• • •

The following article, 'THE INCREDIBLE REVELATIONS OF DR. KUEPPERS,' by Helga Morrow, also appeared in *UFO Review* issue #37, with the following heading: "He Escaped From Nazi Germany At The Height Of World War II And Came To America To Work For The U.S. Military On Top Secret Projects Involving Invisibility, [Time Flow Experimentation], Anti-Gravity Research And Teleportation.":

"*Editors Note:* The following is a highly-abbreviated account of Helga Morrow's recollections of her late father, Dr. Fred A. Kueppers, a German-born engineer who defected to the U.S. during World War II...

"[Helga's Story] I have learned from various sources that my father was one of the scientists who worked on the Philadelphia Experiment; (he) had invented the timing device for the A-bomb; (he) had been chosen by the bomb scientists to represent them to Harry Truman, asking him NOT to drop the bomb; (he) had invented the mathematical formula that brought the astronauts back; (he) had designed the miniaturized electrical system of Sputnik, the first space launching; (he) had worked on Project Blue Book/Black Book, UFOs; (he) had initiated the use of aluminum wiring to replace the heavier wiring in World War II planes; (he) had worked with mind warfare, using psychics to communicate with astronauts in case communication systems failed; and (he) had trained extraterrestrials to fit into human society.

"My head spun; in it wheels were turning, and a thousand things began to make sense. Suddenly the things my father had told me in my childhood and youth snapped into place. It was as if nineteen years after I attended my father's funeral, I began to know him for the first time as only a few others knew him—a man who, for obvious reasons, could never be mentioned in public records, but who had clearly deserved such recognition for the valuable service he had given the nation. My mind began to go back to my earliest remembrances...

"When I was in the second or third grade, I watched him hang up an award from RCA in his room. I asked, 'Why did you get this award?' He told me it was too lengthy to go into. I said, 'Try me!' and he did. He said it was an award for an experiment in time, and then proceeded to put two ashtrays on his bed, and through simple gestures and explanations, show how two objects could transpose in time and return the same way. Then he took me into the cellar, where he put some steel shavings in a cigar box with a large U-shaped magnet taped underneath. He gently tapped the steel shavings, and to my amazement, two distinct series of concentric circles gradually appeared! He then simplified this by saying that if one could transpose these circles, one could transpose time [or 'bend' time such as speed it up or slow it down, or even stop it altogether?].

"He said that alien spacecraft were partly moved by 'reverse magnetism.' He showed me how to get this effect by holding two opposite magnets. I never forgot this lesson. And this was BEFORE anyone really talked about flying saucers. I was Daddy's confidant. I never discussed this information with anyone; he had

sworn me to secrecy.

"My father was not home much—only several times a year. He was completely focused on his work, so normal family life was difficult for him...

"Daddy was a popular innovator in many fields of science and technology. All his patents became the property of either the company that employed him or the U.S. Government [Such patents which were established by various scientists working in antigravity researchers allegedly exist in the patent offices for all to see, IF they know how to find them].

"The winter of 1961 before he died (on February 12, 1962, Lincoln's birthday), my father confided many things to me. He told me that what he was about to tell me was bizarre, unbelievable and might sound absolutely crazy. I was 27 at the time, and thought he had gone off the deep-end (my mother had always thought so). Daddy assured me that by the time I reached 55 or so, all these bizarre statements that he was about to make, as well as everything he had ever explained to me when I was a child, would come back to me and make sense.

"He told me that he had three months to live. 'They' had given him three months to conclude his personal affairs, he said. I asked, 'Who are they?' He said I wouldn't understand. So I realized that I was taking my last walk with him through Guilford. He turned around to see if he was being followed, as always, aware of intrusion. He confided that he had not only been on the moon but INSIDE it, and that he had both spoken to and trained extraterrestrials who looked like us to blend into human society. He had been in spaceships and had traveled in space.

"He told me of the riots where we would kill or be killed in a period of racial intolerance that would occur around 1966—which is now history. He told me that red-baiting propaganda was a lie to keep humanity occupied with worry over 'fighting communism.' And that in reality the two nations were great friends; Russian scientists got along well with their American counterparts and worked amiably together. The Russian 'threat' was nothing but B.S. and a distraction for the public. In the meantime, there were alien bases all over the world and on the moon. He said that whoever controls the moon can target anyplace on Earth; no place would be safe. Therefore, Russians and Americans must remain friends or eliminate each other. He told me he had worked with Tesla, Einstein, Von Braun, Von Neumann and many others.

"My father broke down and cried when I visited him that Christmas. He said, 'If you only knew the real truth!' But as long as I didn't I was safe, he said. He seemed a frightened man alone with his thoughts, afraid to speak out, trusting no one. He rarely spoke on the phone (our phone had always been tapped) and always thought he was being followed.

"My father died in the hospital in the arms of a nun, we were told. When my mother wanted to send flowers and candy to this unknown nun, she was told that there had been no nun in his room (though we had seen her) at the time of his fatal 'heart attack.' She couldn't be traced. At his funeral, I saw two Secret Service men at his coffin (wearing the obvious trench coats)...

"There was something strange about the body in the coffin. I always remember my father's hairy arms and hands. But there was NO HAIR ON THOSE HANDS! His face felt like cold stone, and it had so much makeup that it looked like wax. Was it really my father in the coffin? If so, why had his grave 'disappeared' when I looked for it in the family plot in 1985—a plot that dated back hundreds of years? There was no trace that it had ever existed; there were no grave records!

"And then on May 30, 1962, several months later, he materialized before me and told me he was not dead but only in 'another dimension IN TIME!' I felt his suit, smelled his Molle shaving cream—and his weight pushed down the mattress on my daybed. He was wearing his usual conservative grey suit; I even felt the material as I touched his knee. He told me to continue his work, but not call on him unless absolutely necessary, as appearing to me was painful. He said that he would make himself known to me 'at the crossroads of my life' to help me (and he has kept his promise)."

• • •

The following are several abbreviated excerpts taken from *The Omega Project*, by Kenneth Ring, PH.D. (William Morrow & Co., N.Y. 1972). The following points were brought out in the book:—Most abductions (possibly between 60%-80%?) are conducted by the 'grays' of traditional description.—Many state that

their experiences are often 'dreamlike' yet with evidence suggesting real events. The "grays" (and in some cases black creatures in capes that act as guards during the painful and terrifying medical operations) have a way of blurring their faces in the minds of the abductees, so that the abductee cannot later recall what the aliens' face looked like.

Many abductees experience sleeping problems (not to mention severe social-relational-sexual problems) after being abducted by the saurian-sauroid grays, and these problems often last for years afterwards.—Some abductees who resist are shocked repeatedly with an electric gadget which may induce paralysis and/or unconsciousness.—A majority of the grays seem to be of the gray-white variety, some with opaque black eyes and some with slit (snake or lizard-like) pupils.

Some of the greys are described as 'sinister,' and one abductee stated that when she was taken "one alien was by my head and attempted to frighten me with his large eyes," as three other creatures mechanically performed painful operations, unheeding of her terrified cries to make them stop. She (Clair Chambers) stated that "In my many encounters where I have always been kidnapped from my home, the aliens have shown no compassion. I have several times felt them exhibit FEAR when I have hit them as they do feel FEAR...their reaction behavior patters do NOT indicate an intelligence as high as I would expect from their technology (Due to their "collective-consciousness" nature?)...these experiences have been dreadful, terrifying, and I would like them to stop!"

(*Note*: Four separate doctors have confirmed wounds and injuries in Clair Chambers which she insists resulted from the abductions).—Some 'grayish' aliens, with 3-digit fingers, have been described as being 7 ft. tall (Reptons?). One woman who was abducted by them felt as if the creatures wanted her to have the IMPRESSION that they were 'friendly,' but after being returned to her car from which she was abducted "I then broke to pieces as my whole body shook uncontrollably. I cried 'OH GOD, WHY ME?' I couldn't calm myself as I cried like a baby..."

A woman with an Masters in Social Work (who was at the time of this revelation 51 years old), stated: "The first experience was when I was a child of about five. For years I had a RE-CURRING 'dream' of standing beside a field WHEN A HOLE OPENS UP IN THE GROUND in front of me. The dream ends with me looking into the hole. I was just standing there looking at the hole. Under hypnosis I [recall that I] stepped into the hole and walked down a short tunnel. The tunnel widened into a small waiting area where there was a bench just at the right height for a 5 year old. I sat down and waited. A tall black 'featureless' being came through a doorway, walked to me and held out his hand. I took his hand and went back through the doorway with him. He placed me on a table that appeared to be about three to four feet high.

"He laid me on my back and took one big hand and held my upper body flat on the table. The other beings were behind him looking at instruments on the wall. I was held this way for several minutes. When the being turned to look at the other two, it was as if he lost CONTROL over me and I jerked out from under his hand, fell off the end of the table and ran for the door. When I got to the door, I knew I wasn't supposed to go any further. I stopped and turned around. The being who had been holding me came to me, took hold of my left arm and looked into my eyes. I was looking at where the eyes should be on a HUMAN, BUT I don't REMEMBER actually SEEING eyes. I feel something was communicated, but I don't know what."

The author states that some of the large opaque-black 'eyes' seen by many abductees after being taken by the grays seemed to have been coverings for real eyes which they felt might have been hidden behind or inside of what might have been opaque-black visual coverings. At least this was the impression that some abductees had.

• • •

The following passages are taken from 'LEMURIAN TEMPLE TEACHINGS AND LIFE IN TELOS,' describing some aspects of life in an ancient Lemurian city below Mt. Shasta, which had allegedly been reestablish after the cataclysmic deluge which legend says tore the 'Murian' continent off from the Western shores of North America and sent it towards the bottom of the ocean. The report has been written by Sharula [Bonnie] & Shield DUX. Sharula is

allegedly a priestess of 266 years of age [although physically appearing to be in her mid-30's by 'surface' standards], and one of a number of Subterraneans currently working on the surface, sharing her insights into the antediluvian societies of Atlantis and Lemuria, and her personal experiences with the Confederation Space Fleets, as well as several other aspects of subterranean existence.

Together Sharula and Shield lecture and teach internationally with the assistance of 'Adama,' the High Priest of Telos, who provides them with his own insights into the subterranean 'Aghartan' network and realities of life in this and nearby solar systems. Sharula and Shield reveal the following ideas, with additional comments from the Coscon Research Project:

DISEASE—"The very word means that you are out of ease...Germs, bacteria, must have a consenting environment before they can enter your auric field and your physical body...If a cold manifested, there was a point where you surrendered to it...germs cannot take your self-will from you. Another way to open to germs is sympathy...When you are treating someone who has a cold, for example, and you really feed sorry for that person, you get the cold! Your sympathy has created a door for it to enter in. A 'Master' will treat the person, endeavor to make her feel comfortable, but will never sympathize with her for that reason. [Note: true 'agape' love STEMS from the WILL rather than the empathic emotions, although emotions are nevertheless an important part of a human spirit. If love can be separated into three levels like in the layers of an apple, emotional or COMPASSIONATE love from the heart would be the skin, brotherly or ALTRUISTIC love from the mind would be the fruit, and sacrificial or DEVOTIONAL love from the will would be the CORE from which the other two spring. For instance all of the good feelings in the world will not help a homeless person on the street unless those feelings are backed-up or supported by actions]. "For instance, I guarantee you that if you watch ten horror movies in a row, for example, and eat a whole package of junk food in the process, all of which modulate you downward, you will reach a point where you will manifest something negative. [Note: There is evidence that 'fear' for instance can open the pores of a person's body to the point that they open themselves up to any 'spirit' of infirmity or disease which might be in the air around them. This is why, according to many, intense negative emotions can be tied-in with certain diseases: for instance some claim that fear can actually 'attract' cancer, bitterness can attract arthritis, and so on. This is why it is so important to retain the emotional serenity which only the 'Prince of Peace' can provide]. "Fruit totally cleanses the blood stream. If one stays on a fruit diet long enough, the blood stream becomes so cleansed that it attacks the cancer cells and washes them away. [*Note:* Telosians are usually vegetarians. There are some who argue that the PROTEIN contained in meat is necessary to maintain the protein level in a human body, as well as retain a strong 'spirit-emotional' makeup, and that a deficiency in protein can lead to a weakened spirit and open oneself up to easier manipulation from outside malevolent supernatural forces. If this is true, it would not mean that a Vegetarian give up their lifestyle as various NUTS and GRAINS may provide the necessary protein-level. In fact Sharula speaks of 'artificial' meat later on in the text.] "...Doctors, in their desire for money, simply do not bring these things to the surface. A sure way to never get cancer is to eat almonds every day. Almonds release an acid that is compatible with normal cells, and incompatible with cancer cells. [*Note:* This might tie-in with the alleged wonder-drug Laetrile, which is resident in apricot pits, an anti-cancer substance that has come under a great deal of criticism from establishment Medical Associations. IF laetrile does in fact fight cancer then in light of the desire of the medical establishment to make a profit this 'wonder drug' may have been suppressed. Even if this is not the case and laetrile is not as remarkable as some claim it is, there is nevertheless evidence according to some that the American Medical Establishment in the past HAS suppressed cures for mere monetary reasons.] "...Dis-ease is also very connected to your emotional body....Be aware of the necessity for clean water, clean food, and more importantly, clean thoughts and emotions! [*Note:* In response to the necessity for an 'environmentally clean' earth, Conservatives have often stated that environmentalists are making too much of the alleged 'precarious' balance of nature, and that the earth has a remarkable ability to heal itself. This is true to an extent, but even

nature has a limit. There is evidence, for instance, that pollution and environmental damage does have an effect. Some theories state for instance that the IRREPLACEABLE oil reserves of the world are taking from the earth its natural lubrication, and that at least SOME earthquakes are connected to this 'rape' of the earths natural fluids. This is especially tragic when we realize the possibility that FREE ENERGY—endless and non-polluting—has existed for decades, known only to the most powerful governmental-economic-military elite who would rather destroy the earth to make a profit on natural oil reserves than share such beneficent technology with the masses of humanity].

"The world is so stressed out that they have stressed their immune systems to the point that it does not work anymore. So, the only logical thing is to reduce the stress. An example is how did you feel the last time you went and watched a blood and gore movie? In comparison, how did you feel the last time you went and watched an uplifting movie? How you feel is your example of how it has affected your body. These things actually affect your body! ...It is a proven fact that when a pregnant mother smokes or drinks, it has an effect on her child. A mother who watches horror movies during pregnancy, this has also an effect on her child. [*Note:* Sharula also goes into a lengthy discussion of the effects of certain light rays upon a persons emotional makeup. There is evidence that different colors have different effects on people; some of these color-responses are general and can be classified but the effect a certain color has on a person is often determined by the individuals emotional makeup.]

Sharula states that full-spectrum lighting, the kind used in Telos, has a beneficial effect on a human being. Certain 'colors' can be 'targeted' by bringing out specific colors by painting walls, wearing certain colors of clothing, lights, windows, etc. White light contains all the colors of the spectrum, and scientists state that a wall painted Blue for instance absorbs all the colors except blue, which is reflected off the surface. A white wall reflects all the colors, whereas black ABSORBS all of the spectrum, which is why one feels extra 'warm' on a summer day when wearing black, since none of the light is reflected. This is the opposite of the 'white' light bulb and a 'black' light. A full-spectrum light bulb floods the room with ALL of the color spectrum, whereas a black light allows only the near-invisible rays on the periphery of the rainbow-spectrum into a room. A blue light will allow only blue to flood into the room, and so on.]

"...It is a proven fact that when a pregnant mother smokes or drinks, it has an effect on her child. "A mother who watches horror movies during pregnancy, this has also an effect on her child." [In reference to 'herbal' cures—see: Genesis 1:29] "...Clover and Niacin are good. Niacin will flush radiation from your system....The clover does create a bond around the cells, so the radiation cannot hold the cells themselves. Another thing is bee pollen; it too creates a bond around the cells. Niacin also flushes out heavy metals and toxins....What Niacin does is clean up your bloodstream three times as fast as normal."

PLANET EARTH AND HER PEOPLE—[In reference to the inhabited solar systems in this section of the galaxy] "...The confederation planet (in these systems) is where the temporal government is; the star planet, you might say, for this (solar) system...is Saturn...[there are 'scientific-spiritual' centers in Telos as well as in the inner world of Agartha [and the] temples on Mars, Venus, Saturn, Jupiter [moons?], in the Orion System, the Pleiadean system, and in the Arcturian stations."

Sharula refers to ancient temples "such as those on Atlantis, in Lemuria, in ANCIENT EGYPT, [and] ANCIENT GREECE." [Note: We see the admitted—at least partial—connection between Telos and some groups in the Pleiades star cluster which according to some sources are allegedly now quite extensive and quite varied with different 'branch' cultures. These allegedly run into hundreds of star systems in that cluster, all eventually stemming from an original arrival of refugees from the 'Lyran wars' which took place relatively near our own solar system several hundred or a few thousand years before. The reference to ancient GREECE and EGYPT suggest that Telos does have, along with possibly other subterranean cultures on the West Coast, some connection to the cultural and religious systems which existed in those ancient societies as have been suggested earlier in *The Cosmic Patriot Papers*.

Also, based on other legends of an ancient sunken Island in the Indian Ocean which also might have gone by the title of 'Lemuria,' it might be possible that ancient Hindu-like cultures had some ancient connection with Telos. Whether these were descended from the ancient Aryan 'invasion' of India or part of an entirely different sub-culture is uncertain. However the ancient East Indians ACCORDING TO old records did cooperate with the ancient Greeks in the construction of 'Vimanas' or flying ships.

NEW TECHNOLOGIES SOON—"...Very soon, human beings will be capable of regrowing amputated limbs. A machine will be set up, that will amplify sound waves....What actually will be done is the regeneration of the ethers to such an extent that it will cause matter to form into the shape that is called for. [similar to a Star Trek 'holodeck'?]...This, too, will work for the benefit of man. It is just recently that they discovered that sound will cut through pure rock....I will not say that there are not also the NEGATIVE EXPERIMENTS, such as scientists producing a sound that will kill a human being instantaneously....Also, the day is coming very soon when the ancient technology will be brought back....the Hierarchy [of the Federated Planets?] has now reached the point that they are finding it necessary to break the power of such institutions as the American Medical Association, for instance, and other such organizations on this planet, who have been STIFLING things.

"The American Medical Association has known how to cure cancer for thirty years. The person who discovered a cure, very much like the herb I'm talking about, a simple herb combination which destroys cancer, this person was killed and his formula burnt.

"...There is already a vehicle that will get 150 miles to a gallon of gasoline. There is already a vehicle that will run on water.

"There is a vehicle—the inventor already has a prototype—that will run on nothing but the etheric [electromagnetic] energy such as those used by the Confederation ships. There is already a system being implanted that will make solar panels 1000% more effective, to the extent that they will not only gather the energy; they will hold it in reserve.

"...There are computers now in the works that will create holographic images so real to human beings, that they are right there with them. I'm sure that several people in this room have seen, for instance, 'BRAINSTORM.' That machine exists now, to the extent that if one person has experienced it, everyone who has access to that tape will experience it the same way.

"There are also machines now that are being made into computers whereby you are able to take a vacation anywhere in the world, with all sensory ideas connected to it; this will be released within these coming two years.

"There are computers being built now that will respond to voice control; instead of typing to them, you will talk to them.

"Within ten years...there will be holographic chambers that will create such a sensory atmosphere around you that you can produce any scene you wish and step right into it, as a living movie. You will be surprised how fast this will happen!

"Little by little, the information is RELEASED for a computer that matches those in Telos.

"This computer will work on a crystal matrix. Because it works on a crystal matrix, it works on a system other than the binary system. It will operate off of light itself. It will be capable of taking each portion of information that is locked in each of the individual light rays.

"...You will also find a metal that will be a combination of several metals. It will be stronger than steel, as noncorrosive as gold, and lightweight as plastic.

"This metal will be able to create air ships that can withstand any pressure under water, and any temperature.

"Very soon in the future, you will find cities being built under the oceans. One of the reasons is that you will have the ability to live either on the surface, under the surface, under the ocean, or in floating cities above the planet.

"...Also, by the manipulation of the Light Rays, men will discover the manipulation, for instance, of the Green Ray.

"It will be possible to speed up a tree to grow in one year instead of ten."

At this point a lengthy description of the birth process in Telos is given. In brief, the gestation period of a Telosian woman is only three months and every effort is taken to make the transition of the child into this world as comfortable as possible through warm-water birth, and other methods...

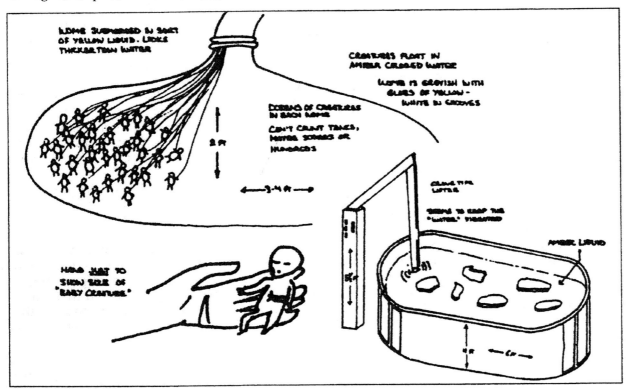

Now part of the "Rainbow Conspiracy," Strange vats filled with eerie liquid is where aliens are being "grown." Dulce's "level seven" is said to be honeycombed with tunnels filled with a variety of genetic as well as breeding equipment.

Chapter 8: Gnomes and the Reality of the Underworld

Nov. 1977 document carried the following article: 'CHANEQUES: MEXICAN GNOMES OR INTERPLANETARY VISITORS? [Veracruz's 'little people' date back to the ancient Totonacs but eyewitness reports do occur today], by Ramon A. Pantoja Lopez and Robert Freeman Bound. Due to their exact human features with exception to their size, could the 'CHANEQUES' be a singular diminutive mutation of the human family who left mainstream society for the sake of their own survival?

"RECENT MYSTERIES and violent occurrences in Mexico's gulf state of Veracruz again have brought into prominence the CHANEQUES (gnomes) who are purported to inhabit this tropical area.

"The name CHANEQUE is indigenous to the state of Veracruz, having been used for centuries by the native peoples, the Totonacs, of this area to designate the 'tiny men' (HOMBRECITOS) who live in the mountainous regions of the state. The Totonacs developed one of the first and most noteworthy Mexican civilizations whose ruins and artifacts still amaze visitors to this part of Mexico.

"Hernano Cortez, conqueror and settler of Mexico, and his armored horsemen, the first Europeans to disembark on the Veracruz coast, were told of the existence of these gnomes by the Totonacs in the early 16th Century. The Totonacs did not indicate the CHANEQUES were mythical creatures but rather talked of them as through they were diminutive flesh and bone beings with extraordinary powers.

"...The legend, which present-day Totonacs say has been passed down through countless generations, is this:

" 'We Totonac women know from many centuries of experience that when we go to wash out clothes or bathe in the river we must guard our small children very carefully. The CHANEQUES are always watching and they love to amuse themselves playing with our children. Although they never harm our youngsters or steal them, they entice them away to play and sometimes we don't see our boys and girls for hours or even days and of course we are distraught with worry until they reappear. However, they are extremely fond of the little heads and statues which we fashion with the smiling faces of the CHANEQUES. If we leave these clay toys near the rivers after a child has disappeared and go away, they always return the missing little ones very soon. These little men have our love and we respect them for their wondrous ['technological' as we will see further on] powers but they do cause us to worry sometimes.'

"Thus ends the ancient legend of the CHANEQUES.

"Today reports of contacts with the CHANEQUES persist in Mexico, not as fantasies but as actual happenings. We talked with more than 20 PERSONS in various parts of Veracruz during our investigation and ALL BUT FOUR of them had stories to tell us about their personal experiences with the gnomes or experiences their relatives, friends or acquaintances have had with the gnomes.

"Sra. Cirila Montero Lagunes, owner of a small store in La Tinaja, told us, 'My three-and-one-half-year-old son Ramiro was found by the CHANEQUES after he wandered away from home in March 1973 and was missing for six days. These tiny people are very timid with adults and instead of contacting us they told a six-year-old neighbor boy Juan who was playing in a far corner of his backyard, that Ramiro could be found in a cave some nine or 10 miles away. We were familiar with the cave and a search party had no trouble finding it and my son, who was asleep inside. Although he'd been missing for some time, he was in perfect health, NOT hungry OR thirsty or the least bit unhappy. Ramiro is talkative in his childish way and quickly advised us he was lost near a 'big water' (river) when five little men found him. They had given him 'sweet food' and milk, then he had gone to sleep. WHEN HE AWOKE HE WAS IN THE CAVE. HE SAID THAT AS LEAST ONE OF THE GNOMES WAS WITH HIM ALL THE TIME AND THEY PLAYED WITH HIM MANY TIMES.

" 'This appears to have a simple solution, Ramiro's mother continued. 'My son, not wanting to be chastised for disobeying my instructions to stay close to home, invented the tale and his six-year-old playmate, of course, vouched for him later.

" 'But it isn't as simple as that. He is just a little young to invent such a tale. More important, the entire hillside below the cave right up to its mouth is covered with an extremely dense spinebearing shrub about five feet in height with limbs extending to the ground. Ramiro's rescuers had to cut their way to the cave in order to reach him. All of these men suffered scratches and bruises; some had puncture wounds on their legs, hands and arms. My son, although barelegged and shoeless when found, hadn't a mark of any kind on him! Besides, its pretty foolish to say that his little playmate carried food and drink to him during those six days, not only because of THE INACCESSIBILITY OF THE CAVE but because of the 18-mile round trip involved. We are so grateful to the CHANEQUES for what they did. We might easily have lost our little boy forever.'

[Note: This account is similar to some which have been related describing similar diminutive humans who allegedly inhabit cavernous regions east of Phoenix, Arizona, below the Salt River Valley, and east into southwestern New Mexico. These have been seen by ranchers standing like sentinels on the tops of ridges; and have reportedly fed lost children and led them out of the dangerous wastelands to safety.

One account which the CRP came across years ago—although we cannot recall the exact source—told of a hunter who spotted a 2 FOOT TALL human in a forest. His dog gave chase and before the hunter could do anything it had torn the poor little man to pieces. The hunter was adamant that the dwarf was HUMAN, and that his internal organs were those of a normal human being, and that he was human in every respect except for his diminutive size. Scientists admit that the first dinosaurs were from six to eight feet tall and that later mutations branched out from this original saurian 'race.' Some degenerated into the small reptilians such as the modern lizards and snakes, while other grew to gargantuan sizes such as the Brontosaurus and Ultrasaurus.

But ALL, most paleontologists admit, must have mutated from this original saurian species. Although not quite as extensive in it's mutability, could the human race have 'branched off' into various other mutations or cultures over the millennia and developed both diminutive races some 2 feet tall to gargantuan races over 20 feet in height according to some sources? Of course it is rare to find full grown humans on the surface who are outside of the four to eight ft. range, suggesting that IF other such societies developed that they may have separated themselves from mainstream society for obvious reasons].

"Another account was given us by Sr. Ricardo Gutierrez. Senor Gutierrez told us that in June 1970 he was walking in the forest, on the Palma Cuata Ranch, near Mixtequilla e Ignacio de La Llave, Veracruz, with his six-year-old nephew Arturo close by his side. Senor Gutierrez said he was suddenly aware that his nephew was no longer beside him. He searched the nearby area, calling the child by name without result. Next, most of the able-bodied villagers made an exhaustive search of the wooded countryside with no success. Somewhat later events took a nasty turn.

"The uncle was accused of murdering his nephew and actually was awaiting trial when, 33 days after his disappearance, little Arturo entered the patio of his home, unharmed and looking well-fed, apparently none the worse for his long absence and appearing as unconcerned as though he'd been gone only a few hours. When asked where he had been he replied, 'Living with the little men. They gave me food and milk with honey in it. We played a lot of games. I was very happy.'

"Of course, charges against the uncle were dropped and another incredible tale was added to the CHANEQUE legend. We checked this story with the authorities and they confirmed that the boy had been missing for the time stated and had inexplicably turned up at his own home, and that the uncle had been charged with murder.

"At about 8:A.M. on May 22, 1973, Manuel Angel Gonzalez was driving a six-ton truck loaded with asbestos sheeting, sacked cement and a small quantity of reinforcing steel between La Tinaja and Tierra Blanca, Veracruz. This is a routine run for him. But suddenly, as he neared the village of Cintalapa he was startled to see five diminutive figures standing with hands in the air ahead of his truck. Manuel, reacting instantly, braked his vehicle in time to avoid running down what he at first thought was a group of small children. He swears they materialized before his eyes, that one moment the straight stretch of highway within his vision was clear and the next instant the figures confronted him. A closer look revealed the 'children' to be miniature adults, well-proportioned and of about equal height, a height Manuel estimates to be no more than two feet. His description of the physical aspect of these 'gnomes' coincides with HUNDREDS of other eyewitness accounts related over the years as to size, light brown complexion, black hair, and the ability to appear suddenly before the viewers' eyes, as through they had come from another dimension.

"When asked to describe their clothing Manuel replied, 'I don't remember what they wore—not even the color of their clothes. I was so shocked and surprised. You see, I didn't really believe in them before this happened.' Later he said, quite logically, 'Perhaps their clothing was so like our own that I didn't pay much attention to it.'

"At the time the perplexed driver descended from the truck cab intent on making a closer examination of them. But before he could take more than a few steps the tiny creatures began to run, scattering into the undergrowth and apparently heading in the direction of a nearby mountain.

"Manuel returned to his truck which to his consternation was completely engulfed in blue flames. In an incredibly short span of time, estimated by the driver and two additional witnesses who stopped to watch the spectacle to be 30 minutes at most, the truck and its normally nonflammable cargo were reduced to ashes and fused metal.

"Not content with the newspaper accounts of this strange happening, we decided to do some on-the-scene investigating. We own and operate a private English school in Mexico City, but fortunately the students were enjoying their spring vacation and we had a few days to drive the 600 miles to that part of Veracruz.

"We arrived in Catemac, Veracruz, headquarters of the Lopez Transportation Company, late in the afternoon of May 24. and went directly to the office of Sr. Abel Lopez, owner of the burned vehicle. He proved to be very amiable and verified everything we had read previously, including the fact that all of the truck's contents were nonflammable.

"Senor Lopez said, 'I still find it incredible that asbestos, cement and steel could be so completely consumed in this fire. It was certainly something out of the ordinary and I want to say right now to those people who have suggested that it was deliberately set afire for the insurance that this truck and its cargo were not insured. Also, I've heard some mention of the fire being cause by a bolt of lightning. This happened on a clear, sunny morning.'

"He then added that Manuel Gonzales, the driver, had proven himself to be one of the company's most dependable drivers, sober, very religious and not given to exaggeration or imaginative flights of fancy. Fortunately, while we were talking with Senor Lopez, Manuel Gonzalez came in. Although he had submitted to repeated questioning by the police and newspaper reporters, he was most cooperative. He gave the appearance of being serious and honest and completely baffled by his traumatic experience. Verifying the statements of his boss, he deepened the mystery by adding that two days after the charred remains of the truck had been towed to their garage, two sections of metal fused to the chassis had suddenly burst into brilliant blue flames resembling huge Fourth of July sparklers and had been reduced to ashes. This was confirmed by Senor Lopez, and later while we were inspecting the ruined chassis these burned out sections were pointed out to us.

"The driver did mention that the newspaper account omitted the statement wherein he said, 'I am as much inclined to believe these small people were space travelers from another planet as that they were CHANEQUES, for two reasons. First, apparently people here in Veracruz have had many experiences with the CHANEQUES but there are no accounts of them having done any harm or committed such acts of violence. Quite the contrary, they have on many occasions aided people in distress; shipwrecked sailors stranded on the beach, lost hikers and lost children have been given food and water and guided to the nearest road or trail. It is said they love the GIANTS' small children and over the years there have been accounts of boys and girls returning home to say that they have been playing with the 'little men.' Second, on May 21 three ranchers reported having seen a large illuminated disc flying very low over this area.'

"Before leaving Veracruz we talked with Police Officer Fernando Aportela Abad who patrols this section of the highway between La Tinaja and Tierra Blanca. He investigated the mystery within an hour after it happened and told us, 'It is certainly true that a short circuit can set a vehicle afire but to me it is incredible that any ordinary fire could have consumed asbestos, cement and steel. I've investigated this thoroughly and have no normal explanation.'

"He told us that a quantity of the carbonized cargo and truck metal was submitted for analysis to José Lopez, industrial engineer and erstwhile professor of physics and thermodynamics at the National University of Mexico.

"After the laboratory tests were completed Engineer de Haro Lopez told the press, 'I am admittedly astonished and puzzled. I've arrived at the conclusion that the burning of this truck and its cargo by an unknown type of light-heat beam with a VERY SELECTIVE WAVELENGTH corresponding to the laser ray but many times more powerful and not known on this planet. The combustion of the asbestos, cement, metals and tires of the truck in such a rapid and destructive way is something I've never heard of before. But almost as amazing was the fact that while the back of the plastic-covered cab seat was completely consumed, the dashboard badly burned and the electrical wiring melted, the bottom of the seat, rubber floor mat and paint on the inside of the cab doors wasn't even scorched. Even more astounding, the fuel in the tank remained intact!'

"Sometime after our visit to Catemac, Veracruz, we received a telephone call from Police Officer Abad who had agreed to call us collect should there be any further developments. He now said two additional trucks had been almost completely consumed by the same inexplicable blue flames in the state of Veracruz, one on the Costera del Golfo Highway, the other on the Cordoba Highway. He added that both incidents were investigated by highway patrolmen with whom he had talked and they had not arrived at any 'logical' conclusion. However, in one of these later cases a motorist who had called the police at Cordoba, Veracruz, three hours BEFORE the fire reported that an oval-shaped UFO hovered over and followed his car for several miles on the Cordoba Highway.

"We are keeping in touch with the authorities, and our friends in Veracruz will inform us of any developments involving the mysterious CHANEQUES. "We both have seen UFOs flying low over Mexico's mountains and now feel that with time and patience we will be able to contact the CHANEQUES. During our two-week vacation later this year we shall camp out in the verdure-clad mountains of Veracruz, probably near volcanic Mt. Orizaba from where the CHANEQUES are frequently reported, hoping to solve the riddle of the CHANEQUES. Are they Mexican gnomes or interplanetary visitors?"

• • •

In her volume, NOTES ON THE UNDERGROUND [An Essay on Technology, Society, and the Imagination], MIT Press., London, England; Rosalind Williams relates some interesting thoughts on the underworld as it is describes in both legends of the past and visions of the future:

"...Houston and St. Paul-Minneapolis [also other cities such as Kansas City] have developed elaborate systems of tunnels and walkways that are virtual indoor cities (the Houston system runs 6 miles; the St. Paul skywalks connect 32 city blocks). These surroundings are comfortable both physically and socially, for they exclude not only summer heat and winter cold but also beggars and other people considered undesirable. Shopping centers, airports, and hotels can be charmed worlds of light and color and music. In these artificial environments, the pain of contrast is absent. Here 'mechanism takes command,' and every detail of construction is planned to comfort the body and relax the mind. Contemporary experience of the artificial environment is therefore contradictory: while we grieve for a lost way of life, we rejoice in a new one...

"Subterranean surroundings, whether real or imaginary, furnish a model of an artificial environment from which nature has been effectively banished. Human beings who live underground must use mechanical devices to provide the necessities of life: food, light, even air. Nature provides only space. The underworld setting therefore takes to an extreme the displacement of the natural environment by a technological one. It hypothesizes human life in a manufactured world...

"...In this century, imaginary underworlds are almost always vast cities and many 'fantastic cities' are buried far below the ground. Even cities on the surface are imagined as being so detached from nature that they resemble caves [Note: the 'artificiality' of a subterranean system would be true in the case of artificially-excavated caverns, but many accounts speak of large natural caverns which have been inhabited and which contain their own 'natural environments' in the way of rock formations, underground streams or rivers, and even flora, fauna and in a few cases of the larger chambers natural illumination].

"...In the decades after writing TECHNICS AND CIVILIZATION and THE CULTURE OF CITIES [1934], (Lewis) Mumford continued to search for images to convey the all-encompassing nature of a technological environment...In his research and writing, Mumford kept pushing the origins of mechanization back to earlier and earlier times—back to ancient Egypt, and eventually to the discovery of agriculture. As he had earlier enlarged his compass from American to Western history, now he embraced the globe. From this sweeping perspective, Mumford concluded that humanity was moving into an unprecedented stage of mechanization, one motivated by a new technological ideal. In the 1960's he invented the term 'megatechnics' to describe that ideal...

"Today, not the city but the spaceship has become the standard image of the megatechnic ideal of complete detachment from the organic habitat. This newer image, however, denies the claustrophobic realities of human life on earth. Although the spacecraft itself may model an all-encompassing technological environment, its mission—hurtling through endless space, going boldly where no man has gone before—suggests the vision of an endless frontier where new varieties of nature wait to be discovered. Unlike the mine, the spaceship fails to convey a sense of permanent enclosure in a finite world. Furthermore, because of the indeterminacy of the interstellar void, space travel lacks the verticality that gives the underworld its unique power in the human imagination.

"Stories of descent into the underworld are so ancient and universal that their fundamental structure, the opposition of surface and depth, may well be rooted in the structure of the human brain. The congruence may be explained by the Freudian hypothesis of an Oedipal experience that splits human beings into conscious and unconscious selves, or by the Jungian hypothesis of a collective subconscious. In any case, the metaphor of depth is a primary category of human thought.

"...If we imagine going underground, we not only imagine an environment where organic nature is largely absent; we also retrace a journey that is one of the most enduring and powerful cultural traditions of humankind, a metaphorical journey of discovery through descent below the surface.

"...Long before Virgil's Aeneas was guided by a Sybyl to the infernal regions through a cave on the leaden Lake Avernus, long before stories of Proserpine's abduction to the underworld by Pluto or of Orpheus's descent to the Stygian realm to brink back Eurydice, and long before recorded history, when the earliest humans drew the bison and bears they hunted on the walls and ceilings of caves, they must have told stories about the dark underworld lying even deeper within the earth.

"...Beginning in the Renaissance, the epic tradition of the journey to the underworld was transformed into narratives that were written and secular rather than oral and sacred. In these narratives, an adventurous, unlucky, or half-mad traveler sets forth and discovers an underworld, which he enters and from which he may or may not emerge.

"...In the nineteenth century, however, another type of underground story also began to be written—one quite different in its fundamental structure. Instead of being a place to visit, the underworld becomes a place to live. Instead of being discovered through chance, an underworld is constructed (or a natural underworld is vastly enlarged) through deliberate choice.

"...Then and now, JOURNEY [TO THE CENTER OF THE EARTH] is one of (Jules) Verne's most popular books. Far less famous, and quite different in its premise, is another Verne book on a subterranean theme, published thirteen years later. LES INDES NOIRES (1877) [variously translated as THE BLACK INDIES, BLACK DIAMONDS, UNDERGROUND CITY, or THE CHILD OF THE CAVERN] is a story not of intrepid explorers and guides but of hard-working engineers and miners, and not of an exciting journey but of a permanently functioning underground society.

"...One novel describes an imaginary subterranean journey, the other an imaginary subterranean society....As technology advanced, on the other hand, the idea of building an inner world became more and more credible.

"...According to the eminent geologist Archibald Geikie, who wrote the article on geology in the ninth (1887) edition of the *Encyclopedia Brittanica*, various themes ('most fanciful') about the inside of the earth had been propounded, but only three merited serious consideration: the earth might have a solid crust and molten interior; a liquid substratum might lie BENEATH the crust [that is, BENEATH THE MOHO or the lower extremity of the crust which ranges from a few miles to a few dozen miles in thickness depending on the locality—as the crustal caverns are those most often associated with the ability to maintain physical life whereas the lower 'Magmatic' caverns of the lower Mantle are certainly regarded by scientists and theologians alike as being much too 'infernally' hot to support such life], the rest of the globe being solid; or the planet might be solid and rigid to the center except for 'local vesicular spaces.' The last theory was favored by the eminent Lord Kelvin, codiscoverer of the second law of thermodynamics.

"During the winter of 1863–64, Verne had a series of conversations with Charles Sainte-Claire Deville, a geographer who had explored European volcanoes and who theorized that they might be connected by passages under the earth [*Note*: This was the theory presented not only in the original Jules Verne volume A JOURNEY TO THE CENTER OF THE EARTH, but the three movie versions of the book which came much later. The first movie version, starring Pat Boone and James Mason, was filmed in Carlsbad Caverns and was the most accurate of the three, even though it departed slightly from Verne's original story line. The second version dealt with explorers who entered a volcano in the Hawaiian Islands and was rather campy and non-serious and did not even come close to the quality of the original version of the movie in regards to story-line nor visual impact. The third version, a re-make by NBC, appeared on that network in March of 1993. It surpassed the other two in special visual and technical effects, yet was still slightly inferior to the original 'classical' version in both story-line and plausibility. For instance, whereas the other two movie versions—true to the original work—had the explorers descend into extinct volcanoes, the third version had them descend into a live and active volcano. However the third version had a rather open ending, possibly giving it a chance to redeem itself in the areas just mentioned if and when it is continued into a television series].

"Verne became so excited by Deville's ideas that he dropped his work on CAPTAINE HATTERAS and quickly wrote JOURNEY TO THE CENTER OF THE EARTH. In that book he described the underworld in a way compatible with Kelvin's theory of 'local vesicular spaces.' Furthermore, since geologists of his day agreed that the earth's interior must be hot (citing as proof the eruption of volcanoes and the thermal gradient in mine shafts), Verne took care to explain how his explorers could descend so far without burning up. JOURNEY is farfetched, but NOT too much so.

"Over the next three decades Verne continued to write his memorable 'imaginary voyages,' including several more on subterranean themes....much actual excavation—from the digging up of ancient Troy to the digging of railway tunnels through the Alps—was going on in the period when Verne, Wells, and Forster were writing. They could not avoid seeing some excavation projects and hearing about many others. Even more important, they knew the same was true of their readers. This assumption of shared experience allowed Wells to have the narrator of THE TIME MACHINE explain to his readers of the 1890's that, although the evolution of an underground species might seem grotesque, 'even now there are existing circumstances to point that way.':

" 'There is a tendency to utilize underground space for the less ornamental purpose of civilization; there is the Metropolitan Railway in London, for instance, there are new electric railways, there are subways, there are underground workrooms and restaurants, and they increase and multiply. Evidently, I thought, this tendency has increased till Industry has gradually lost its birthright in the sky. I mean that it had gone deeper and deeper into larger and larger underground factories, spending a still-increasing amount of its time therein, in the end—! Even now, does not an East-End worker live in such artificial conditions as practically to be cut off from the natural surface of the earth?'

"...the social implications of subterranean life, especially the concern that humans living in an enclosed environment might degenerate into feeble, brainless hedonists or cruel, heartless barbarians." [*Note:* This need not always be the case however. One could say that an underground environment might provide the safety and privacy for a peaceful society to exist unmolested by outside cultures. Then again it might also provide the privacy necessary for a hedonistic society to carry on their cruel activities in secret without coming into condemnation from 'mainstream' society. Both sides may in fact exist, as have been suggested in numerous accounts]

• • •

'COMMUNISM' vs. 'CAPITALISM'—There have been many who state that Communism as well as Capitalism has failed in its attempts to bring equality of power and wealth to the citizens of the world. In essence, both philosophies may have their good as well as their bad arguments. Capitalism establishes the right to own private property while Communism advocates the free distribution of wealth, which is seen more in principle than in practice. The problem is that hard-core adherents to each philosophy have refused to accept the precepts of the 'opposing' philosophy (then again there are those who believe that BOTH Communism and Capitalism have been forced by the 'powers that be' into artificial conflict with each other to keep the masses in a state of fear and confusion which would allow them to become more easily controllable).

The truth is that the earliest cultures instinc-tively utilized a societal form which combined the equal distribution of wealth with the right to own private property. This pattern is also seen in the first Christian Church as described in the book of ACTS. COMMUNIST-SOCIALISM has enforced the distribution of wealth, but has been intolerant of ANY right to own private property and has even destroyed those who have done so.

In former Communist Russia wealthy farmers were slaughtered by the hundreds of thousands. In Communist China 'ownership' rights have been enforced to the point of allowing for only one child per family, and since boys are often more economically desirable to a family mass infanticide of females is rampant and the female-male ratio in that country has been affected tremendously as a result.

DEMOCRATIC-CAPITALISM believes in private property ownership but frowns upon the equal distribution of wealth and private property, as is practiced in Communist countries, allowing for unfair and even criminal exploitation by multi-millionaires or billionaires and an often violent division between the upper and lower classes. One cannot say that Capitalism nor Communism is entirely wrong in every aspect, but we must come to the realization that the more palatable ideals of both philosophies have been used as bait by the Illuminati or 'Cult of the Serpent' in order to recruit both sides into the game-plan which is being orchestrated by PAGAN-ILLUMINISM.

It was apparently decided long ago by the Serpent Cult (that is, the Illuminati AND the Serpent Race) that 'half truths' were more effective in destroying human individuality and replacing it with the draconian 'collective conscious' techno-dictatorial society where all human thought, emotion and will would be controlled by a Central Command.

In other words, man's free agency would be taken away from him, and with it his soul. Opposing PAGAN-ILLUMINISM (not necessarily Communism or Capitalism which are apparently mere 'tools' used by the serpent cult to manipulate the masses) is CHRISTIAN-REPUBLICANISM. We see the perfect pattern for this system in the book of ACTS, wherein the first Christians under Divine influence WILLINGLY fused the ideals of Communal sharing with the right to own private property, a unity which the Illuminati would erroneously have us believe cannot be possible.

• • •

Now back to the subject of encounters with 'reptilian' entities, John A. Keel in his book *Strange Creatures From Time and Space* (Neville Spearman., London, England 1975), refers to a 'giant four-legged dragon-like creature' which reportedly stepped out of South Dakota's Lake Campbell one day in 1934 and forced a farmer's tractor off the road.

• • •

In earlier files we reported on a group of 'hairy giants' or humanoids seen by a British Embassy worker in now-sealed-off catacombs below Malta's 'Hypogeum.' What we did not relate however was the remarkable claim that these white-fur clad hairy giants were upwards of 20–25 ft. tall according to the British woman who claimed to have seen them. Even if she, in her panic, misjudged the size of the creatures it is obvious from her description that they were a great deal taller than the average human being.

With this in mind we quote from the following account which appeared on in a submitted letter on p. 150 of the Dec. 1969 issue of FATE magazine, under the heading 'MYSTERY MAN.' Since the account is of a rather incredible nature we leave the readers to make their own determinations as to it's reliability, in light of the documentation which has been given throughout the *The Cosmic Patriot Papers*. Is the following a 'tall tale' or an actual account of the discovery of a freak gigantic mutation of the human race—possibly the remains of a father, a mother and their child!?

"Last year in Washington State I met a man who told me that years ago (1902, if I remember correctly) he worked around Thermal, Calif. He said that at that time some workers opened a mound eight miles from Thermal and discovered three HUMAN skeletons, 24 feet, 22 feet and 12 feet in length. He did not see them himself but said the grave was closed by ORDER OF THE PRESIDENT.

"He MAY have been pulling my leg but he seemed sincere and honest...If the skeletons are still there they certainly would be a valuable find now—William Hoggatt., Perry, Okla."

• • •

In earlier Files we have written much on the alleged Federation which allegedly ties together such human colonies as those in Tau Ceti, the Koldasian system, Epsilon Eridani, Erra-Taygeta in the Pleiades, Vega in Lyra, various colonies in the Hyades, the alleged Solarian Tribunal on the moons of Saturn, and the UMMITES in Wolf 424 [all of which have incredibly and repeatedly been described by numerous and apparently separate contactees]. One additional allegation is that the UMMITES, a Scandinavian-appearing race who live on a planet with a magnetic field much more intense than that of earth, have apparently made contact with scientists associated with the French government.

It is interesting that M.K. Jessup's annotated version of *The Case for the UFO* contains comments by alleged members of an ancient terran race who have access to interplanetary craft technology. They have stated that France has been the subject of much interest among exterran cultures because of it's unique social atmosphere. The UMMITES allegedly come from the star system we know of as Wolf 424, a star which they themselves refer to as IUMMO. Their insignia resembles an 'H' with an extra vertical bar in the middle and the four corners of the 'H' tapered into an outward curve. This symbol has been PHOTOGRAPHED on the underside of some UFO's which have been encountered in this century. Also the UMMITES speak of themselves as belonging to a large Federation of planets, possibly more or less consisting of the interstellar regions described above.

• • •

In *The Cosmic Patriot Papers* we referred to an incident involving hair and flesh which had allegedly been dredged up from an underground well. C.R.P. was not familiar with the exact source of the story at the time, however we were fortunate enough to come across the full account at a later date. The incident in question appeared in the Sept. 1966 issue of *Fate*, pages 25 and 28:

"FROM 'DOWN UNDER'—We suspect this story may be a hoax but we can't resist reporting it. We have TWO DIFFERENT clippings from Darwin, Australia, concerning the discovery of animal flesh, hairs and hide during a well-drilling operation at a depth of 102 feet.

"An experienced well driller, Norman Jenson, was boring for water 15 miles from Killarney homestead, about 350 miles south of Darwin.

He had penetrated seven layers of limestone, clay, red soil and sandstone when, at 102 feet, the bit of the drill struck something soft and quickly dropped to 111 feet. Jensen thought the drill had penetrated an underground water course and lowered a pump to make tests. His pump brought to the surface a bucketful of what he believed to be flesh, bone, hide and hairs. Jensen told Constable Roy Harvey he never had seen anything like this before. Some of the material was given to chickens at Killarney station. They ate it, apparently without ill effect. Several days later the rest of the matter HAD NOT putrefied, although it had been left EXPOSED in the open air.

"Dr. W. A. Langsford, Northern Territory Director of Health in Darwin, stated that microscopic examination revealed the material to be hair and tissue. Samples were to be forwarded to forensic laboratories in Adelaide for further tests. There is even a possibility, he said, that the matter is human. Possibly romancing, Australians report that for many years overland drovers have DISLIKED TAKING CATTLE ALONG THAT PART OF THE ROUTE because of FREQUENT STAMPEDES."

One might wonder if the material allegedly recovered from the well might have been from a 'Sasquatch' like creature or an animal unknown to us. It would seem logical for living matter, once dead, to remain relatively free from petrification for long periods of time within the cool and unchanging environment of an underground cavern system as opposed to the often hot, degenerating and debilitating environment on the surface. Could a type of natural mummification have also taken place underground, possibly explaining why the hair and flesh had not putrefied after several days?

• • •

William Halliday, in his book *Adventure is Underground*, records an affidavit submitted by a Mr. Earl P. Dorr, describing vast caverns he and an associate allegedly discovered and explored in Southern California. Portions of the sworn testimonial are quoted below:

"...These caverns are about 250 miles from Los Angeles, California. Traveling over state highways by automobile, the caverns can be reached in a few hours.

"Accompanied by a mining engineer, I visited the caverns in the month of May, 1927. We entered them and spent 4 days exploring them for a distance of between 8 and 9 miles. We carried with us altimeters and pedometers, to measure the distance we traveled, and had an instrument to take measurements of distance by triangulation, together with such instruments convenient and necessary to make observations and estimations.

"Our examinations revealed the following facts, viz:

"1. From the mouth of the cavern we descended about 2000 feet. There, we found a canyon which, on our altimeter, measured about 3000 to 3500 feet deep. We found the caverns to be divided into many chambers, filled and embellished with the usual stalactites and stalagmites, besides many grotesque and fantastic wonders that make the caverns one of the marvels of the world.

"2. On the floor of the canyon there is a flowing river which by careful examination and measurement (by triangulation) we estimated to be about 300 feet wide, and with considerable depth. The river rises and falls with the tides of the sea—at high tide, being approximately 300 feet wide, and at low tide, approximately 10 feet wide and four feet deep.

"3. When the tide is out there is exposed on both sides of the river from 100 to 150 feet of black beach sand which is very rich in gold values. The sands are from four to 11 feet deep. This means there are about 300 to 350 feet of rich bearing placer sand which averages eight feet in depth. We explored the canyon sands a distance of eight miles, finding little variation in the depth and width of the sands.

"4. I am a practical miner of many years' experience and I own valuable mining properties nearby which I am willing to pledge and put up as security to guarantee that the statements herein are true.

"5. My purpose of exploring the caverns was to study the mineralogy in order to ascertain the mineral possibilities and actualities of the caves, making such examination in person with my engineer necessary to determine by expert examination the character and quantity of mineral values of the caverns, rocks and sands.

"6. I carried out about 10 lbs. of the black sand and 'panned' it, receiving more than $7 in gold. I sold it to a gold buyer who offered me at the rate of $18 per ounce. 2 ½ lbs. of this black sand I sent to John Herman, assayer, whose as-say certificate shows a value of $2145.47 per [cubic] yard, with gold at $20.67 per ounce.

"7. From engineering measurements and observations we made, I estimated that it would require a tunnel about 350 feet long to penetrate to the caverns, one thousand feet or more below the present entrance, which are some 3 miles distant from my property.

"8. I make no estimate of even the approximate tonnage of the black sand, but some estimate of the cubical contents may be made for more than eight miles and the minimum depth is never less than three feet. They are of varying depth—what their maximum depth may be we do not know.—Sworn by E. P. Dorr., 309 Adena St., Pasadena, Calif., November 16, 1934."

It is of interest that this river, which is referred to by Earl Dorr, allegedly rises and falls with the tides. Could it be that somewhere near the source of this underground river—possibly beneath the great western desert of Utah-Nevada-California where little surface water escapes by way of streams and rivers—there is a subterranean body of water large enough to be influenced by the tidal forces of the moon? One might consider such a possibility with a grain of salt if it were not for the fact that there is, in an extension of Death Valley National Monument near the California-Nevada border, a low-lying cave which is known as "Devil's Hole."

There are at least two surface openings to this cave, which is also described in detail in William Halliday's book. This cavern is filled with water and, according to some sources, rises and falls slightly with the tides! This may indicate that the underground water-courses of California such as described by Earl Door AND by other researchers as well, might connect with extensive underground lakes or small underground freshwater seas. Whether this theory proves accurate or not remains to be seen... when and if future adventurous Speleonauts make their way once again into Dorr's secret caverns and to the SOURCE of the 'alleged' underground river. "Devil's Hole" contains a rare species of cave-fish found nowhere else in the world (at least nowhere that marine biologists are aware of).

This, including the fact that two professional, some say Navy, divers disappeared in this apparently 'bottomless' aqua-cave some years ago, led officials to put the cave under government protection by making it an exten-

sion of Death Valley National Monument, much of which lies well BELOW sea level. The existence of, or possibility of the existence of, such underground 'seas' beneath the California- Nevada regions seems to be supported by other accounts.

We will now quote from William R. Halliday's professional observations of the claims made in Dorr's affidavit, which also appear in his book *Adventure is Underground*

"...What is the gimmick? "This was probably the question in the mind of every reader of the *California Mining Journal,* when this affidavit appeared in it's November, 1940, issue. The question still arises whenever a caver first hears the remarkable story of this still more remarkable cave. Furthermore, the answers to the other obvious questions are not those which might be anticipated.

" 'Is this just an imaginary cave?' No, the cave certainly exists. I have been in it.

" 'Did Dorr keep it's location secret?' No. Dozens, perhaps hundreds, of people know it's exact location, high on the side of Kokoweef Peak in the Mojave Desert.

" 'Has anyone tried to find this river of gold?' Yes, indeed. The prosperous Crystal Cave Mining Corporation owns the property.

" 'Then what is the gimmick?' That's quite a tale.

"The beginnings of the story of the cave of gold are shrouded in the mists of the minds of old-timers. For a long time, prowling prospectors have known of the existence of the wide mouth of a deep cavern on the limestone flank of a peak which forms part of the east face of IVANPAH VALLEY—Kokoweef Peak. Even though only four miles by dirt road from the highway between LAS ANGELES and LAS VEGAS, the area was so desolate that, in the 1920's, weeks might elapse without the passing of more than an occasional prospector and his burro. The opening of the cavern was several feet in diameter and the cave was obviously much larger farther down. There were local stories that it was bottomless, although it took 'only a few seconds' for a rock to strike 'bottom.'

"Then someone found a narrow crack leading to ANOTHER cave, high on the east face of the peak. Maybe it was Dorr. The stories vary. One version repeats the common story of two Indians with a treasure map, which in this case was supposed to have showed the entrance to the cave. Dorr was well known in the area, having a claim across the valley, several miles southwest of Kokoweef Peak. Like any experienced prospector, he certainly prowled every ledge of the area. In any event, the new cave seemed even deeper than Kokoweef Cave. Like at least seven other caves in California, it eventually became known as Crystal Cave.

"Later, in 1934, another old prospector, Pete Ressler, was resting near the bottom of the southwest slope of the barren peak. He idly tossed a rock into a crack. To his surprise it rattled back and forth for a long time until the sound died away into the depths. He strapped his load on his burro and headed for Mountain Pass Station for dynamite.

" 'What do you think it is, Pete?' the men at the station asked him.

" 'Quien sabe?' he shrugged. Pete's Spanish, however, was horrible. It sounded like 'Kin Savvy' or 'Kin Sabe,' and this name stuck to the cave he dynamited open. It wasn't much of a cave. It slanted downward, but was filled with rubble [rubble from the dynamite blasts, perhaps?] to a level not far below the entrance. Old Pete dropped out of the story. Dorr is the main character.

"Dorr must have been a strange person. No one else was particularly interested in the caves, but soon he was telling of an enormous cavern into which he was gradually making his way, trip after trip. The main part of the cave was a series of vertical drops from one small chamber to another. In several areas there were small, dry pools which contained sharp little crystals. From one of the small rooms a tight tunnel led a relatively short distance to a huge cavern containing a chasm 3,000 feet deep. He told of a stalactite 1,500 feet long.

[Note: The underground cavern allegedly ran south beneath Kokoweef Peak and continued southwest under Dorr Peak. Both peaks are near the southwest flank of the Ivanpah Mts. on the northern flank of which is an area where U.S. Highway 91 goes west and makes a sudden northerly turn toward the Boulder Dam area. Dorr alleged that he and the engineer who explored the caverns with him followed the upper tiers or shelf rock ledges to a place where they could make their way down to the shore. They also allegedly discovered a huge cataract or waterfall cascading down the side of the 'canyon' in one area beneath—what they judged to be—

Dorr Peak. They allegedly followed the shelves for 8 miles. According to a map of the caves drawn by Herman Wallace Jr., under the personal instruction and supervision of Earl Dorr, the stalactite was only 500 feet long and was located adjacent to the underground waterfall which flowed into the underground river at the bottom of the canyon as one of its many tributaries].

"The cavern went on for miles. He had walked to the brink of the chasm, but had not found a way to it's bottom. There were places where air came into the cavern, so other caves on the peak must open into it. And there ought to be an entrance somewhere on his claim, too. That was the direction the cave headed. Before long Dorr was claiming to have found a way down the wall of the subterranean canyon. Down below the wonders were even greater. He had found great deposits of placer gold. By this time he had the other old-timers half convinced. Still, THEY weren't going into that awful-looking hole for all the gold in the U.S. Mint.

"One day in 1928 Dorr again told his friends that he was going into the cave for another trip. Two days passed, three, four. His friends became worried. Gold would not tempt them to go into the cave, but they were his friends and the code of the desert is stern. Dorr might be trapped there, hurt, dying. A rescue party climbed to the mouth of the cave, where Dorr's ropes were still fixed.

"Hardly had they all entered the cave when they met a raging Dorr they hardly knew. Although disheveled and wild-eyed, he was obviously in no need of rescuing. Nervously they shrank away from his needless fury. Had he gone mad from his long stay underground? [More likely it was the dreaded 'gold fever' which has affected the minds of men throughout the centuries and has often motivated them to acts of cruelty and irrationality.] They were trying to help him, yet he was accusing them of trying to steal his gold.

"Before they quite understood, they felt the dull impact of a HEAVY charge of dynamite. Then Dorr calmed down. 'You'll never get it now,' he smirked.

"That blast finished the tunnel to the river of gold.'

"We do not know whether Dorr was ever convinced that his friends were only trying to rescue him. For several years he was a familiar figure in the Mojave Desert. Continually he attempted to persuade people to run a tunnel into the cave of gold from the lower slopes of Kokoweef Peak. He would go shares with them. If they were willing to pay for the tunnel, they could have part of the profits.

"On·this basis few investors were willing to consider the project. Finally, however, a small group headed by a Los Angeles capitalist was willing to speculate on Dorr's proposition. First, they tried the easy expedients. Kin Sabe Cave was the most accessible. Dorr thought it connected with the great chasm. They installed an inclined railway track and began to remove the rubble which filled it. Before long they had quite a respectable cave, 125 feet deep, but the air in it was completely stagnant. Over Dorr's protests, they abandoned the attempt. If there was an entrance to the great cavern from Kin Sabe, it was too deep to bother with, at least until all easier possibilities had been investigated. Next they turned their attention to Kokoweef Cave, the first cavern discovered on the peak. A road was built to a nearby ledge and a short tunnel was drilled, connecting the bottom of the cavern to the surface of the peak.

"Again, much rubble was removed without encountering the true bottom. Operations were in full swing when someone discovered a mineral vein in the wall of the peak a few dozen yards from the tunnel. It was zinc, and high-grade ore. Because of the war, zinc was at a premium. The Crystal Cave Mining Company promptly went into the zinc business. Dorr was disgusted. He abandoned the project.

"Occasionally someone would hear of him, still telling his story of prowling the hills near his old claim, still seeking another entrance to the cave of gold. A fantastic story? Yes, but this version is mild in comparison with the one related to us at the first meeting ever held by the Southern California Grotto[of the National Speleological Society].

"The Kokoweef story and that of the Cave of the Winding Stair were obviously firmly entangled in the folklore of the desert. Just in case there might be something behind the unbelievable tale, however, three of us obtained an appointment with D. Foster Hewitt, an eminent geologist who knew the Mojave Desert better than his own back yard.

" 'You cavers should know better than that,'

he reproached us. 'Dorr may have found more cave, but certainly nothing like what he claimed. Such a thing is geologically impossible. Why don't you go over and see Herman Wallace? He's an officer of the company and can tell you all about the caves.'

"Mr. Wallace did so, most cordially. He told us the story as Door had told it to him, stressing that he thought there was only a chance in a thousand that the cave of gold existed. He showed us a copy of Dorr's affidavit, and a sketch of the caverns made by his son under Dorr's direct supervision. He gave us exact measurements of the caves and ended up by asking if we would like to visit the caves and see if we had any ideas.

"Would we? Thirty-four cavers and their friends and families showed up at the Carbonate King Mine camp on the morning of November 13, 1948. Many had come along only for a glorious autumn outing in the Joshua trees, but the bare flanks of the rock-ribbed peaks were swarming with people. We had to divide the group into several parties and establish strict traffic regulations. The group I led took a quick look at Kokoweef Cave, noted the rubble on the floor, nodded wisely, and took off for Crystal Cave like a herd of bighorn sheep which are sometimes seen in these mountains.

"The company had placed a gate over the narrow entrance to Crystal Cave. We unlocked it and fixed a 250-foot climbing rope to the frame. Squeezing into the tight orifice, we surveyed the wooden ladder that had been installed several years previously. To be safe, we relayed the first man down the 70-foot descent. He kicked the supports hard, found them solid, and the rest of us poured down.

"We found ourselves in a small, irregular chamber about twenty-five feet in diameter. Several short extensions led off, but they were too tight for us to advance more than a few feet. The walls were richly embellished with flowstone, and we admired them vaguely. Our business lay deeper, however, and we approached the second descent of seventy feet.

"Here, again, ladders had been installed by the company. The lower part of the chamber we had just examined, however, was moist, and the wood of these ladders had deteriorated. A strong kick brought most of the supports down in crashing ruin.

"As we lined up for the descent, someone

shouted. He had found the name DORR smoked boldly on the wall. We gathered around the signature. Here was our first proof that Dorr had actually been in this cave.

"One by one we worked our way down the pit. It was not quite vertical, and the descent was easy until we came to an overhanging 10 feet high. We climbed down the rope hand over hand, and called back for a rope ladder so that we could get out again.

"Here was a second small chamber, even more richly decorated with dripstone and flow-stone than the one above. It, too, was quite irregular and there was considerable broken rock on one side. We found Dorr's name, again splashed boldly across the wall in soot from his miner's lamp.

"There were several small pits in the floor of the chamber. One of us popped into each. Mine went nowhere. Someone else found that his pit continued down at a steep angle. We followed him. Alas! Thick flowstone deposits narrowed the passage, and we came to the end of the cave about sixty feet below the second chamber, just as Mr. Wallace had told us. Furthermore, it was obvious that no other passage had ever opened along these smooth flowstone walls. We would gladly settle for a hidden opening to just a little more cave, but it would not be found here.

"We pulled ourselves back up to the second chamber and began a detailed examination of every corner and pit. In a small alcove we found a long, thin trail of ash. It might have been from a long dynamite fuse. BROKEN ROCK and flowstone at one side of the room caught our eye. Could it have been shattered by dynamite, closing off the entrance of a small passage? It had the distinct look of blasted rock.

"We lingered long at the spot, taking turns studying the broken wall. We talked, and looked again. Certainly someone MIGHT have set off a blast of dynamite here.

"Was there enough evidence that we should tell Mr. Wallace that we believed Dorr had actually blasted this wall? No one was willing to say yes. It looked possible, but who could be sure?

"Another group was waiting to descend. We returned to the brilliant sunshine of the desert, sought out Mr. Wallace, and told him exactly what we believed. He nodded. The officers of the company had reached the same conclusion. They, too, were bothered by the question that had puzzled us ever since he had first heard the story of the cave of gold. If there was no gold beyond that shattered wall, why would any rational person set off dynamite in the cave?

"Perhaps someday somebody will go to the heavy expense of digging this section of the wall, slab by slab. It is very doubtful that his efforts will be rewarded with any financial return. Caves such as Dorr's simply 'do not exist,' as Foster Hewitt reminded us. Nevertheless, we all hope that someday someone will solve the mystery of this shattered wall. There is a nagging worry in the back of the minds of even the most skeptical speleologist who has visited this spot. Until that day, no man knows what may lie beyond this wall, for Dorr carried his secret to his grave. Maybe—just possibly maybe— Dorr was right and the geologists were wrong. Such things have happened before in the Mojave!"

In relation to the above, Ray Palmer, during his editorship of AMAZING STORIES science fiction/science fact magazine in the 1940s, published some findings which were submitted to him by one researcher who claimed to have personally investigated the Dorr account. The researcher confirmed that years ago some Paihute Indian boys (some accounts say two, others say three) had discovered a cavern in the same area and almost of an exact description as that given by Dorr, including the alleged existence of the multi-leveled rock 'shelves' which ran the length of the cave and were set at various heights along the 3000 foot height of the cavern/canyon walls.

These Indians, according to AMAZING STORIES, had caused quite a stir among the Bankers in Needles, California, as they reportedly entered the town on several occasions with bags of black alluvial sand which was assayed and found to contain high concentrations of gold. They reportedly accumulated over $50,000 worth of gold ore in their bank deposit at one point. However, tragedy apparently ended their operation when one of the boys slipped off of one of the upper 'tiers' or 'rock shelves' which ran along the edge of the subterranean canyon, falling to his death.

• • •

From time to time encounters with homi-noid 'saurians' take place. Usually these encounters leave the human victims [presuming they return to tell the story] in a state of fear and trauma. Occasionally however some have shown incredible courage, at times insanely so, in their encounters with these hominoid or sauroid 'lizards.' The following account describes one such encounter, one which may have turned out far worse than it did had not the saurian hominoid been apparently an infant or child of its infernal race.

The creature was seen entering and leaving the sewer 'drains' near a small Pennsylvania town. The May, 1982 issue of *Fate* carried the following personal investigation made of the incident, written by Robert A. Goerman and titled 'THE LITTLE GREEN MAN WHO GOT AWAY': "ONE SUNDAY evening, March 1, 1981, I was watching THE AMITYVILLE HORROR on my 12-inch black-and-white television screen when the telephone rang. I immediately recognized the voice as that of Arnold, Pa., Police Sgt. Jim Dargenzio, an old friend.

" 'Bob, where were you last night?' he asked. 'I tried to reach you on this situation we got here. Seems some boys encountered some really weird creature by the railroad tracks...less than three feet tall, all green, wrinkled skin, long arms....

" 'The rub is that one of the boys picked the damned thing up and tried to carry it home! The thing wriggled free. Didn't hurt him or anything. It fled into a drainpipe and got away. But it's been seen since. Seems to be sticking around.'

"In Arnold (PA) is Roosevelt Park, a block-long playground complete with amphitheater and war memorials as well as an auxiliary policeman who oversees safety.

"But safety never was a teen watchword. Kids crave adventure, especially when there's the slightest hint of danger associated with it.

"Small wonder then that four brothers—Bobby Johnston, 16, Marvin, 13, David, 12, and Chris, 11—and their friend Randy Uhler, 12, sought out the Penn Central switchyard, with its even rows of boxcars and tankers, bunkers and trees and the like, just as they did every other Saturday afternoon. Here was a battle field strewn with enemy tanks, a fortress to be assaulted by commando forces, a Martian landscape and more.

"As they were playing, young Chris saw what he thought was a green trash bag. Curious, he approached it. Now it looked more like a statue, a big green statue. Of a man? But what kind of man?

"The statue moved.

"Not much. But it moved.

"The thing was squatting down along the railroad track beside a gray tank car loaded with salts. Its back was to Chris, who was a mere 50 feet away.

"I just had to take it home,' Chris would tell me, 'or nobody would BELIEVE me!'

"His mother added, 'That boy is always bringing something home and hiding it in our basement—anything he can get his two little mitts on and carry home.'

"Chris ('Bring 'Em Back Alive') Johnston edged forward, carefully stepping only on the railroad ties, avoiding the crackling cinders and gravel. He could not call for help now. The thing might run.

"His arms snaked under the thing's armpits, lifted up and locked his fingers against the back of its neck—the standard wrestler's full-nelson grip.

"Now Chris screamed for help. 'Bobby! Marvin! Help me carry this home!' he shouted. His brothers and friend rushed to his aid.

"Bobby, Marvin and company froze in their tracks. They could handle turtles, even snakes, but THIS was something else. Later, when interviewed separately, the boys agreed that the 'something' was green in color with NO HAIR OR FUR. Humanoid in SHAPE, it had wrinkled 'elephant' skin, stood JUST UNDER THREE FEET TALL and WALKED UPRIGHT ON TWO LEGS. It also had a muscular chest and distinct nipples, a tiny ONE-INCH TAIL and large ears. Chris told me that the skin felt dry and rubbery, stretched like elastic.

"Bobby! Help! It's too strong!' Chris shrieked.

"It wriggled and twisted and squealed and wriggled. Older brother Bobby, five years the wiser, offered this advice: 'Drop it and get out of there!' That sentiment having been expressed, Bobby took to his heels.

"If the others thought to help Chris, it was too late. The thing broke free of the boy's grasp and shot into the drainpipe less than eight feet away.

" 'Those boys were really excited and upset when we arrived on the scene,' Sergeant Dargenzio said. 'We were checking a robbery in the area when we saw them running. They thought we were the reinforcements, so to speak, that someone had called us to help them capture this green thing.'

"Mrs. Johnston told police her son's coat had a foul odor 'like a dirty fish tank' where it came into contact with the creature.

"The next morning I met with Chief Clark and received a copy of Chris' sketch of the thing made under rather harried conditions in the back of à patrol car. The Arnold police are hard-nosed, cynical cops who have seen and heard every tale in the book. They are anything but gullible; yet they were convinced that the boys had seen something far out of the ordinary.

"At 11:45 A.M. I drove to the scene and checked it out. Before I left, I inspected the drainpipe. Lying there on my stomach while I stuck my head and lantern into the pipe, I half-way expected to come eyeball-to-eyeball with the twilight zone's answer to Kermit the Frog. But the pipe was empty. In addition, the ground was rocky, eliminating any possibility of tracks.

"...Later that afternoon I returned to find the site surrounded by teenagers...Minutes later, upon my arrival at Arnold police headquarters, I saw a scowling desk officer inform a caller that an investigation into reports of a 'green thing' was under way. He put down the phone long enough to tell me that calls were flooding in.

"By seven o'clock that evening dozens of teenagers were prowling the site. Many were ARMED with rocks, pellet guns, clubs and flash-lights. Cars slowed and paused on the road above, their occupants jeering. So much for my low-key investigation.

"The next day pandemonium ruled. The local newspaper, VALLEY NEWS DISPATCH, was working on a 'green monster' piece. I met the reporter, Mike Burke, and urged him not to ridicule the witnesses.

"...I also talked with Marvin Johnston over the phone. In the afternoon I came back to the site, which was overrun with kids. Knowing that serious investigation was impossible under these circumstances, I returned home until 9:00 P.M. Then I drove back and began to patrol a mile-long stretch of railroad tracks. It was a miserable experience. The rain was turning to snow and the temperature was dropping. Seven hours later, at 4:00 A.M., I finally got to bed.

"Late the following morning, March 4, I was back patrolling the tracks. This time I found something: seven branches, about one inch thick and seven inches long, broken off evenly

with bark chewed off like corn-on-the-cob. This was nothing deer would have done, but as evidence of anything it wasn't much.

"But if hard evidence was difficult to come by, wild rumors were all too abundant.

"...At 9:00 A.M. on March 5 I talked with reporter Burke at the DISPATCH. He told me his first story draft had been REJECTED because his editors feared it would further 'INCITE PUBLIC HYSTERIA.' The word came down to keep it light and humorous. I had to agree.

"I later interviewed Sandy Uhler, the attractive and articulate mother of 12-year-old Randy, one of the original witnesses. 'My son isn't lying,' she declared emphatically. 'He and the other kids were all genuinely frightened and upset by this experience. I'd rather not believe his story because I don't like the idea of that creature lurking about. I hope you CATCH it—to end this ridicule.

"Halfway through my interview Chris Johnston walked into the Uhler home on his school lunch break. I showed him a sketch of the creature I had drawn. He confirmed its accuracy.

"From there I journeyed to the Arnold police station, where I was handed the logbook. At 7:40 the previous evening, it reported, two police officers had searched the 1600 block of Horne Boulevard for a 'THREE-FOOT LIZARD.'

"I talked with the patrolmen who interviewed the witness, a Glen C. (name withheld by request), A MAN IN HIS 40's AND THE FIRST ADULT WITNESS.

"At 3:00 P.M. the VALLEY NEWS DISPATCH hit the stands complete with a front-page story, headlined 'GREEN THING' SPARKS RUMORS, that made light of the scare. Reading it, I reflected that not only would no witness in his right mind EVER report a sighting after this, but previous witnesses would probably begin reneging their testimony.

"By the next day...on a final visit, I found a crowd of excited men bent forward and staring at something on the ground: a six-inch print WITH THREE TOES. The men began pouring the plaster for the cast.

"...'IT WAS A DINOSAUR-TYPE THING, BUT YET—' Sherry Coover paused as she sought the right words. 'It was human, a child. Definitely not an animal.' (Or rather, possibly humanoid or hominoid—not like any 'conventional' animal known or recognized by the zoological establishment.)

"I was impressed. I had done nothing to lead my star witness. I had not placed words or impressions into her mind. But her remark that it was human [i.e. humanoid], not an animal,' substantiated what OTHER WITNESSES had said.

" 'It must really fear people, the way it took off so quickly when we approached it,' THE 23-YEAR-OLD BRUNETTE SAID when we talked after her sighting. 'I won't give you their names but I saw some kids DOUSE IT WITH GASOLINE AND SET IT AFLAME...most of the gas went everywhere but on this creature.

"...Sherry Coover, her brother Mike, 18, daughter Sandy, four, and acquaintance Robert Stoner, 17, had THEIR ENCOUNTER on that fateful Sunday, March 1, at approximately 11:00 P.M. Until now they had told no one but close friends and family.

"It was fortunate that Sherry and I have a mutual friend: Joe Spano, owner of Spano's Tropical Breeze, Arnold's finest and only pet store. Spano steered me to this all-important, MULTI-WITNESS episode.

" 'My daughter saw it first—and screamed,' Sandy related. 'It was STANDING UPRIGHT in one of those large garbage-dumpster thingamajigs—you know, those square jobs with twin lids. It was picking up food, I guess.

" 'We all got a good look at it before it jumped out of the dumpster and took off on all fours. Could it ever move fast! We followed it as fast as we could. The whole area is lit up pretty good to cut down on the crime rate. It disappeared down this drainpipe.'

"The 'dumpster' was located right along Fifth Ave., right in the heart of town, alongside a housing project—and, yes, right along a single railroad line, a spur leading from the industrial district bordering the ALLEGHENY River to a convenient railroad switching area frequented by bored adolescents nearly every Saturday."

As we have said, the witnesses alleged that the 'sauroid' was probably a small 'toddler' among its reptilian race, and the residents of Arnold, Pennsylvania might consider themselves fortunate that it was not a life-threatening [according to some who have survived such events] encounter with the full-grown variety.

• • •

According to the PBS series 'TRAVELS,' which aired on February 15, 1993, over 5,000,000 Quiche Maya of Guatemala (including women and children) were slaughtered by the Spanish ROMAN Catholic Conquistadors. Piles upon piles of historically priceless Mayan books were burned during this reign of terror in Central America. Only one of them survived, the POPAL VU, which was later found hidden behind an alter.

There are still accounts of lost cities inhabited by modern-day Maya's deep in the jungles of Yucatan and Guatemala which have existed undisturbed since the ancient decline of the rest of the Mayan kingdom. The stories say that they are very protective against encroachment by white man. If such rumors are true, can you blame them for being so paranoid?

• • •

From *The UFO Encyclopedia*, by John Spencer (Avon Books., 1993), under the heading 'DR. OTTO STROVE,' we read how this astrophysicist assisted Frank Drake in establishing Project OZMA, and it's very mysterious conclusion: "...the project began its search by focusing on the star TAU CETI. According to claims made at the time, AS SOON AS the project got underway STRONG INTELLIGENT SIGNALS were picked up, leaving all the scientists stunned. "Abruptly, Dr. Strove then declared Project OZMA had been shut down, and commented that there was no sensible purpose for listening to messages from another world." [*Note:* Or, was this merely an 'excuse' used to keep the Project and it's findings SECRET?]

• • •

In April, 1972 a reader submitted a letter to *Fate* describing what, if true, may be one of the most remarkable 'encounters' with a subterranean civilization. The letter, which appeared below the heading 'SPIRITS OR SUBTERRANEAN BEINGS,' stated:

"Two years ago my small son Danny and I were playing in his bedroom when we heard a sharp metallic sound as if a large steel hammer had struck the concrete BASEMENT floor three times. It took us so by surprise that Danny began to cry. I was merely curious because I had heard a noise like that several months earlier in or beneath the living room.

"I decided to lie down on the bedroom floor with my ear to it. I clearly heard the roar of

MACHINERY or I should say a 'hum.' As I listened I heard something or somebody moving around and fidgeting with what sounded like machinery.

"I quickly got up and fetched a small hammer from my husband's tool chest and began to tap the floor, 1-2-3, 1-2-3, etc. I had continued for about five minutes when to my surprise the 'being' beneath the floor began to tap back, 1-2-3, 1-2-3. As I listened I heard a series of noises and knocks and then a MAN'S voice began to speak, not to me but to someone else. His words were too muffled to understand.

"I called the local police and asked if there were any underground installations in our town and they said there were not. "Frequently after that I would place my ear to the floor and always I could hear the hum of machinery but never again the man's voice. "It is my opinion that races of people live far beneath the earth in vast networks of caverns and they have access to miracle machinery that can project sound and even images to the earth's surface. I wonder if we are confusing these subterranean beings with spirits?—WANDA LOCKWOOD, BAKERSFIELD, CALIF.?

Appendix 1:
A Petition Against Government Harassment of UFO Percipients of the Visitor Experience

Are you ready to stand up and be counted for your beliefs? The time has come when we must stand together to make a difference! If we keep to ourselves and do not say anything against the atrocities that are being committed on innocent persons, then we have no right to complain. Only through strength in numbers can we make a peaceful demonstration as to where we stand. *If you disagree with the harassment and the threat on the lives of individuals, please sign the petition.* It will be brought to the news media's attention, our congressional representatives and senators. Together we can make the difference!

The following list will give you an idea of what has been happening to percipients. There are many more, but they have not spoken up because they are frightened—and with good reason! There is something more at work than we know, but the government does know and it is time it supported its people instead of trying to annihilate them.

- **Contact.** Military personnel in woods chased him. MIBS, Sasquatch encounters.
- **Contact.** Military incarcerated him in mental asylum. "German" sounding doctor ordered seven shots of Haldol to be administered all at once without antidote—tried to kill him.
- **Contact.** CIA worked him over and had slow poison administered to him. Many poisons can cause seizures and ever since contact he has had seizures when someone tries to put him in hypnosis.) Cannot work due to nervous condition and extreme allergies which developed after contact. On government assistance.
- **Contact.** Taken into underground base at Site 51—kept for 26 days—did experiments on him. Military wore black uniforms and red insignias. Put in special forces so he could not talk.
- **Contact.** Put in prison for seven years because of seeing too much at site 51. Three men taken there blindfolded to see crashed UFO. One went to prison, one died and one missing.
- **Contact.** Hounded by military and FBI because of contact in North Carolina. She and her father constantly on the move to keep away.
- **Contact.** Policeman in Ashland, NC held for 21 days by military under hypnosis with arm In air and needles stuck in him to ascertain if he was telling truth and really under hypnosis. He had been chased for one year. Lost everything.
- **Contact.** Followed by a Captain Morgan. Implant that came out of nose and two artifacts given to him by aliens confiscated by military. Held by armed guard in room. Constantly on the move to keep away.
- **Policeman** took pictures of aliens. Hounded—house burned down, lost job,

wife left him. From Greensboro, S.C.

- **Contact.** FBI came to house and demanded to see flies on his Soviet Parapsychology research.
- **Contact.** Three attempts on life by C.I.A. Water system on ranch sabotaged and his cattle mutilated. Bank account tampered with. Lost everything.
- **FBI harassed** town of "Blue Diamond" searching for Pleadeans. Made things hot for L. so he moved. Knows lots of cases of military harassment.
- **Contact.** Abducted on military and Indian reservation near underground base site.
- **Contact.** In Metro Mall—Phoenix, AZ. taken by a "security guard" to his office in basement. Saw a picture of herself on wall. Let her go. Asked if she knew anyone else's picture on wall!
- **Contact.** Harassed by Army to retire. Refused. Worked on "Project Snowbird" research for last three years.
- **Contact.** ELF wave beamed at her house (or something akin to it). Made her hus-band and herself sick and her teeth started turning brown. This happened after they became involved In the "Psychotronics" organization.
- **Contact.** On military plane enroute to Europe. Hit by "lightning" (plane lit up). Next thing he remembers he was on steps of barracks. Many gaps in memory—felt he was drugged. Next on a farm where everyone laughed. Next in a hospital In South Africa. From there sent to New York where he was incarcerated in "mental" hospital with people who had "big" heads and looked strange. Said they squeaked. They were kept behind a fence from him. Psychiatrist wanted to know what he was doing there, that there was nothing wrong with him. Let him go. Now has seizures and a nervous condition that prevents him from working. On assistance.

Please return your signed petition to: UFOCCI, 3001 S. 288th, Federal Way, WA 98003.

Petition

Appendix 2:
This Information Can Save Your Life and Freedom

The Coming "Official" Announcement of the Alien Presence on Earth

Why "Star Wars," the Hubbel Space Telescope, the Sudden Fall of Communism?

WHAT IS GOING ON? Something very SINISTER is going on. Polls reveal that over 90% of the American people believe in UFOs and 95% of these people believe the government is keeping this knowledge from the public. But why? Are they afraid the people will panic if an "official" announcement were made? Hardly. Such announcements would create interest and excitement and many questions, particularly by the churches, but not panic. Why then the continued cover-up?

There is overwhelming evidence in the past several years from "whistle-blowers"—retired military officers who have finally said, "Enough is enough! It's time the government told the people the truth!" These officers, such as Navy intelligence officer William Cooper, Major John Lear (whose father found the Lear-Jet Corporation) and Air Force officer William English, to name but a few, have all discovered the truth, and at the risk of their very lives, are trying to alert YOU to the secrets behind the UFOs and the Alien Presence on this earth. These people worked on secret projects, had access to classified Top Secret documents, had seen with their own eyes captured aliens or extraterrestrial entities, UFOs and the incredible technology they brought with them.

Sightings of "UFOs" (unidentified flying objects) have been reported throughout history, and biblical and historical references to "flaming chariots," huge flying "birds" and odd-looking beings predate our history by thousands of years. In the 1940s, several alien spacecraft were recovered by the U.S. and other countries, along with a few dead aliens and one live one they named EBE (a name suggested by Dr. Vannever Bush, and was short for Extraterrestrial Biological Entity).

In 1953, astronomers discovered large objects in space that were moving toward Earth. At first they believe these were asteroids, but later evidence proved that the objects could only be spaceships. Project Sigma and Project Plato intercepted alien radio communication and using the computer binary language, was able to arrange a landing that resulted in face-to-face contact with alien beings from another planet. Meanwhile, a race of human-looking aliens contacted the U.S. Government, warning us that the aliens orbiting the equator were hostile beings from Orion. These human-type aliens demanded we dismantle and destroy our nuclear weapons, that we were on a path of self-destruction and we must stop killing each other, stop polluting the earth, stop raping the earth's natural resources and learn to live in harmony with one another. President Eisenhower rejected those demands.

later in 1954, the race of aliens, known as Grays, from Zeta Reticuli area in space, who had been orbiting the equator, landed at Holloman Air Force Base. They stated their planet was dying and they needed quarters on earth to conduct genetic experiments that might allow their race to survive; this in exchange for certain technology. President Eisenhower met with the aliens and a formal treaty was signed. The treaty stated the aliens would not interfere in our affairs and we would not interfere in theirs. We would keep their presence on earth secret; they would furnish us with advanced technology. They could abduct humans on a limited basis for the purpose of medication examination and monitoring, with the stipulation that the humans would not be harmed, would be returned to their point of abduction, that the human have no memory of the event. It was also agreed the alien bases would be constructed underground, beneath Indian reservations in the Four Corners area of Utah, New Mexico, Arizona and Colorado. Another was to be constructed in Nevada in the area known as S-4, about seven miles south of an Area known as "Dreamland." A multi-billion dollar secret fund was organized and kept by the Military Office of the White House, supposedly to build secret underground sites for the President and staff in case of military attacks.

By secret Executive Memorandum, NSC 5410, Eisenhower established a permanent committee known as "Majority Twelve" (MJ-12) to oversee and conduct all covert activities with the aliens. This included FBI director J. Edgar Hoover and six leaders of the "Council on Foreign Relations," known as the "Wise Men" and later others from the Trilateral Commission, George Bush, Gordon Dean, and Bryzinksi were among them.

A major finding of the commission was that the aliens were using humans and animals for a source of glandular secretions, enzymes, hormonal secretions, blood and in horrible genetic experiments. The aliens explained these actions as necessary for their survival, that if their genetic structure was not improved, their race would cease to exist.

The ruling powers decided that one means of funding the alien project was to corner the illegal drug market. A young ambitious member of the Council on Foreign Relations was approached. His name was George Bush, who at the time was president and CEO of Zapata Oil Company, based in Texas. Zapata Oil was experimenting with offshore oil drilling, and it was arranged that the drugs could be shipped from South America to the offshore platforms by fishing boats, then transferred to the U.S. shore by normal transportation, thus avoiding search by customs agents. The plan worked better than anyone expected, and today the CIA controls all the world's illegal drug markets. One should remember: It was George Bush who first started selling drugs to our children. The drug money was used to finance the deep under-ground alien bases.

Conclusions; The Bilderburgers, the Council on Foreign Relations and the Trilateral Commission are the SECRET GOVERNMENT and rule this nation through MJ-12 and the study group known as the Jason Society.

Throughout history, the aliens have manipulated and/or ruled the human race through various secret societies, religion and the occult. The CFR and the Trilateral Commission are in complete control of the alien technology and the nation's economy. Eisenhower was the last president to know the entire overview of the alien problem. Succeeding presidents were told only what MJ-12 wanted them to know, and it was NOT the truth. MJ-12 presented each president with a picture of a lost alien culture seeking to renew itself, build a home on this planet and shower us with gifts of technology. Each president has bought the story hook, line and sinker. Meanwhile, innocent people continue to suffer unspeakable horrors at the hands of alien and human scientists who are engaged in barbarous research that would make the Nazis pale in comparison. And if that is not enough, many people end up as food for the insatiable alien appetite for biological enzymes, hormonal secretions and blood. At least one in every 40 Americans have been implanted with alien devices that are used to control them if necessity calls.

By 1989, over three million "Grays" were occupying these deep multilevel underground complexes. Level 7 at Dulce is called 'Nightmare Hall." They have welched on their agreement on abducting humans; today over 25 million citizens have been abducted and implanted, a literal army awaiting orders to march! (Whitley Strieber has written bestselling books on his personal experience as have many others). For this reason, other nations were informed. Within five months, the communist monolith Russia was dismantled to unit with the U.S. and its technology to fight the invasion. The Hubbel Space Telescope was created to keep a watchful eye on the invasion fleet; Star Wars technology has been developed to hopefully stop them in outer space before they can get on earth.

Today, the government is on the horns of a dilemma. Too many sources are releasing alien information. The public could get angry at continued secrecy. So MJ-12 plans soon to make an "official" announcement, under controlled conditions, probably Area 51. Network TV will be called to meet the staged "landing" of the aliens, these being the Greys. They will come bearing gifts, technology that supposedly will heal cancer and AIDS, retard aging, etc. They will tell us they are the "saviors of humanity" who have come to defend the earth against an invasion of man-eating aliens called Reptoids. The story is a LIE. They already work for the Reptoids! Their plan is to unify the world into a One-World Government, a "New World Order" with the argument that only this can defeat the invasion by Reptoids. This is a trap to enslave the world's population. Control will be accomplished through the money system, a universal currency controlled by certain international bankers, who for years have been lackeys of the aliens, who seized upon their greed and lust for wealth and power as a means to bring about their evil plan to control the earth. (This also being the scenario predicted in the Bible's *Book of Revelation*, wherein only those who accept the Mark of the Beast (the aliens being the "Beast" and the "Mark" being some sort of laser tattoo or Credit Card they will use, which will allow people to buy and sell goods). Those who do not accept this "Mark" must live outside the money system and survive somehow on their own, through barter, etc.

SO BE AWARE! ONLY YOUR KNOWLEDGE OF THIS FAKE INVASION AND FAKE RAPTURE CAN PREVENT IT FROM HAPPENING. DEMAND THE TRUTH FROM YOUR GOVERNMENT. TELL THEM YOU KJNOW ABOUT THE ALIENS AND THAT THERE ARE GOOD ALIENS AND BAD ALIENS AND THAT MJ-12 IS PROMOTING THE BAD ALIENS AND THE ONE WORLD GOVERNEMNT THEY HOPE TO CONTROL.

INSIST ON THE TRUE STORY OF THE ALIEN PRESENCE! YOUR LIFE COULD DEPEND UPON IT, AS WELL AS YOUR FREEDOMS!

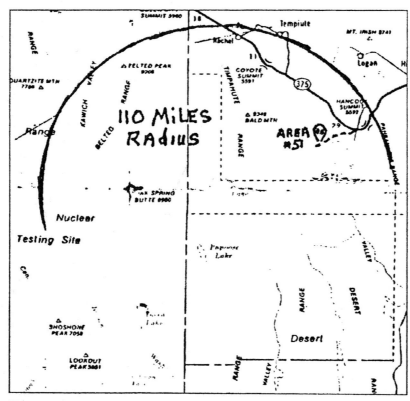

The mysterious Area 51, where Top Secret testing, perhaps using an alien technology, is rumored to be taking place.

Appendix 3: Area 51 Update: The Government Screwed Up!

The White Sides Cover-Up!

In 1984, in a highly publicized and bitterly contested action, the U.S. Air Force seized control of over 89,000 acres of public land in the Groom Mountain Range in Nevada. They had no use for the land itself; they only wanted to keep people from climbing the mountains to look down on the top secret Groom Lake air base, home of secret aircraft and Star Wars projects. The only trouble is, they failed to seize one critical hill, called White Sides, where visitors can still look down on the Groom Lake facility.

In other words, the Groom Range land seizure served no purpose.

Now, there are only two choices open to the government:

1. They can seize White Sides and close off this window into Groom Lake, or
2. They can give back the land they seized in 1984, returning it to public use.

No other option is logically consistent. If they do not take White Sides, then the 1984 seizure was useless, and the public has the right to demand the land back. If they do seize White Sides, then the military has bigger questions to answer: What is being tested at Groom Lake, and why, since the Soviet threat has ended, are these projects so important to national security?

The world has changed in the past few years. The U.S. is no longer engaged in a technological race with a sophisticated enemy, yet many of the top secret projects meant to keep pace with the Soviets continue to be pursued this day, at a cost to the taxpayers of billions of dollars. Secret projects like the rumored Aurora aircraft are the darlings of the military, because they can be conducted without oversight, outside the view of the public and beyond the inspection of Congress.

Now the situation has reached a crisis—at White Sides. If the military takes this land, then it must explain to the American people why the continued secrecy and official nonexistence of Groom Lake is justified. Why must America spend billions of dollars to find a facility designed to keep pace with the Soviets? Most of us agree on the importance of a strong military, but the world has changed, and Nevada is no longer crawling with spies. The practice of conducting huge projects in absolute secrecy is questionable now. Today, the secrecy seems intended only to protect these projects from Congressional review and reasonable oversight by the American taxpayer.

Our goals, here, are small but symbolic. The original justifications for the Groom Range land grab have vanished now, and we want the military to return what it has taken.

WE WANT OUR LAND BACK!
The White Sides Defense Committee
May 1993

Address correspondence to: The White Sides Defense Committee, c/o Glenn Campbell (Secretary), P.O. Box 448, Alamo, NV 89001.